Software Quality Assurance & Testing For Beginners

Nitin Shah

Copyright © 2019 Nitin Shah

All rights reserved.

ISBN: 9781097280445

ABOUT THE AUTHOR

Nitin Shah has more than 35 years of experience in the area of software Development, Implementation, Training, Software Quality Assurance, Pre Sales, Testing and Project Management. While working with training, in-house and export oriented multinational organizations, he acquired extensive knowledge and experience in all stages of SDLC and STLC phases.

He was a Key Contributor in starting and growing new accounts and building high performing team in the area of Verification and Validation in general and also setting up automation and performance testing practice team for a location of the company. He was also instrumental in conceptualization and mentoring software Test Automation Framework/ Code generation tool development. As a delivery manager he held responsibility for all testing projects being executed from that location and have successfully performed techno-functional, managerial and support roles in various large accounts.

He successfully managed delivery for an SLA based engagement supporting plenty of release based testing projects with a team of 170+ Resources and contributed in significant cost savings on customer side by consolidation of team, high offshore leverage of 82-85%, continuously increasing productivity, automation, and reusability.

He Presented a white paper at international conference organized by Practical Software Quality & Testing (PSQT) at Minneapolis in September 2005 and Co-authored a paper which was published during Step-in summit held in Bangalore in January 2006.

He also has 5 years of full time training experience in a reputed software training institute in India. Evan today he is associated with educational institutes to deliver expert lectures and as external faculty for conducting viva. He is also a visiting faculty at a reputed university in India and contributing in syllabus design and conducting training on Software Quality Assurance and Testing.

PREFACE

Quality is meant to be built into any software

Defects are bound to be part of any development

Assuring quality and controlling defects is an unavoidable activity

Software applications have crossed the boundaries of the organizations and have reached to almost all the people helping them in their day to day activities. It is assumed that more than 90% of people use one or other software in some form. In this highly competitive world, the focus on quality of application is becoming more and more critical from end user perspective.

From development perspective, technical complexities, continuously changing and enhancing requirements, technology advancements and non-availability of skilled resources, makes it difficult to produce error free application. Every application developed or enhanced will contain many errors. While it is impossible to develop error free application, it is critical to identify and remove defects before software moves to the next development phase and ultimately bring them down to 0 or bare minimum level when application moves to production environment for end-user use.

Software testing has not just remained as one of the phases of Software Development Life Cycle but has become a full-fledged engineering involving detailed processes and techniques. For large and complex projects even independent testing teams having thorough understanding of processes, techniques and tools are involved. Independent software testing is considered to be a fastest growing market and hence many students aspire to build career in Software Testing.

Lot of material is available in the market but most of them focus on theories with an objective to impart as many testing related jargons and aspects as possible. In the process of covering so many aspects useful not only to beginners but also to project leads, managers and strategists, it becomes complex and irrelevant for many beginners. The content of most of the books are organized concept wise rather than the sequence in which the concepts should be utilized / implemented. In absence of any industry experience of large and complex project development, students really find it difficult to understand these concepts well and just mug up for clearing exams. They find it difficult to apply the knowledge when they really get in to industry.

This material sets the context by explaining importance of Software Quality Assurance and Testing With an objective in mind that the reader should not just read the book because of compulsion (of exam) but for applying in real life projects. The explanations of concepts and examples are aligned to Software Development Life Cycle process and hence it becomes very clear when and where specific concept can be applied. It also focuses on identifying and removing issues and defects at every stage of software development life cycle and hence it is not just for those who are aspiring to build career in SW testing but also for those who are aiming to become quality developers.

This material explains all the concepts, processes and techniques with practical industry examples and hence beginners who do not have any experience in developing business applications can easily grasp and apply their learning immediately.

Rather than covering each and every aspect which they may not use for many years in the beginning of their career, it focuses more on the clarifying concepts and developing ability to apply the knowledge. It is for all the students / beginners aspiring to be good developers or testers.

ACKNOWLEDGEMENTS

I would like to thank Mr Mohit Shah for reviewing material as a student and providing valuable feedback and suggestions that can make the contents even simpler and relevant to students.

I am very thankful to Dr Satyen Parikh (Executive Dean, Prof. and head AMPICS, DCS, Ganpat University) for giving an opportunity to design the course and conduct training sessions on 'Software Quality Assurance and Testing' for their BSC IT and BCA programs in Ganpart University, Gujarat.

I am also very thankful to my previous employers who provided ample opportunities to enhance my practical knowledge and experience to practically implement various concepts, practices on software development and quality assurance.

Last but no he least, I am extremely thankful to family members for all the support given to make me capable and adjusting to all the inconvenience caused during my work and book writing.

REVIEW COMMENTS

"I found all the chapters to be really well written and the book covers all the important topics. Overall the entire book is really good with chapters that are clearly and concisely written. The examples provided makes each of the topics really easy to understand".

Mohit Shah,

B Tech in CS, CHARUSAT, Changa, Gujarat

Student of MS in CS, University of Southern California, L.A

Table of Contents

1. **SOFTWARE TESTING IMPORTANCE** 1
   - 1.1 IMPORTANCE OF TESTING 1
     - 1.1.1 Impact of defects 2
     - 1.1.2 Why Software Systems have defects 3
     - 1.1.3 Increasing Customer Expectations 6
     - 1.1.4 Cost of Quality 6
     - 1.1.5 Conclusion 8
   - 1.2 CHALLENGES / LIMITATIONS OF TESTING 9
   - 1.3 DEPTH OF TESTING / TESTING RIGOR 11
   - 1.4 SW TESTING QUALITY 11
   - 1.5 IMPORTANCE OF TESTING KNOWLEDGE TO SOFTWARE PROFESSIONAL 12
   - 1.6 SUMMARY 14
   - 1.7 EXERCISE 16

2. **SOFTWARE TESTING OVERVIEW** 18
   - 2.1 CONCEPTS AND KEY TERMINOLOGIES 18
   - 2.2 SW TESTING VS OTHER PRODUCT TESTING 30
   - 2.3 SOFTWARE DEVELOPMENT LIFECYCLE PHASES 34
   - 2.4 SDLC – V MODEL 38
     - 2.4.1 V Model 43
     - 2.4.2 Verification and Validation 44
     - 2.4.3 Who should do Validation / System Testing 46
   - 2.5 SEVEN TESTING PRINCIPLES (ISTQB) 46
   - 2.6 SUMMARY 48
   - 2.7 EXERCISE 51

3. **VERIFICATION OF DEVELOPMENT DELIVERABLES – QUALITY ASSURANCE** 52
   - 3.1 INTRODUCTION 52
   - 3.2 REQUIREMENT ANALYSIS AND AMBIGUITY REVIEWS 52
     - 3.2.1 Challenges of Requirements 52
     - 3.2.2 Requirement verification, Ambiguity Reviews 54
     - 3.2.3 Requirement Analysis Guidelines 60
   - 3.3 DESIGN REVIEWS 61
     - 3.3.1 Database Design Reviews 61
     - 3.3.2 User Interface Design Reviews 64
   - 3.4 CODE REVIEWS 65
   - 3.5 STATIC TESTING TECHNIQUES 67

    3.5.1 Informal Reviews 68
    3.5.2 Formal Review 69
    3.5.3 Comparison: 73
  3.6   Summary 74
  3.7   Exercise 75

4 UNIT AND INTEGRATION TESTING WITH STRUCTURAL BASED TEST DESIGN 78

  4.1   Introduction 78
  4.2   Unit Testing 79
  4.3   Integration Testing 83
  4.4   Structure Based / White Box Testing 90
    4.4.1 Statement Coverage 95
    4.4.2 Decision / Path/ Branch Coverage 97
    4.4.3 Condition coverage 100
    4.4.4 Loop Testing 102
    4.4.5 Approach, Advantages and limitations of White Box Testing 106
  4.5   Summary 108
  4.6   Exercise 110

5 BUSINESS FUNCTIONALITY TESTING – SPECIFICATION BASED TEST DESIGN 113

  5.1   Introduction 113
  5.2   Business Testing Levels 114
    5.2.1 Business Unit / Function Testing 114
    5.2.2 Validation and System testing 118
    5.2.3 Acceptance Testing 121
  5.3   Specification Based/Black-Box Test Design Techniques. 122
    5.3.1 Equivalence partitioning 123
    5.3.2 Boundary value Analysis 128
    5.3.3 Decision Table 132
    5.3.4 Use Case Based Test design 142
    5.3.5 State Transition 149
  5.4   Experience Based Test Design 156
    5.4.1 Error Guessing 156
    5.4.2 Exploratory Testing 157
  5.5   Gray / Grey Box Testing 158
  5.6   Summary 159
  5.7   Exercise 162

6 SW TESTING PROJECT EXECUTION PROCESS 165
6.1 SW Testing Quality – Testing Metrics 165
6.1.1 Coverage Metrics 166
6.1.2 Productivity Metrics 167
6.1.3 Process – Quality Metrics 168
6.1.4 Effort /Schedule Metrics 169
6.1.5 Metrics – Summary and Benefits 170
6.2 Software Testing Life Cycle Phases (STLC) 171
6.2.1 Requirement Analysis and Ambiguity Reviews 172
6.2.2 Test Design 179
6.2.3 Test Case creation 184
6.2.4 Test Execution and Defect Management 195
6.3 Test Plan 204
6.3.1 Testing Scope: Example 205
6.3.2 Testing Strategy 205
6.3.3 Milestones and Timelines 206
6.3.4 Quality Assurance Gates 206
6.3.5 Entry / Exit Criteria 207
6.3.6 Resource Requirements 209
6.3.7 Communication - Status Reporting 209
6.3.8 Defect Tracking and Resolution Process 210
6.3.9 Risk Management 211
6.3.10 Assumptions 211
6.4 Summary 211
6.5 Exercise 213

7 SW TEST OPTIMIZATION – TEST AUTOMATION AND RISK BASED TESTING 215
7.1 Test Automation and Automated Testing 215
7.1.1 Introduction 215
7.1.2 Test Automation Tools 216
7.1.3 How the tool works? 217
7.1.4 Automation Process 220
7.1.5 Test case selection for automation 221
7.1.6 Automation Benefits 222
7.2 Risk Based Testing 223
7.3 Summary 225
7.4 Exercise 226

8 TESTING TYPES 227
8.1 Functional Testing 228
8.1.1 Bases for Functional Testing: 228
8.1.2 Functional Testing Process 230
8.1.3 Testing of Error Messages 230
8.1.4 Report Validation 233
8.1.5 Localization/Internationalization Testing 234
8.2 Non-Functional Testing 236
8.2.1 Usability Testing 236
8.2.2 Performance, Load, Stress Testing 242
8.2.3 Security Testing 248
8.2.4 Compatibility Testing 253
8.3 Regression Testing 256
8.4 Summary 258
8.5 Exercise 260

9 REFERENCES 262

1 Software Testing Importance

- Before we get in to details, it is critical to know its importance in today's market scenario and importance of acquiring necessary knowledge on software quality assurance and testing.

So, this chapter describes following topics in details

- Importance of Software Testing
  - Impact of defects – What could happen if the software retains some defects in production environment
  - Why all software applications are bound to have defects
  - Increasing customer expectations in terms of quality and cost of software
  - Cost of Quality and Cost of Poor quality
- Importance of testing knowledge required by software professionals – why all who are starting their career as software professionals need to have good understanding of all the software quality assurance and testing concepts, processes and techniques.

This chapter will set the stage to move further.

1.1 Importance of Testing

When we are testing something, we are checking whether it is OK or not as per our expectations. We all do testing knowingly or unknowingly in our day-to-day life. We do some amount of testing before we buy – pen, TV, vehicle or any such product - small or big, cheaper or expensive. We do only basic testing as in most cases; company provides confidence to us by way of giving assurance on the quality through warranty/guaranty. We tend to buy branded products even at a higher cost because we are sure of the quality. This is because manufacturing companies with good brand do very thorough testing of the product they manufacture before delivering the product in the market.

Similarly, whenever we develop any software, we need to do thorough testing to ensure that there are no defects/issues in the system and we can give confidence to the customers / users of the system.

In simple terms, **Software Testing** is the process of executing the program or application with the intention of finding errors/bugs in the software application.

A survey conducted few years back for the success rate of various projects revealed that

  - only 34% of the projects were successful,
  - 51% projects were completed but they were challenged for some of their functionalities and
  - 15% projects were completely failed.
  - The cost of failed projects was as high as $38 Billion.
  - The survey also revealed that 52% of required functions do not make it to final product.

Every product can have defects due to various reasons and; if not tested properly; can impact negatively to the customers and customers can move to competitors providing similar products with good quality. Same is the case with software application.

Following sub sections provide details on why all software applications have defects, how unresolved defects could negatively impact the customers and why customers can move to other competitors. The importance of testing can be derived from this understanding.

1.1.1 Impact of defects

Like any other product, quality of software is equally or sometimes, even more important than price in the current competitive world. Today, software is used for very critical applications and even a small issue can result in very heavy loss. Let us see some of the Industry examples.

- In November 2003 a defective baby-food formula resulted in the deaths of three babies in Israel. Due to wrong formula in the dispensing system, the food contained less vitamin B1 than required by babies and shown on the label.
- 3140 medical devices were recalled between 1992 and 1998 in US, because, 242 of them (7.7%) were attributable to software failures. 79% of them were caused by software defects that were introduced when changes were made to the software after its initial production and distribution.
- Between January 4th and May 24th, 2000, 158 women had been told that they need not worry about having a child with Down Syndrome, even though four of them were carrying foetuses with the abnormality.

    An investigation into the incident had revealed that the software automatically assumed that patients weighed zero pounds if an actual weight was not known.

- Ariane 5 was designed by the European Space Agency (ESA) as a replacement for the successful Ariane 4 launcher. On June 4, 1996, this US $500 million space craft was launched. Shortly, it suddenly veered off its flight path, broke up, and exploded.

    Sadly, the primary cause was found to be a piece of software from the previous launchers systems was not required but was not removed.

- In 2010, Toyota had to recall 9+ million cars worldwide as the cars had a software bug that caused a lag in the anti-lock-brake system.

- In 2012 US based Knight Capital Group Inc, mistakenly sent out more than four million stock orders in less than an hour, costing half a billion dollars to reverse.

    The reason was a code change was not deployed to all the servers

- October 2017: Digital Payments firm MobiKwik loses over Rs 19 crore due to technical glitch

This happened because the software erroneously allowed user to use money beyond their balance amount.

As you can see in the examples above, the mistakes could be very small

- Wrong formula
- Regression effect: Defects are introduced in the working software/product when the changes are made in the software for any enhancements.
- Retaining unwanted piece of code from previous version
- Incorrect/missing assignment to the variable – and the software assume 0 value
- Missing some specific condition of maximum allowable limit for money withdrawal.

So, the software is developed for benefits but defects in the software results in loss.

And there are many instances where the loss may be much more than the benefits.

1.1.2 Why Software Systems have defects

One may argue that having these kinds of errors (as describes in previous section) and impact in the software may be a rare case. We as human being, most of the time do not feel or agree that there are issues in us or our creation. So, as a developer, we always have (over) confidence that the program we have developed is right and meets the requirements.

Unfortunately this is not true. Mistakes happen because of many reasons such as

- Time Pressure
- Low capabilities – of the team members involved
- Complexity – of requirements, design or technology to be used
- Wrong understanding of requirements
- Communication gaps between the team members and/or
- Due to Environment Conditions

So, all software applications have defects/bugs because people (Analysts, Designers, developers, users) make mistakes. Some may be unimportant but some may be critical / dangerous also.

For any software development project, multiple teams and multiple members within the team are involved

- Business users who need the software with specific requirements,
- Business representatives who explain the requirements to the Business Analysts.
- Business Analysts who explain the requirements to designers to design the system.
- The designers provide design and program specifications to different programmers.
- Programmers who developed programs.
- Senior programmers integrate all these programs to build software.

At every stage the miscommunication / misunderstanding can happen and issues may get introduced.

In fact, in the real life scenarios, the issue starts from Requirement gathering phase itself. There are gaps between the actual requirements needed by the end-user and what is understood by Analysts.

Let us take one industry example to understand why every software application is expected to have defects when built.

Case Study

Requirement: A Software product was to be developed which can be used by any educational institute providing following high level modules and functionalities

- Learner & Staff setup
- Statutory Attendance and requirements
- Progress Tracking (Assessments & Exams)
- Behaviour Management & Detention
- Site management (Rooms, Equipment etc.)
- Automatic Timetabling/ Scheduling
- Manual Timetable updates
- Portal view for parents, learners, staff etc

Key expectations and measures:

- To be built and delivered in 14 calendar months
- Software product size: 21,000 Function Points (FP) and around 2 million lines of code (LOC)
- Note: Function Point is a well-known unit to measure size of the software application. It considers various aspects of the software to come up with number of function points.
- It had 2000+ database objects
- 55,000+ person days of effort was spent
- At peak it had 175+ team members including Architects, Development & Quality consultants. More than 60% of the team members were freshers (without any major industry experience)
- 150,000 test cases were built with an estimation of 18 defect per 1000 lines of code

There are many other reasons such as

Large projects, Large teams. – Most applications are much larger than the exercises being done during college education and requires large teams.

For large and complex applications, there are always communication issues/gaps, where multiple people are involved. There can be Inconsistency between components developed by different people

Technical / Logical complexities - The system may have to be implemented in **heterogeneous environment** (Desk top, Mobile, ATMs or any other such) making it difficult to maintain quality.

Time Pressure – To meet deadlines, facing more issues than planned or due to any other uncontrollable reasons.

Limited Knowledge / Experience level of developers. People with low knowledge / experience level will have understanding gaps and unclear end-users perspectives

Changing Requirements: The requirements can change due to changes in business rules, government rules or any other reasons. Many times the implications of requirements are not foreseeable in the initial stage.

Exceptions are ignored: All business processes have some exceptions which are generally missed out during analysis and design and only come up during testing/implementation

Typical communication issues.

- **Missing information** (Sender misses to communicate or receiver misses to listen even if sender communicates)
- **Untold assumptions** – Receiver makes some wrong assumptions even if some aspects are not communicated to him/her.
- **Misunderstanding** – Sender provides some information, receiver receives the information but understands differently.

These gaps between Business to Business Analysts, Analyst to designer, Designer to developer results into issues. So, issues are bound to be there in the software.

Some statistics reveal that 20 to 50 errors are found for every 1000 lines of code and 1 to 4 errors remain even after system testing is done.

There can be no software in the world which does not have any issues.

1.1.3 Increasing Customer Expectations

The customer expectations are also continuously increasing because of the various industry trends as provided below

Trend	Consequence	Customer Expectations
Newer Areas of applications	Continuously increasing volume	Increased Support
Continuously increasing user base	Transactions directly done by end user	Improved quality, performance, security
Increased Competition	Increased features, Newer techniques / processes	Quicker Deployment Customer Satisfaction
Technology Advancement	Grid Computing, Mobile Services, Cloud Computing, Big Data, Analytics….	Manage Complexity, Varied Interfaces
Globalization	Mergers and Acquisitions	More Complexity
Economic Slowdown	Budget Cuts	Reduction in Project Costs

Customer wants best quality at lowest price with latest features possible.

Such demands require dedicated focus and specialization in testing also.

As we have seen, every Software System will have errors. Impact of many of these errors could be very high and even if not; in a current highly competitive world customer expectations are continuously increasing for quality.

1.1.4 Cost of Quality

Maintaining high quality requires time and effort and hence cost. Although testing is itself an expensive activity, the cost of not testing is potentially much higher. For example if you are saving an effort of 2 days by not testing a specific functionality but if the application had some error in that functionality which was found by user then it may take much more time of user, customer care representative, developer, tester and all. If you quantify that effort, it could be 5-6 days (more than 2 days of testing and debugging).

Cost of **Quality** is a means to quantify the total cost of quality-related efforts and deficiencies.

While calculating cost of quality, we need to consider following three types of costs

1. **Failure Cost**: any effort or cost involved in Rework / replacement / Prestige / business loss. These costs are incurred only because there was a defect. So, it is also known as cost of **poor Quality.**

   Internal Failure Cost are incurred when the defects were detected before the application is moved to production environment. It includes direct cost

   - To reproduce, analyse and fix the problem
   - Retesting to determine that the defect is removed
   - Reimplementation of the corrected code
   - Costs involved in mitigating the risk of any possible side effects due to rework done for fixing the problem. Any effort of regression testing to ensure that the corrections/changes have not impacted other working module. If by chance it has introduced new defect then additional effort may be required to identify and remove that also
   - Costs related to collection of quality metrics based on which organization can do assess the modes of failure

   External Failure Costs are associated with the defects found after the product has been shipped to customer. It includes all the above costs and additionally include

   - analysis of issue / Complaint resolution
   - Product return and replacement
   - Help line support
   - Labour costs associated with warranty work
   - Indirect costs such unsatisfied customers, loss of reputation, and loss of business

2. **Appraisal Cost**: Cost of reviews (of all the work products such as Requirements, Design, Code), testing and debugging (removing defects) and cost associated with data collection and analysis. In order to reduce failure cost, we need to spend time and effort for reviews and testing before the application goes into production. This is known as Appraisal cost.

3. **Prevention Cost**: Cost involved in Training, Process implementation, planning etc. So, if the organization spends enough time and effort to train the people, implement some standards and follow various processes, the overall number of defects introduced in the application will be less and hence will reduce appraisal cost and failure cost.

   Total Cost of Quality = Failure Cost + Appraisal Cost + Preventive Cost

Find below four different stack bars indicating total cost of quality with different levels of effort in prevention and appraisal cost.

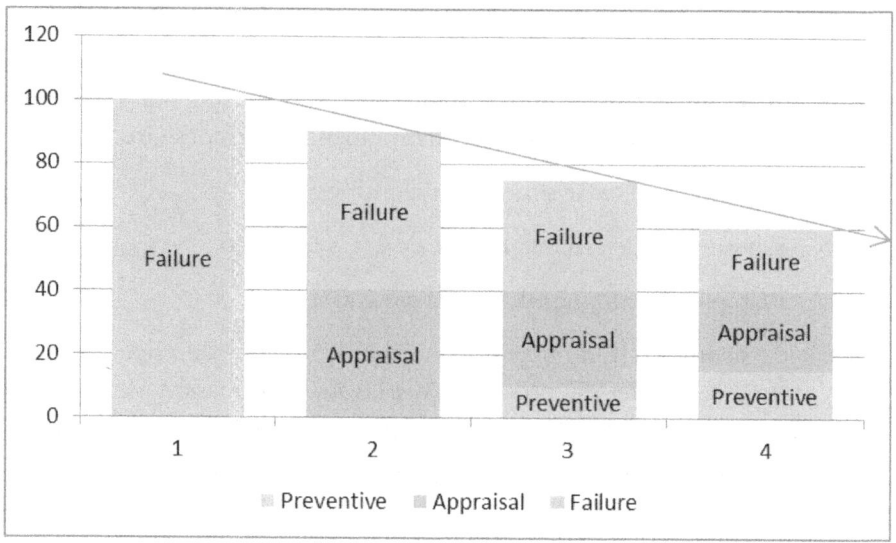

Stackbar 1 indicates no effort was spent for prevention and appraisal

Stackbar 2 indicates some effort was spent on appraisal because of which not only the failure cost reduces but the total cost of quality also reduces.

Stackbar 3 indicates that some effort was spent for prevention by following various processes and standard etc. This reduces appraisal cost and failure cost to the extent that the total cost of quality also reduces.

4th stackbar indicates that higher the prevention and appraisal cost, lower the failure and overall cost of quality.

1.1.5 Conclusion

It has been observed that if you increase time and effort for appraisal (testing and reviews), failure cost will reduce resulting into overall reduction in total cost of quality. It has been statistically proved and experienced that testing the application at the right time reduces the overall cost.

Hence, improving quality of the software system by way of testing (finding the defects) and debugging (removing defects) is very essential.

Every software system hence needs to be **tested** before it goes in to production for use. In fact overall project cost could be reducing if you spend time on quality assurance activities rather than acting on the defects found in the field.

1.2 Challenges / Limitations of Testing

Can we demonstrate to our customer that there are no errors in the software?

If we have to demonstrate that the software is completely error free, we need to test the software with all the possible permutations / combinations, which is practically impossible.

Let us understand this with an **example**

A 6 character text field is supposed to accept a character code of which 1st character should be numeric and all other characters should be alphanumeric.

> 1st character can be filled up in one of 10 ways. Rest can be filled up with 62 ways (digits -10, Lower case characters - 26, and Upper case characters - 26)
>
> Total combinations would be $10*62^5 = 9,161,328,320$
>
> Now, if we have to test each combination, it would require approximately 2,905 Years for testing (assuming it takes 10 seconds for testing each combination)
>
> If we include 10 Punctuation characters – it would require 44,176 years of testing

Additionally, when the requirement says 1st character can be numeric which means the requirement indirectly also tells that 1st character cannot accept any character other than numeric digit. So, we need to also try with other characters and check that the program should not accept any such character and throw's an error message. Such tests will increase effort requirement even further.

The application may have many such requirements leading to large number of possible input values, possible output values, and possible paths to move from input to output. So, it is practically impossible to cover all these combinations in testing. Also, the software specification is subjective. Hence, No one can prove that the computer code is **error free.** But **can be proved wrong if evidence** is collected (errors are found). So, we need to learn how to reduce huge domain of possible tests (large number of combinations) in to manageable set.

Testing an entire application for all the requirements is a very intense activity. It will not be possible to be effective and efficient if the tests are not planned and documented.

Limitations of Testing

- Testing shows presence of errors and not their absence
- It is impossible to detect all the errors
- The domain of possible inputs is too large for exhaustive testing
- Number of paths could also be too many to do exhaustive testing

Benefits of Testing

Testing of systems and documentation (test cases and results) can help to

- Provide information and confidence about level of quality to the customer/user by providing traceability of requirements to results.
- Reduce the risk of problems occurring during use, as the defects are found and corrected before the system is released for operation. Hence, proper testing contributes to the higher quality of software.
- Provide sufficient information to the stakeholders to make informed decision about release of Software. They may postpone some functionality, which have errors, or can provide some work-around till the defects are resolved.

Since testing needs to be completed in limited time and effort, the primary **objective** of the testing techniques and process is

"To find the **greatest** possible number of **errors** with a **manageable** amount of **efforts** applied over a **realistic time** span with a **finite** number of test **cases**."

We need to implement Testing process and activities that include planning & control, choosing test conditions, designing and executing test cases, checking the results, evaluating exit criteria (customer's acceptance criteria), reporting on testing process & results, and finalizing and completing closure activities after test phase is completed

1.3 Depth of Testing / Testing Rigor

All applications need not be tested with same rigor. There may be some software applications where the impact may be very low even if there are major defects in the software. For example a static website providing static details of any city, cannot be considered as a critical application. Even if there are some errors in the application, the impact may be very low.

Sometimes, the impact for a single instance may be low, but, if it occurs **more frequently** then also the overall impact becomes very high.

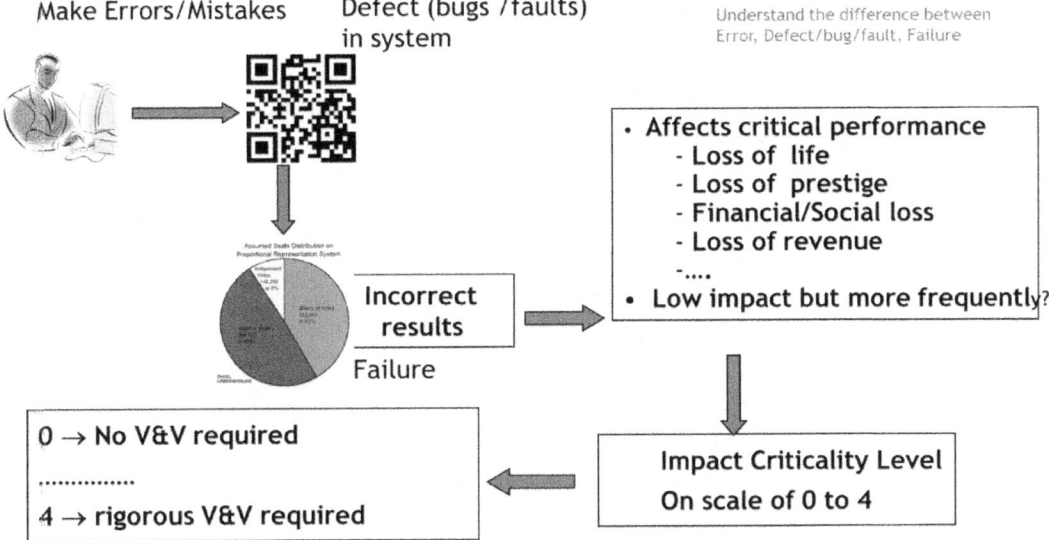

The cost of not testing is potentially much higher than cost of testing.

We as developer make mistakes/errors while requirement understanding, designing and coding which results in to defects (bugs/faults) in the software system due to which the results are incorrect. These incorrect results can impact some or the other way.

The rigor at which the testing should be done depends on the criticality of application or the impact level due to failure. Very rigorous testing should be done for the applications where impact criticality is very high but one may do very superficial testing for the applications where impact criticality is very low.

1.4 SW Testing Quality

As quality of product is important, quality of testing is also important. Like, people can make mistakes during development; people can also make mistakes during testing. So, the testing process and output needs to be reviewed and quality of the process and quality of team should be measured. This should be done such that the testing quality continuously improves.

Organizations collect various data during and after the project and generates various metrics for the same.

A metric is a quantitative measure of certain aspects. While there are many different metrics generated, some important metrics generated by most organizations include following categories.

Coverage Metrics: This checks how much % of requirements, % of test cases are covered in testing

Process/Quality Metrics: It conveys % of defects could be found before moving the application to production

Productivity Metrics: It conveys how many test cases can be prepared per hour or how many test cases can be executed per hour.

These and many others such metrics help to continuously monitor the quality of testing and help to improve on an on-going basis.

1.5 Importance of testing knowledge to Software professional

Testing the application just randomly with some inputs as we feel appropriate will not meet high quality expectations. In last couple of decades SW testing has moved from art to engineering. As an art, testing was based on only individual person's skills and experience without involving any methods and processes. The results depend on mood of the artist. Today testing is engineering and involves methods and techniques, follows well defined process for test creation and hence the results are predictable and verifiable.

One needs to understand various testing types, techniques and processes in order to do effective testing.

Every software professional hence need to have good understanding of SW QA and Testing fundamentals along with mind-set change because

- The understanding helps implementing various techniques during developer testing that can help improve quality of software
- The understanding of System and Acceptance testing process helps how developers become part of overall process
- The knowledge becomes stepping stone for those who want to build career in SW Testing fields.

In fact we will learn that validation and system testing which is done for the entire system before delivering the developed application to users, need totally different testing team requiring user-like mind-set and thorough understanding of testing processes and tools. This has emerged as a career path for many.

When as a developer we test our own code, our primary objective is to prove that it works (we test with a mind-set that it does not have any defect). Unfortunately we do not find real defects in the system with this mind-set. Hence, testing should be done with a mind-set to prove that it does not work, (it has defects and we need to somehow find it). One also needs an aptitude towards identifying problems and work until the problems are resolved. As a developer we also may have taken wrong assumptions and understanding which only independent team can find out.

So, Testing can be taken **as career** as the demand for test professionals is continuously increasing with increased focus on quality.

It is also important to note that this knowledge is applicable for any software, developed using any technology. All the types, processes and techniques one learn, can be used for any application developed in any technology.

Skills acquired/required by the team involved in testing

Apart from conceptual understanding and application of the various processes and techniques of SW testing, one can acquire following skills

- Analytical ability
- Desire to dive into detail
- Aptitude towards problem identification
- Ability to work with a problem until solved
- Applying testing methodology; testing tools and techniques
- Creative thinking to find maximum defects in minimum time
- Domain and application knowledge.
- Effective communication
- Curiosity / Willingness to ask questions
- Maturity

In addition to the courses being conducted in colleges, there are industry accepted certifications that help aspirants to build career in testing

1.6 Summary

We discussed that **every software applications will have defects** due to multiple reasons such as a) complex business requirements or technology, b) communication issues in the large teams, c) ambiguous or incomplete requirements provided by customer, d) quality and experience level of team members involved in the development of software and e) every human being is prone to make mistakes however good the developer is.

These **mistakes** results into **defects** in the software solutions and if not detected and removed from the software before it goes into production for customer/end-user use, can lead to **failure** of the system. The **impact** can be small or in some cases it **can be very high** – loss of life, prestige, money, social loss, time etc. In today's world, customer can move to competitors if they are not satisfied with the quality. We also discussed that **cost of quality** can be divided in to 3 categories – **Failure Cost** (cost of rework, replacement, business loss etc), **Appraisal Cost** (cost of reviews & testing), and **Prevention cost** (cost of training, process implementation, reusable components etc.). Total cost of quality can be reduced if we focus more on appraisal and prevention.

Customer expectations are continuously increasing and in highly competitive environment, customers expect high quality software applications with latest features implemented quickly and at lower cost.

SW testing requires time and effort. It is hence best to avoid any mistakes so that defects are prevented. But since defect cannot be prevented completely, they need to be identified and removed as soon as possible and certainly before it goes into production environment.

SW testing hence is an unavoidable activity for any software developed. The level of depth with which the testing should be done will depend on the criticality of the application and potential impact due to defect.

So, testing / reviews are extremely important though all applications may not be tested with equal importance. It is however practically impossible to test each and every possible combination of data. We may have to apply some techniques and guidelines to limit our combinations and hence it is practically impossible to detect all the defects. There are also some other aspects one need to remember that testing shows presence of defects and not absence. So, no one can prove that a specific application is completely error free.

So Primary objective of testing techniques and processes is

"To find greatest possible number of errors with a manageable amount of efforts applied over a realistic time span with a finite number of test cases".

Lastly we also discussed that, there could be quality issues in testing also. Hence, quality of testing also needs to be measured. Accordingly we discussed about some metrics such as coverage metrics (% of requirements / test cases covered), Process Metrics (% of defects could be found at each level/phase), Productivity metrics (eg. Number of test cases created, Executed, automated per hour).

Anyone who is aspiring to become a good developer or tester needs to hence understand and implement **testing techniques** at different **testing levels and processes** along with various soft skills.

1.7 Exercise

Sr.	Question
1.	One cannot test a program completely to guarantee that it is error free. T/F?
2.	Why is SW testing important?
3.	If testing is done by independent team, it is possible to say that the SW is error free or not. T/F?
4.	We should not do much testing because it takes lot of time and effort. True/False? Why?
5.	Why all software applications have defects. Provide reasons.
6.	Name 4 important skills required by tester
7.	What is the basic purpose of testing?
8.	What is the objective of using SW testing Techniques and processes
9.	Name 4 typical types of errors found in SW along with possible reasons for those defects
10.	What are the typical challenges in SW testing (why exhaustive testing is not possible)?
11.	If there are good programmers, software may not have any defect (T/F?)
12.	There is a two character code. The 1st character can contain alphabetic values and the 2nd character can contain alphanumeric values. This can result into _____ valid combination of data inputs.
13.	A software defects may result in loss of life also (T/F?)
14.	Mistake is same as failure (T/F?)
15.	The word 'bug' is synonymous with which of the following words? a) Incident b) Defect c) Mistake d) Error
16.	There is no harm if a piece of code remains in the program even if not required in the updated version (T/F?)
17.	No software code can be proved to have no errors (T/F?)
18.	Objective of V&V process is to find the _____ errors with a manageable amount of _____ applied over a realistic time span with a finite number of test cases.
19.	Explain Cost of quality
20.	Briefly explain limitations of Testing?
21.	All software applications should be tested with very high and equal importance (T/F?)
22.	Testers need to have good logical reasoning skills (T/F?)

Sr.	Question
23.	Is Exhaustive testing possible? Why?
24.	Briefly explain why one can choose software testing as a career
25.	Briefly explain why a developer should also have testing knowledge

2 Software Testing Overview

2.1 Concepts and Key Terminologies

Let us quickly understand meaning **of some key terms.**

System: is a collection of components organized to accomplish a specific function or set of functions. [IEEE 610]

Business function & Transaction is an elementary process or a smallest unit of activity expected to be performed by user at a given time and is meaningful to the user. For example, viewing flight schedule, booking ticket, cancelling ticket, printing ticket etc.

> Business function can be classified as External Input, External Output, or External Query or combination of any of them. A business function in general may not update any data in the system (eg only viewing schedule) but some business functions can change the data in the system (eg. booking a ticket). Such functions may be called business transactions. Business transaction could be combination of functions. Each transaction has a beginning and an end. If the transaction is terminated in between for some reason, the application state does not change (and it does not trigger any action or does not change any data).
>
> All software applications are built to perform set of business functions and transactions. Software applications hence can be considered as collection of functions or transactions from business perspective.

Defect: A flaw in a component or system that can cause the component or system to fail to perform its required function or it wrongly performs the required function or it produces wrong result is called defect. A defect, if encountered during execution, may cause a failure of the component or system.

A **mistake/error** made by a human being (any of the team members) produces a **defect/bug** in the design/ code/ document and results in to **failure** when such system is executed. These incorrect results may impact critical performance such as Loss of life, Loss of prestige, financial loss, and Social loss.

Severity: The degree of impact that a defect has on the development or operation of a component or system. [After IEEE 610]

Testing Types: We test what is required. Testing types depend on requirement types and there are two major types of requirements

- Functional Requirements – **Functional Testing**.

    Functionality and Features: What the system should do or how it should work. So, it includes Business Processes; rules and constraints, User Interface (Forms, Reports), Interfaces with other systems. For example, Bus Reservation, Accounting, etc. The document which describes what the system should provide and how it should provide is called **specification document**

    The **Objective** of functional testing is to verify that each functionality and feature of the **software application / system** operates in accordance with the **functional requirement specifications**. To check that it delivers **what** is expected. It has only one of the two possible results –**met or not met**

- Non-Functional Requirements – **Non Functional Testing**

    This comprises of qualitative aspects of the system such as security (not allowing unauthorized persons to access the system or data), performance (respond very quickly to customer requests), usability (easy to use with good look & feel) etc. Even if system's functionality and features work perfectly fine but if it gives response for a simple request after say 30-40 seconds or the unauthorised user is able to get into the system and disturb some processes or get access to some secured data, user will not like it. Testing of such non-functional requirements is called non-functional testing.

    Non-functional issues are derived based on the experiences encountered while running the software in an environment similar to production environment. The outcome of these tests is not just 'met or not-met' but 'the extent to which the expectation is met'.

    It also includes System management issues such as Installation, Portability, Backup & Recovery, Start-up and shut-down etc.

There is a separate chapter dedicated to explain testing types and particularly non-functional testing types in detail.

Work Products: Software development and Software testing is an intensive activity requiring many phases as discussed in previous section. At the end of each phase some documents are generated such as Requirement specification document at the end of Requirement Analysis phase, Function specification document at the end of high level design, UI design, database design, program specifications etc.at the end of detailed design phase and actual program code, database etc at the end of development phase.

Similarly, Test plan, test design, detailed test cases etc are documented and delivered at the end of test design phase. Test reports, defect reports etc are documented and delivered at the end of test execution phase.

All these documents are termed as work products. These are kind of intermediate deliverables from different teams and generally used for further project execution.

Testing: Testing; in simple terms; is a process of executing the program or application with an intention to find errors. However we had seen in section '1.1.4 Cost of Quality', and as we will discuss in detail in subsequent chapters, we can't wait for the application to be fully ready for testing. We need to focus on each and every stage to identify all possible issues which could result into defects/bugs in the application. Technically speaking Testing has a limited scope but it is also normally used as a term that covers all the aspects.

So, **Testing** is the process consisting of all lifecycle activities, concerned with planning, preparation and evaluation of software products and related work products to a) determine that they satisfy specified requirements, b) demonstrate that they are fit for purpose and c) detect defects

Hence, Testing is a process not only done on code but on all software work products across all life cycle activities, requiring proper planning, preparation and evaluation. Activities done to ensure that defects are prevented in the code are also termed as **Quality Assurance** activities.

At the end of testing process, we are expected to check that

Software requirements are implemented completely and correctly. Requirements include, Contractual or legal requirements, Functional, Non-Functional, Operational and procedural requirements or Industry specific standards

And it performs no unintended functions —system does not do what it is not supposed to do.

If any of the above does not meet, means there are defects in the software. The most damaging defects are the ones, which could not be discovered during the testing process and therefore remain when the system goes live. So, testing does not restrict the execution of program in a normal manner to see it works but involves some tests with some abnormal inputs and actions to see that it does not behave in unexpected manner with those inputs/actions.

In simple terms, Testing is a process of finding errors. It can involve

Positive Testing (Tests-to-Pass): check that the application behaves normally as expected with normal and legal input data. We can also term these tests as test-to-pass testing

Negative Testing (Tests-to-fail): Check that the system does not do things that it is not supposed to do when invalid or illegal data provided. And also check that system responds with required error messages for such abnormal or illegal data inputs. It has been observed that most errors are found here. We can term these tests as Test-to-fail testing. Tester has to be destructive who can make the system fail.

Let us understand positive and negative testing in detail.

Aspect	Positive Testing	Negative Testing
Objective	To prove that application functionality is as expected	To try and break the system.
What to check	To check that the product does what it is supposed to do	To check that product does not fail or does not do what it is not supposed to do, when an invalid/illegal input is given or unexpected action is taken
Test cases	Mostly derived from Requirement specifications. The conditions are known.	Not all tests are derived from requirement specifications. These are either derived based on techniques, or some unknown conditions for the product.
Coverage	If all requirements and test conditions are covered, we can say that we have achieved 100% coverage	There is no limit to negative testing. We can never say that we have achieved 100% coverage for negative testing
Example	Input valid value within the boundary for any field	Skip the input for a mandatory field and try to proceed Embed Single Quote on URL when it tries to query the database
Example Scenario	Password textbox **should accept** - 6 character length - 20 character length - With 10 character length - Including at-least one special character (as per rule)	Password textbox should not accept - 5 character length - 21 character length - 10 characters with no special character

Generally requirement specifications do not include any specifications related to what should be done when invalid data is entered. However, it is expected that system does not behave unpredictably and rather handles such exceptions properly. So, it is important to include test cases related to negative testing.

We can make application more stable and reliable by doing both positive and negative testing.

Priority: Test-to-Pass test cases could get higher priority with an assumption that application must provide required functionalities correctly. **Test-to-Fail** test cases could take lower priority.

A test condition is simply something that we could test. Tests or test conditions are derived from requirements, a technical specification, from the code or from business process. For example, Password must contain between 6 to 20 characters and must have at least one special character. These source documents are often known as **test basis**. Sometimes tests can be based on an experienced user's knowledge of the system, which may not have been documented.

Test case: A set of input values, execution preconditions, execution steps, expected results and execution post conditions developed for a particular objective or test condition, such as to exercise a particular program path or to verify compliance with a specific requirement. [After IEEE 610]

For every test you need to prepare and document a **test case** covering

o What is the purpose of the test – Eg. Ensure the validity of password as per rule
o Precondition: In which state the application should be before we carry out the test. Eg, application is already invoked, and login page is displayed.
o Which input details to be provided – Eg. 'abcde'
o What is the expected output/response from the application – Eg. The system should display error message saying password must contain at least 6 characters.

You may have multiple test cases for a given test condition (requirement). For example, to test that number of passenger field inputs only numeric value, we will prepare a test case as given below.

Purpose: To Ensure that field number of tickets do not accept any character other than number

Precondition: Application is successfully logged in and ticket booking form is already opened

Inputs and expectations

Input	Expectations
4	System accepts the input
Blank	System Displays Error message

Test cases could be documented in Excel or using any other tool. Please also note that test cases may include many other details apart from what is described above. Those details are explained in Test design section of chapter 6 – Testing execution process.

Test cases need to be developed, reviewed and managed (keep updating as required) on an on-going basis.

Test Design: A process of creating/developing effective and efficient test cases

Test Execution means, we have to establish the necessary preconditions (bring the application and data in a state before we actually proceed further), provide necessary inputs as documented, observe the output and compare with the expected output to determine whether the test has passed or not.

If the expected output and actual output do not match, we conclude that test case has failed and there is a bug in the system.

Testing (or Test execution) technique: The method used to perform the actual test execution, either manual or automated.

There are two testing techniques applied as given below.

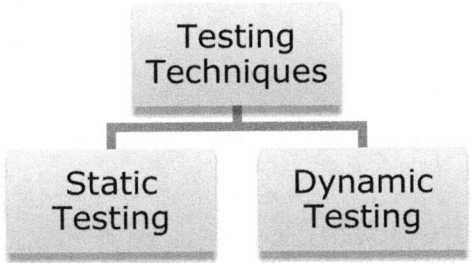

Static testing: Testing of a component or system at specification or implementation level **without execution** of that software.

So, Static testing is done during requirement Analysis, Design and Coding stage and involves analysis of software artefacts/work products such as requirement specification, design or code. Even if static testing is done on code, it is done without execution of code.

Dynamic testing: Testing that involves the execution of the software of a component or system.

With dynamic testing methods, software is executed using a set of input values and its output is then examined and compared to what is expected. It involves executing the software – provide inputs, process and validate output.

We will study each of the techniques in detail in subsequent sections.

Test Design Techniques

As we had seen earlier that exhaustive testing to ensure that there are no bugs in the system is not possible. We saw in section 1.2, Challenges and limitations of testing, that considering all permutations and combinations for even a single input field are enormous and may take years.

In order to meet objective of finding maximum defect in minimum time and effort, we have to select a subset of all possible tests (combinations) and still, it has to have a high probability of finding most of the defects in a system. It should also avoid any redundant test case that can find same defect which could be found by other test case.

The test design techniques provides guidelines through which we can focus on all potential errors and restricts number test cases to essentially required for testing. They help us to optimize the testing – Not too much and not too less testing.

Note that every application can be viewed from developer's angle and from business angle.

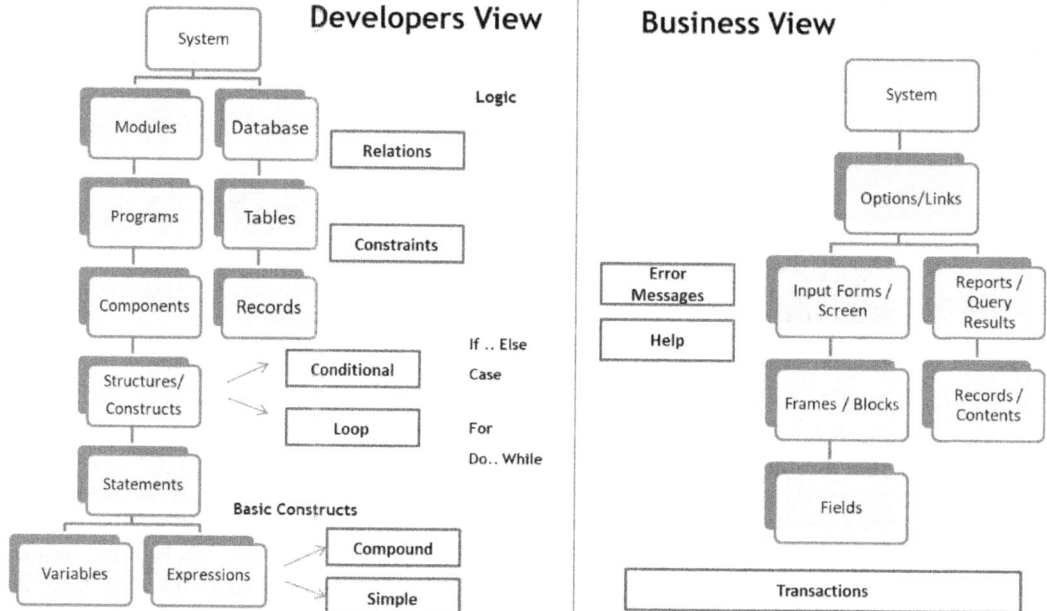

Developers View – the way developers look at the system focusing on how the requirements are implemented in terms of modules, programs/functions/classes, constructs and statements used.

Business View – the way the end users look at the system for the usage. They see Application home page, links menu options, forms and reports etc. They do not see what is behind and how the content of the pages, forms and reports are done.

The items which are to be tested hence depends on both these views

Testing from a Developer Point of view

    Function Specification and Design documents

    Various Code components

        Data structures

        Control structures

        Constraints and business logic implemented in code

    Interfaces between components / modules and outside applications

Testing from a business point of view

    User Interface:

        Layout, alignment, consistency, Sequence

    Inputs to be taken – Forms / Pages

    Constraint on field – Length, type, Minimum / maximum value, Mandatory?, Value in relation to other value

        How to handle wrong inputs-   Error Messages

    Process:

        Calculated / Derived fields

        State Transition – Updates

        Business process Rules and Constraints

    Output: Query Results, Reports, Details to other applications

The **Test design techniques** are catering to both the views and aspects so that the issues are found from all angles at the earliest possible time and at the right place within the application.

Different techniques offer different ways of looking at the software under test. Each technique provides a set of rules or guidelines for the tester to follow in identifying test conditions and test cases. Test conditions should be able to be linked back to their sources in the test basis - this is called **traceability**.

So, <u>**Test design technique/ Test Specification Technique**</u> is a procedure used to derive and/or select test cases.

White-box testing: Testing based on an analysis of the internal structure of the component or system.

White-box test design technique: Procedure to derive and/or select test cases based on an analysis of the internal structure of a component or system.

It is Logic Driven, focusing Internal Design – Sequencing of statements, Decision structures, Loop structures

black-box testing: Testing, either functional or non-functional, without reference to the internal structure of the component or system.

Black box test design technique: Procedure to derive and/or select test cases based on an analysis of the specification, either functional or non-functional, of a component or system without reference to its internal structure. It is Business Driven.

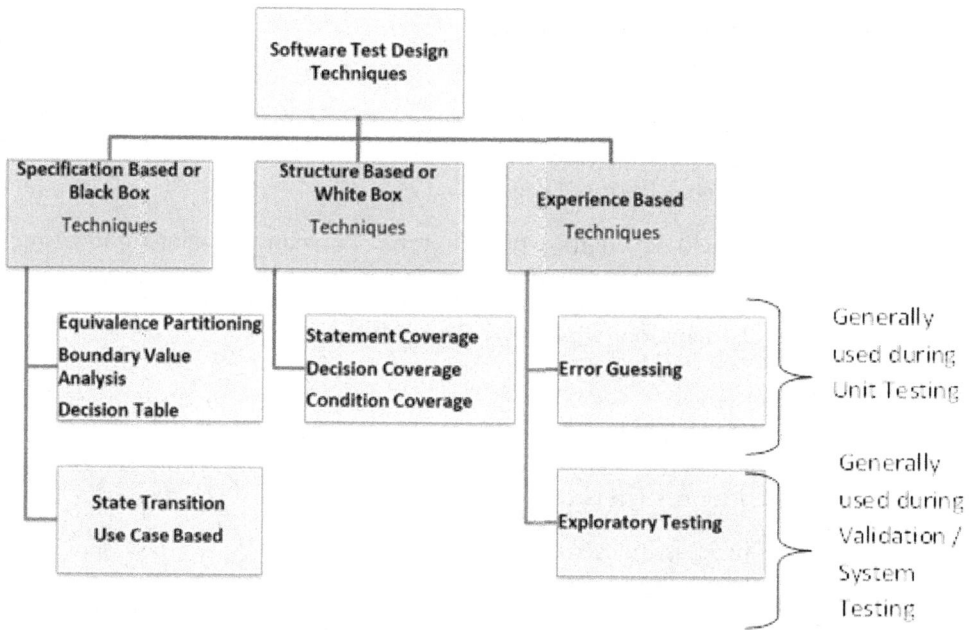

Please note that test design techniques showed at level one are generally used during Unit and Integration testing and shown at level 2 are generally used during Validation, System and Acceptance Testing. We will discuss all these techniques in details when we discuss testing levels - Unit, Integration, system and acceptance testing.

Test level: A group of test activities that are organized and managed together. A test level is linked to the responsibilities in a project.

Unit Testing, Integration Testing, Validation and System Testing and Acceptance Testing are called **levels** because they describe level at which the testing is done. You start with Unit Testing which is lowest level and keep moving at higher levels to integration, Validation and system testing and finally Acceptance Testing.

To reduce cost of testing, it is suggested that as soon as any component is developed, **unit testing** for that component should be done. As soon as some integration of two or more than two components take place, **integration testing** should be done and **system testing** should be done when entire system is ready. Users should carry our **User Acceptance Testing** only after Unit, Integration and System testing are completed.

Testing at each level helps to identify and fix as many defects as early as possible so that next level gets cleaner code and one can focus only on the specific aspects of the next level when next level testing is done.

All testing activities at each level are organized and managed together and generally activities of two different levels are not organized together. However, Test levels can be combined or recognized depending on the nature of the project or system architecture. For example, for the integration of a commercial off-the-shelf (COTS) software product into a system, the purchaser may perform integration testing at the system level (integration to infrastructure, and other systems or system deployment) and acceptance testing (functional or non-functional and user and / or operational testing)

Refer to the design phase of SDLC where it is depicted how business functions are realized using technical components. Also refer to Developer's view and Business View depicted above. Keeping that in mind the testing is suggested to be done in following sequence.

1) **Technical testing** – This is generally done using White box testing techniques
    a. Technical Unit Testing – Testing of each procedure, class, methods or any such unit
    b. Technical Integration Testing – Testing of interfaces between various technical components
2) **Business functionality Testing** – This is generally done using Black-Box Testing techniques
    a. **Business Unit / Function Testing** – Testing of each business functional unit such as view flights, book ticket, cancel ticket etc.
        - **Field level testing** (testing of each element on the input screen) – Testing of each field / element on the page/screen/form
        - **Business Function / Form Level testing** – Testing that a specific form is successfully saved, can be edited, can be cancelled/deleted successfully. For example a ticket can be booked, can be viewed, edited and or cancelled successfully as per the process and rules defined.
    b. **Validation & System Testing**: testing an integrated system to verify that it meets specified requirements. This is done after all the components/units are developed and tested. When individual business functions are tested, we do not worry for any of the upstream components or downstream components as they may or may not be ready. However when we do system testing, all the units are available and hence possible to carry out testing.

Practically I propose following approach to carry out system testing.

- **End-to-End Testing** (many times this is referred to be same as system testing but I consider a minor difference). This covers actual flow through a system in an end user scenario. For example, we test ticket booking process end to end with following steps with an assumption that individual functionalities are tested separately.

  Login to the application

  View Flight options

  Book a ticket – Select a flight, select date of travel, Provide passenger information, make payment etc

  Print a ticket

  Check the availability for updates

- **Life Cycle Testing** – This refers to the testing all functions required under different situation for the life of a specific entity or a transaction – from birth (initiation) to death (completion/deactivation). For example an entity 'ticket' comes into existence by booking and cease to die (become inactive) once the passenger has travelled on the ticket or cancelled it. There can be multiple functions in between for a given ticket such as Update, Print, Email, Upgrade, Check-in and so on.

c. **Acceptance Testing** – similar to business functionality testing with some real-life data done by the users before they accept the system.

We will discuss above levels in detail with corresponding test design technique in next few chapters.

Regression Testing: Every application undergoes changes during development and after implementation due to various reasons (including defect fixing). These changes may introduce new defects in the areas which were working fine earlier.

So, we need to test previously tested programs or functionalities in order to ensure that defects are not introduced and functionalities continue to work fine. This is known as regression testing.

Test Automation - Automate repetitive executions of the testing steps with the use of **special software** (separate from the software being tested). It helps to **set up test preconditions, control the execution of tests and the comparison** of actual outcomes to predicted outcomes and **report**.

Test automation is very useful for regression testing as the same tests are executed multiple times as and when the changes are done in the system.

Risk Based Testing – Even after applying various testing and test design techniques, teams may not have enough time to complete all the testing. In such case, functionalities and tests are prioritized based on various risks associated with those functionalities in to a) Must test b) should test c) could test and d) won't test.

Complete testing for functionalities, which must be tested, and then focus on other functionalities as per priority if time permits.

Software Testing Life Cycle

Testing is an immense activities and like there are Software Development life cycle (SDLC) phases, there are SW Testing Life Cycle (STLC) phases that covers

Test Strategy development: Considering scope and expectations of the application under test, strategy is prepared that answers questions such as - which type of requirements will be covered, what level of testing to be done, the rigor at which the testing to be done, which testing techniques to be applied, which tools to be used, whether to use automated testing and risk based testing or not etc.

Test Planning involves, people, schedule, roles and responsibilities, communication process etc.

Requirement Analysis and Ambiguity Reviews: Analyze the requirements, itemize them into individual testable requirements and identify if there are ambiguities in requirements.

Test Design: Identify and list down all test scenarios for each test type and test level

Test Construction/Test Case development: Derive and document detailed test cases describing the state in which the system should be for a specific test, various steps to be followed and various inputs to be provided at each step and the result expected at the end of each step or the entire test case. Develop Automation scripts if automation to be done and carry out risk analysis and prioritize tests, if in case risk based testing required.

Test Execution and Defect management: Run the application and execute each test case to actually check whether the actual result is as per expectation or not and if not report defect. Continue the process till all known defects are fixed, retested and closed.

Debugging means removing errors from your programs. Before we debug the program, we need to find errors and that is testing. So, Testing is different from **Debugging**.

2.2 SW Testing vs Other product testing

SW testing is no different than testing any other product. All manufacturing companies would test their product with respect to functional and non-functional requirements before launching their product in the market. Not only the final product, but all individual components of the product are first tested before they are assembled together.

Let us take an example from other industry.

Requirement: Assume that one of your relative has recently started a manufacturing unit to manufacture a pen which they plan to sell across the country. You are asked to do testing of the pen

Exercise: List down what are the aspects you will consider for testing

Answer: You will come up with 5 to 10 different aspects for testing. However if you really see, there would be plenty of aspects to be covered

Type:

Pen: Ball point, Ink, Scatch..	Reservation: Airline, Hotel, Bus…

Functionality

• Ability to write	• Ability to register
• Has a cap	• Ability to view various options
• Ability to hold and put in pocket	• Ability to book and cancel reservation
• Ability to put cap on the back side (depending on type)	• Ability to Print ticket or save for future purpose
• There is no bloating, fading or leakage	• User should be able to customize appearance
• Ability to put cap on the back side (depending on type)	• Ability to hold the transaction on halfway and continue after some time.
• Gripper to plug it on shirt	
• Effect on Paper – dries quickly, No bloating, no fading.	

Secure

• no leakage	• No unauthorised person can use • Information stored within the system should not be leaked outside.

Compatibility

• Should be able to write on different types of paper (Smooth, rough, card boards) • Standard refills can be used and replaced • Ability to keep it in standard size compass box	• The system can be access using any browser • It should support all mobile OS and device sizes

Usability – User interface

• Ink Color • Look and feel – Design, print color (of name) • Ability to hold properly - Firm grip, comfortable to hold for a longer time • Dimensions – length, weight – Do not get pain when use for long • Ability to be used by people of all age, all types of people • External material nontoxic (No risk for small children) • Ability to write from different angles – same quality, • Odour of ink • Writing – smoothness	• The UI of the system should be attractive, with consistent color and fonts • The font colors and contrast should be such that it does not give strain to eyes • It should easy to operate • Should use colours which can be recognized by colour blind people • The user should be able to reach to their specific task within 3 clicks. • It should provide multiple options to use /access a functionality – Type in, touch, click • Moving from one screen to other screen or directly moving to a specific option should be easy

Performance, Load and Stress

• Ability to quickly open and close • Works in extreme temperatures • Ability to write continuously (say for 5 hours) • Same quality even if you write very speedily • Ink does not dry up when it is kept open for long • Can it bear reasonable weight? • Should not break when you press it hard to surface while writing • Drop open pen from distance and check that it is not broken • Gripper does not break easily	• Application should respond very fast for all requests. • Even if number of users increases performance should not be degraded drastically • It should not create any issues with high volume of data inputs or fast actions. • System should not hang if user takes some more time for inputs unless to be halted due to security reasons • Even in case of power failure or abrupt interruption, it should not lose any data.

This example shows that, even for a very well-known product, that we use from our childhood, we are not able to come up with all the aspects to be covered for testing.

You will also see that many aspects are related to specific component of the pen and may not require the entire pen to be assembled before we do testing of those aspects

Unit Testing: Checking / Testing of individual component of the product or application

• Individual body parts • Ink, Refill, ballpoint (pointer thickness) • Pen Body, Spring (depending on type) • Cap • Pen Box	• Individual code components • Login Form • Registration form • Enquiry form • Ticket booking form • Ticket printing

Integration Testing

• Refill fits properly in the pen body • Cap fits properly on both the sides • Pen size is standard to be able to fit into compass box	• Registration information flows properly to further modules • Travel details entered in while booking is flown to ticket printing.

Conclusion:

SW is no different than pen or any such product. You need to do all types of testing for software as mentioned for pen

- o Requirement Coverage is key for any product. You need to get clarification if was not provided by your relative
- o There could be some explicit requirements and some implicit requirements (which will not be conveyed by customer)
- o There are functional (able to perform it's basic task properly) and non-functional requirements (qualitative aspects)
- o One need not wait till the final product is out for testing - Intermediate components should be tested before it goes into final product

2.3 Software Development Lifecycle Phases

Software testing could be well appreciated if we understand how large projects are developed in the industry. This will help us to understand when and how defects introduces (are injected) in the software and also to realize why and what kind of quality assurance activities could be done alongside the development phases.

Unlike very small assignments you do in college, real-life business applications are reasonably large requiring multiple modules and multiple programs within each module. Refer an industry case study given in section 1.1.2. Such application development takes lot of time and effort and hence requires not only large team but also a well-defined approach for entire development project. There are various approaches also known as 'Software Development Process Models' defined and used by different companies. For example, Waterfall Model, Incremental Model, Iterative Model RAD (Rapid Application Development) Model, Agile Model, Spiral Model, Prototype Model. Each process model follows a particular life cycle in order to ensure success in process of software development.

Software life cycle models describe phases of the software cycle and the order in which those phases are executed. However, every model uses following phases

- Requirement Understanding & Analysis:
- Design : Functional Design, Detailed Design, Program Specification
- Development / Coding:
- Testing: Unit Testing, Integration Testing, System Testing, Acceptance Testing
- Implementation

Notice that, Design and Testing phases are subdivided due to specific objectives.

Each phase produces deliverables required by the next phase in the life cycle.

Since our current focus is on testing newly developed application, we will not consider Implementation and Maintenance phases in our discussion.

Requirement Understanding & Analysis: All the business and functional requirements are gathered during this phase. For example, for an airline reservation system, you understand in very detail, all business functions such as passenger registration process, ticket booking process, cancellation process etc. Understand various business rules for each process such as maximum number of seats can be booked in single ticket. Refund rules for cancellation etc.

Design: Once the requirements are gathered, designers will design the computerized system. This will include Module design, User Interface Design, Database Design and so on. Subsequently, detailed specifications are developed for each program or a webpage to be developed.

Functional Design / Functional Specification Document: Defines how user requirement to be implemented by the software solution (functions and features such as view flights, book ticket, cancel ticket etc.). It may additionally include set up processes such as flight set up, staff set up, agency set up etc. It may be in one or more of various forms such as descriptions, use cases or user stories to explain what software does (or should do) to support business user for carrying out various functions.

For example, Function Specification for the ticket booking process could be as follows

- First time users will first register by giving all required personal details
- Registered user will login with valid user ID and password
- System will ask for travel date, class preference and number of passengers and based on that display various options.
- User will select a specific option and provide basic travel details.
- System will then ask for all passenger details. Subsequently it will allow user to make payment either through debit card/credit care/net banking.
- On successful payment, system will reserve the ticket and provide confirmation.
- User will be able to print the ticket immediately or at a later stage

Detailed Design: Detail design is more technical and would describe in detail covering procedural components, Data Model, User Interface, APIs, Web Services and Configurations and Parameters, etc. One other objective of the details design is to decompose the overall application function into various modules and various individual functional or technical components. Business function components are visible to the users and technical components are designed for simplicity maintainability and reusability. These components could be used / called by other calling functions.

Look at the following diagram that shows how reservation functionality is decomposed into various business functions and technical functions (boxes which are highlighted).

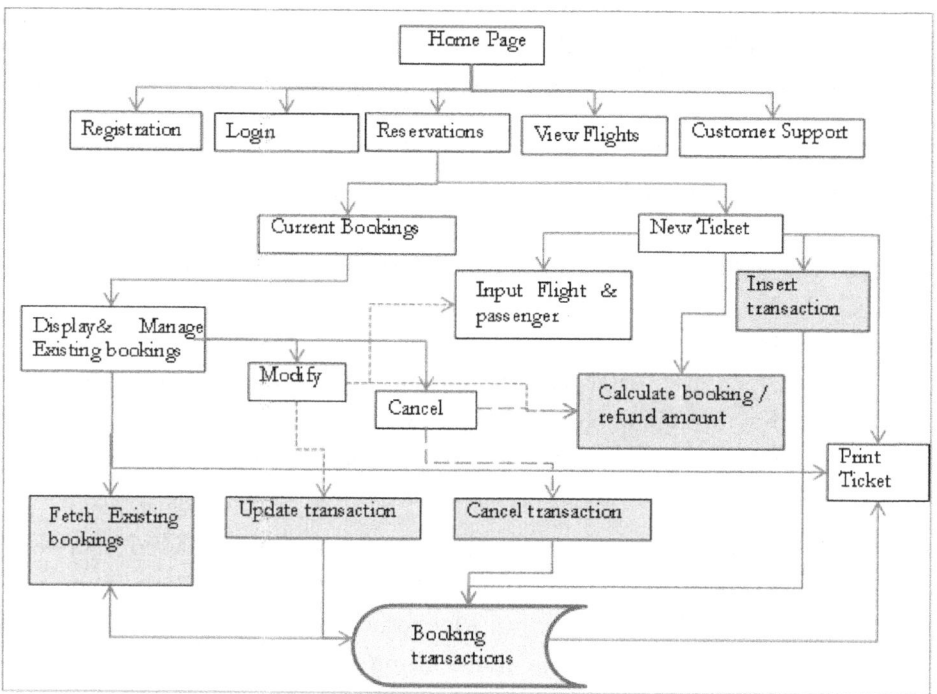

You can notice that many technical components are reused for different business functions. These are just sample business functions. There could be even more business functions such as register boarding of a passenger can call many of the components. Since each component needs to satisfy requirement of calling function, it could receive some parameters from the calling function to actually work as required.

So detailed design will also include how different components are integrated with each other (Through parameter passing or back-end data storage and retrieval or direct calls) to complete one specific task.

There could be integration with other modules also. For example, Ticket reservation module will internally call accounting module for the payment made by the user. It can also be integrated to Agent module if the booking is done by an agent on behalf of the passenger so that commission processing can be done accordingly.

Program Specification: Once detailed design is completed, program specifications are prepared for each program or a technical component we discussed above with the use of details described in detail design. It provides foundation for the programming methodology to the developer and gives details of what the computer program is expected to do. It covers user interface, what inputs to be taken, what processing to be done, what is to be stored in internal/external storage, interfacing details, what output to be generated and presented. For example, Program Specification for login page will provide

- o UI screen design for Login page covering User ID, Password, Submit button, change Password button
- o Rules for password, changing password etc
- o Where to check (which database table) correctness of password
- o What to do if details are not valid and which page to be displayed when details are valid

Development / Coding: Actual coding of various programs done using a specific programming language. Here as a developer you use syntax of the language and various programming constructs such as If... Then ... Else, Loops (While, Do ..Until, For), in a specific sequence.

Also note that whole application cannot be developed at a shot. Application is collection of different components integrated together for a specific purpose. As part of development process, first individual small components/programs/routines (called units) are developed. Integration of these components happens as more and more components get developed and when all components are developed and integrated, we get a full system.

Testing: The software is tested for it's correctness and completeness from requirement perspective during this phase.

SW Testing requires effort and hence cost. The amount of money we spend on testing should not be more than the benefit (or the cost we avoid due to faulty software) we receive. It is hence important to see that the cost of testing is as low as possible.

So instead of waiting for coding to be completed for entire application, Unit / component testing should be done as soon as specific unit or component/program is developed. Integration testing should be completed when two or more units are developed and individually tested. And System testing should be done once the development is completed for entire system. Finally, User Acceptance testing should be done by users or user representatives.

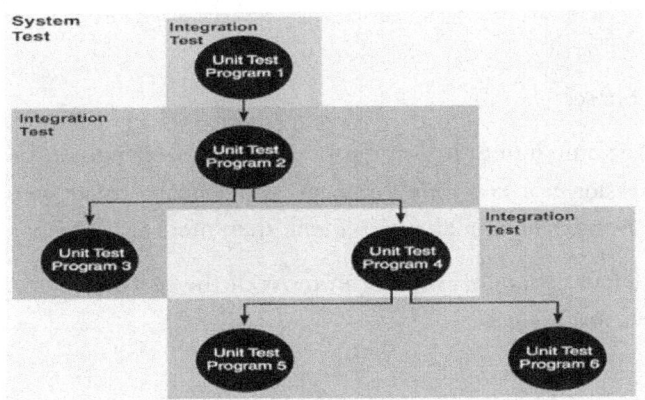

Unit testing / Component Testing: The testing of individual software components (smallest testable part of an application). To demonstrate that their smallest pieces of executable code function suitably. It is done based o program specification.

It is the most **'micro'** scale of testing and can be at a level of program, subprogram, subroutine, procedures, function or code modules, a class, or a stored procedure. The unit constitute of various statements, loops, if-then-else control structures, functions / procedure calls, assignments and related data – records, variables, constants etc.

Integration Testing: Testing performed to expose defects in the interfaces and interaction between integrated components. It verifies inter-component interfaces, external interfaces and user and business workflows. Testing of combined parts of an application to ensure that components of module or modules of an application are integrated properly and **function together** correctly. So, it focuses on the interfaces specified in detailed (low-level) design.

Validation testing: The process of testing an integrated system to verify that it meets specified requirements.

It demonstrates that the system works end-to-end in a production-like environment for all business functions specified in high level function design.

Primary focus is on checking that various functions / transactions expected to be performed by different users are working as expected.

Acceptance testing: Formal testing with respect to user needs, requirements, and business processes conducted to determine whether or not a system satisfies the acceptance criteria and to enable the user, customers or other authorized entity to determine whether or not to accept the system.

Acceptance testing done after the system testing is completed and almost all the defects found up to this stage are fixed. It verifies whether development team has met all the obligations and whether the system can be released or not. It also checks specific non-functional characteristics, e.g. usability, of the system.

2.4 SDLC – V Model

Defects introduced at all phases

Every application will take some input, do some processing and generate output. If inputs not taken properly, processing not correctly done or output not correctly generated and presented for any of the specific functional requirement, then there are defects

Let us see some typical defect generally available in most of the software systems with an example of Airline Reservation System

Sr.	Defect Description	Possible Root Cause
1.	Full name of one passenger did not appear on the ticket as his full name contained 34 characters but system printed only 30 characters	Maximum length of the name was never discussed during requirement gathering and assumed to be 30 **OR** Front end ticket booking form accepted 35 characters but database table contained only 30 characters for passenger name
2.	Number of tickets booked for a specific passenger was 0 instead of 4.	The input form allowed alphabetic character and user entered a space character along with number of tickets as 4 and hence database stored only 0.
3.	Passenger entered number of tickets as 12 but system allotted only 10 tickets	As per rule, more than 10 seats cannot be booked in a single ticket. The ticket booking program did not restrict but the seat allocation routine implemented the rule
4.	A passenger by mistake entered past date while booking a ticket and he faced lot of difficulties in recovering the amount as company had a rule that full payment can be refunded only if ticket is cancelled before travel	The input form for ticket booking did not check the date. As per rule booking can be done only for current or future dates but not before three months of travel date.
5.	The aircraft used for Ahmedabad-Mumbai flight did not have business class, but it allowed to book ticket for business class	The system did not have a proper check for the same. It should have either disabled the business class option or should have checked and displayed proper error message
6.	As per the functionality, user can enter various details for travel and save it without confirming the booking so that he/she can complete/modify the details at a later stage and confirm. But system did not allow to 'Edit' the details	The 'Edit' button is disabled in the initial stage. Only after ticket-booking details are submitted, it is enabled. However the program was wrongly coded to enable the 'update' button only when ticket booking is confirmed and not when the booking details are just saved without confirmation.
7.	Some passengers wanted to book ticket for Diwali vacation but when they were not getting response even after waiting for 2-3 minutes and they were closing the browser	During peak time, the server was overloaded and the response time drastically reduced as the reservation program was not optimized with release of unwanted memory, parallel processing and proper indexing of database
8.	One passenger complained that he being	As per discount calculation rule, Gold

	a frequent flyer (and hence was given a gold card) should have got 10% discount but he actually got only 5% discount	card members get 5% discount and gets additional 5% discount if they book more than 3 passengers in single ticket. The program was not coded properly to implement this rule correctly.
9.	The airline once realized that information of their passengers including their contact details etc were leaked to competitor.	Their registration process was weak and someone could inject a full query (to access passenger details) through UI of the registration form.

In general, some typical defects we notice in many applications are as given below

- Defects related to input
  o Allowing characters for fields accepting numeric values
  o Allowing more number of characters to be entered than system actually allows
  o System assumes some value when user do not input
  o Some inputs which are mandatory are not taken resulting in wrong process
- Defects related to Processing
  o Processing logic or formula not correct (Eg. Loan processing, Balance processing, Seat allocation process etc.)
  o Business rules are not correctly taken care of (Eg senior citizens should be given discount but not given)
  o Application not properly interfaced with other application correctly (Eg. Payment interface)
- Defects related to Output
  o Required information not printed completely or correctly
  o Details not organized properly or in consistent manner

As you can notice from above examples, defects may be related to Functional or Non-Functional requirement (eg. Speed, Security etc). Defect could be due to incorrect understanding and implementation of business processes and rules or due to incorrect coding – logical issues

Errors could also be due to environmental conditions, use of the system by hackers.

Defects are introduced in every phase of phase of SDLC. As per 'Defect Amplification Model' described by Pressman, errors get amplified by some factor if that error is not removed in that phase only. In fact the cost of removing error will keep increasing if the gap between introduction of error and removal of error increases.

Also note that some bugs are just the tip of the iceberg. So, if you find one bug and when you really do root cause analysis, you may find many more bugs.

Cost of fixing the defect increases when it is found later as root cause analysis and correction may be required at all previous phases. For example, if it was discussed during requirement stage about maximum number of characters to be allowed for a passenger name or could have been reviewed at the time of design, the 1st defect related to truncation of name could have been avoided. Similarly, if it was tested immediately after development of ticket booking program that number of tickets should accept only digits, defect number 2 regarding system storing 0 tickets could have been avoided.

Let us understand why impact of the defect introduced in one phase becomes more and more expensive when the gap between defects introduction phase and identification phase.

	Defects introduction and identification stages.	Implication
Req 1	Requirement was wrongly understood and the issue was reported only after implementation	Effort for design, coding testing, implementation waste. Will impact prestige also.
Req 2	Requirement was understood correctly, Design was correct but there was a bug in coding but defect found in implementation	Additional effort will be required to change the code, functional testing, regression testing and implementation. Could also impact prestige
Req 3	There was a defect in coding and was found during testing	Only coding and testing effort will be waste. Additional effort required for changing the code and testing the functionality again after correction
Req 4	There was a requirement issue and coding also was not proper. Only Coding defect was found and then requirement defect was found during implementation	1st time effort will go for debugging, testing and implementation and 2nd time additional effort will be required for all the phases.
Req 5	There was a design issue and defect was found during testing phase	Additional effort will be required to identify root cause, redesign, recode and retesting of the functionality

As you would have noticed in above example, if the defect is introduced in a specific phase and is found in much later phase, rework may be required in all the phases in between and hence the cost of fixing defect in such case is higher than the defect which is found in same or immediate next phase. Many times even more effort goes in testing some other functionality again to ensure that these functionalities are not impacted due to changes done in system to solve some other defects.

It is also important to consider that a relatively minor error left early in the process can be amplifies into a major set of errors later. Study following diagram showing increase in cost based on data collected by Bohm and Basil [Boe01b] and illustrated by Cigital [Cig07]. The cost is an industry average cost

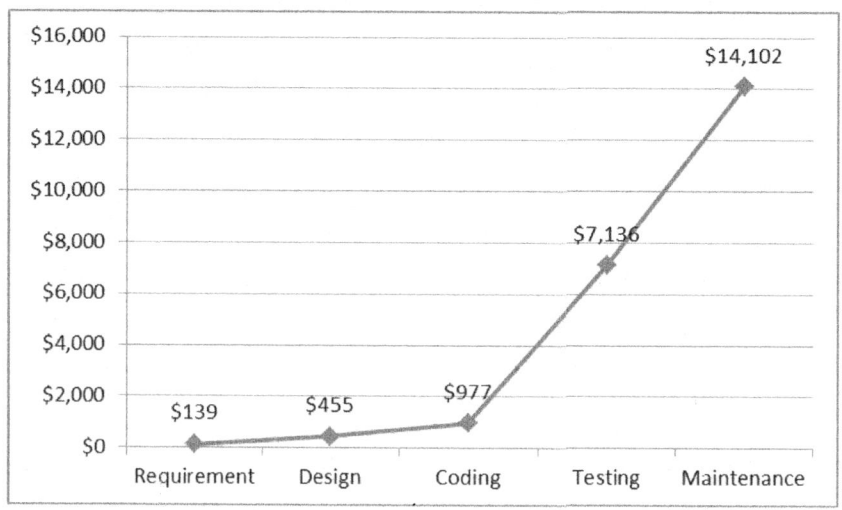

While the actual cost may vary from project to project, it is important to know that cost of testing (finding and fixing defect) later is much higher (some time exponentially higher) than cost of testing and finding defects early. There is tremendous intangible loss if customer faces defects. We may lose customers to competitors

The cost of testing itself should be lower than potential loss of not finding the same. So, Testing must end when the economic returns cease to make it worthwhile i.e. the costs of testing process significantly outweigh the returns.

It is hence important to reduce cost of testing by discovering and removing defects early in the life cycle and also reduce overall cost by taking measures to prevent the defects getting introduced.

2.4.1 V Model

The diagram given below which depicts SDLC phases on the left side, Testing levels on the right side and relationship between them through.

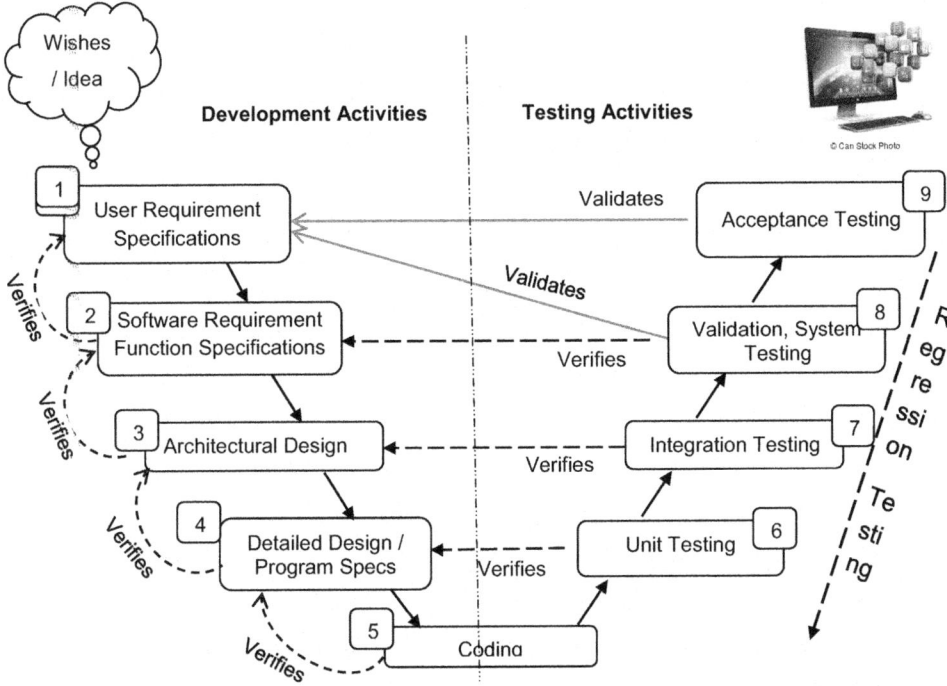

We will discuss Verification and Validation, Testing levels and testing techniques used at each level in next two sections keeping this diagram in mind.

As you can see in the above diagram there are four main SDLC phases. After each phase you carry out low level checking or verification to ensure that the phase is completed accurately in accordance with previous phase and as per the defined processes. For examples, once all the user requirements are collected and documented, a review takes place to ensure completeness, clarity and correctness of the requirements. This is known as verification for requirements. Users will be accepting the final application based on these requirements and hence, Requirement Specification documents become input to Acceptance Testing which is the last phase/level from testing perspective.

After requirement analysis is completed and documented, function design or Software Requirement specification is done for the application being developed. Again detailed review takes place to ensure that design is being developed in a right manner as expected, taking Requirement Specification Document as input. The system once fully developed will be tested based on this functional design. Hence, Functional Specification document becomes base for Validation testing.

Similarly Architectural design phase delivers high level design document which becomes input to program specifications for development and input to Integration testing phase for testing.

Program specifications or detailed design are prepared based on architectural high level design and are referred for unit testing.

In general, you start from upper left SDLC phase on top and move down to next phase below and once coding is completed based on program specifications, all testing levels starts from Unit Testing and then moves up on the right side to Integration testing, Validation & System testing and finally Acceptance testing.

As you can see, this forms V shape and hence this model is popularly known as V model. The V proceeds from left to right – top to bottom, depicting the basic sequence of development and then once coding is completed it proceeds from left to right – bottom to top, depicting basic sequence of software testing levels and their dependence on SDLC phases

You can notice several characteristics of good testing in the V model.

- For every development activity there is a corresponding testing activity
- Each test level has test objectives specific to that level
- The analysis and Design of tests for a given test level can begin during or immediately after the corresponding development activity
- Testers can be involved in reviewing documents as soon as drafts are available in the development life cycle.

2.4.2 Verification and Validation

Verification and Validation is a disciplined approach for assessing software products throughout the product life cycle and employs various reviews, analysis and testing techniques to ensure that quality is built into the software and the system developed meets the user requirements.

Verification - Are we building the product right? This refers to the processes involved to verify that all the activities performed before completion of development are proper as planned and expected (as per specifications defined in previous phase).

In a typical software development life cycle, there are many human resources (Analysts, Designers, Coders, Testers and Customers) involved at each phase to perform lot of activities and create a work product that is used as an input in the next phase. This may lead to inconsistency, incorrect conduct/implementation of specific activity, which can result into an issue in the final product. So, Various reviews at each stage are very important.

So, **Verification**

- Is a set of activities to ensure that the work product correctly reflects the expectations specified
- Examines the work product of each development activity to ensure that it meets the pre-defined set of requirements and standards. So, at each stage, the team needs to ensure that whatever they do is in conformation to previous stage – Design should conform to requirements, Program specifications should conform to design and Code should conform to program specification. Integrated components should conform to architectural design.
- In general review/analysis of all the phases shown on the left side of the V model and even unit and integration testing shown on the right side can be termed as verification. Refer section 2.4.1.
- Related activities are considered to be lower level of test activities as they are done before the code construction is completed.
- It primarily uses static testing methods such desk-checking, inspection, walk-through and does not involve execution of code. Some amount of execution do take place during unit and integration testing.
- It is also called a **Quality Assurance/improvement** process as the issues are identified and resolved before the development/coding completes, preventing defects getting into the fully developed code.
- Activities are normally conducted by development team – generally by expert, lead or any other senior person
- Is an approach for ensuring that we are doing things rightly through the process and it answers the question – **"Are we building the product, Right?"** – Is our construction process correct?

Validation (Have we built the right product?) – This refers to the processes involved to ensure that the *product already developed* meets customer requirements. Even if the current product developed, does not have any issues (as all issues were resolved based on verification process implemented) may not meet the exact/all customer requirements. Validation testing starts once the development activity is completed.

So **Validation**

- is a Dynamic process (by executing the code) of validating/testing the actual product developed against customer requirements
- targets actual product developed – generally the entire system depending on the test conditions
- is known as **Quality Control** process, as the defects were already there in the code developed but are found and removed before the application goes into production.
- is aimed to ensure that the software is traceable to customer requirements by testing under actual or simulated user conditions. It confirms that the product will fulfil its intended use and answers the question – **"Have we built the right Product?"**

- These tests are generally conducted by independent test team and users also get involved.
- It can catch errors that verification process cannot

2.4.3 Who should do Validation / System Testing

All the reviews, Unit testing and Integration testing is done by development team but validation/system testing is generally done by independent team. The primary reason is to bring unbiased checking of the software developed and also to bring in specialized yet independent perspective about the system functionalities. There are many chances that if developer himself/herself does testing, he/she is likely to miss many aspects which he/she has already missed while development.

There are key benefits of having independent testing teams as given below.

- Mindset Change – To prove that SW does not work and not to prove that it works – Aptitude towards identifying problems and work until resolved

- Technical Independence.
    - Expertize with techniques, tools, processes and best QA practices.
    - Business/user perspective
    - Unbiased review
    - Managerial Independence. Testing activities managed and controlled independently
    - Independent appraisal and growth path. Reporting hierarchy not leading to managers from development team
    - No influence from Development

- Financial Independence. Budget for V&V is not in anyway controlled by those responsible to design & development.
    - Budget set aside for QA is not cut just because AD eats up more budget
    - Investments on tools and processes can be made even if returns come at a later part of the project

2.5 Seven Testing Principles (ISTQB)

After getting overview of Software Testing and before getting into lot of details, let us understand 7 principles of Software Testing derived based on past 40+ years of experience. These principles offer general guidelines common for all testing projects.

Principle 1: Testing shows presence of defects

Testing can show that defects are present but cannot prove that there are no defects. Testing reduces the probability of undiscovered defects remaining in the software, but even if no defects are found, it is not a proof of 100% correctness.

Principle 2: Exhaustive testing is impossible

Testing of everything (all combinations of inputs and preconditions) is not feasible except for trivial cases. Instead of exhaustive testing, techniques and / or risk analysis and priorities should be used to focus testing effort

Principle 3: Early Testing

To find defects early, testing activities should be started as early as possible in the software or system development life cycle, and should focus on defined objectives at that stage.

Principle 4: Defect Clustering

Testing efforts shall be focused proportionately to the expected and later observed defect density of modules. A small number of modules usually contains most of the defects discovered during pre-release testing, or is responsible for most of the operational failures. So, more focus should be given to those few modules.

Principle 5: Pesticide Paradox

When farmers go on using same pesticide repeatedly, insects become immune to the pesticide after some time. Similarly, if the same tests are executed over and over again, they will no longer find any new defects. To overcome this 'pesticide paradox', test cases must be regularly reviewed and revised and new test cases need to be written to exercise different parts of the software or system to find potentially more defects.

Principle 6: Testing is context dependent

Testing is done differently in different context. For example safety critical software is tested differently and with in-depth focus as compared to an informative website.

Principle 7: Absence of errors fallacy

Finding and fixing of defects does not help if the system built is unusable and does not fulfil the user's needs and expectations. It is hence important to first ensure that software system provides functionalities required by the customer/user before ensuring that these are designed and developed correctly.

2.6 Summary

In order to ensure that quality is getting built from the beginning of the software development, we need to align softer testing activities to Software Development Activities.

All the software development models (Waterfall, Incremental, RAD...) include some standard **phases** of software development executed in specific order as specified by the model. These phases include – **Requirement Analysis, Design (Functional Specification, Architectural detail design, Program Specifications), Development/Coding, Testing and Implementation**. Most applications are decomposed in to module and components (business or technical) (Procedures / functions / objects / APIs / Web Services…).

Similarly Testing is again divided into different **testing levels – Unit** Testing, **Integration** Testing, **validation & System** Testing and **Acceptance** Testing.

Software testing is very similar to testing of any other product such as pen.

We then covered various standard terminologies used – Software, System, Business Function/transaction, Defect. Etc.

In simple terms testing is a process of finding errors so that we get confidence that the software has implemented all the required functions correctly and completely and does not give unexpected output.

Testing can involve positive testing (application should behave as expected when valid data provided) and Negative Testing (application should not do things when it is not supposed to do when invalid data provided).

We also discussed some important terms in little more details such as

Testing Types: It indicates what (Which aspects) do we test. There are two primary types

    Functional: To check that all the functions (business functions) are working correctly as expected

    Non-Functional: To check qualitative aspect – How good these functions are implemented. So it covers Security, Performance, Usability, compatibility etc.

As part of the testing process, we need to develop test cases based on test conditions. **Test condition** is something that we could test and **test case** covers a set of input values, execution preconditions, execution steps, Expected results and execution post conditions.

Testing Techniques: Testing can be done without executing the program (by reviewing the document/code) which is known as **Static Testing** and by executing the program which is known as **Dynamic testing**.

Test Design Techniques: Testing is an immense activity and requires lot of time and effort. Primary objective is to find defect and if hence it is important to ensure that we **cover all possible scenarios** that can result in defect and avoid unnecessary tests which do not have potential to find new /different defects. There are various **techniques** (guidelines) developed keeping in mind two different angles of the software. The internal view and the external view. Techniques based on internal view (focusing on actual system architecture and code) are known as **White-Box** test design techniques and the techniques developed for the external / business view are known as Black-**box** test design techniques.

In order to find defects early testing should start as early as possible. **Testing Levels: Unit testing** is done as soon as specific program or unit of the application is ready, **Integration testing** is done when more than one unit-tested programs are integrated for their interface related requirements and **validation and System testing** is done when the entire system is ready for ensuring that various business functions are correctly implemented through more than one interfaced programs. Lastly Users do **Acceptance Testing.** Unit and Integration testing is again done from technical perspective and from business perspective.

We also briefly introduced **Regression Testing** which is done to ensure that any changes/enhancements done in the application does not introduce new defect and because of that any functionality which was working earlier does not work now as expected.

Even after applying various techniques, we may not get enough time and effort to cover all the test cases in our testing. We need to hence either **automate** some tests which are expected to be run more frequently with every release or we may have to do **Risk based testing,** whereby we prioritize the tests in order of importance so that we can skip non-important tests if time is not available.

Like Quality of development is important, Quality of testing is equally or even more important. Process oriented organization collects various product and process related data to generate some **quantitative measures known as metrics** to check the quality of testing. This includes coverage metrics, Process Metrics and productivity metrics.

Since entire testing process needs to cover all types, all levels, apply various techniques, it become a huge project and needs proper planning and monitoring of various activities. Validation and System testing particularly requires various **SW Testing life Cycle phases** to be followed in a planned manner. These phases include - Requirement Analysis and Ambiguity Reviews, Test Design, Test Construction, Test Execution with defect management and closure activities.

While planning and implementing all these activities we will keep the seven principles in mind.

In order to ensure that the system is being built correctly, we do various verification activities at the end of each phase or testing level (Are we building the product right?) and once the full system is developed, we do **Validation** against customer requirements (Are we building the right product?). Verification covers reviews / inspection of all the deliverables of each SDLC phases. Validation is a post development testing activity to ensure that whatever we develop is as expected by the user. Each SDLC phase on the left side of V model is linked to the testing level depicted on the right side.

There are seven generic principles one need to keep in mind for any type of project

1) Testing shows presence of defects, 2) Exhaustive testing is impossible, 3) Early Testing, 4) Defect Clustering, 5): Pesticide Paradox, 6) Testing is context dependent, 7) Absence of errors fallacy

2.7 Exercise

Sr.	Question
1.	Give at least 4 difference between positive and negative testing
2.	Testing which checks what system should not do is known as _____ testing.
3.	What is the difference between Functional and non-functional requirements? Explain with examples
4.	Cost of testing later is _____ than cost of testing early.
5.	It is not necessary to check that the software does not do what it is not supposed to do (T/F?)
6.	There are two testing techniques _____ and _____
7.	In a quick testing you have done, if you find more defects in one specific module, you can conclude that further testing will reveal more defects in other module. True/False?
8.	What is the difference between testing and debugging?
9.	Testing is in a way a destructive process. True/false
10.	The probability of the existence of more errors in a section of a program is proportional to the number of errors already found in that section. True/False
11.	Unit testing is done based on program specifications. T/F?
12.	Verification is other name of Validation
13.	Discuss Verification vs Validation with suitable example
14.	_____ means to check Are we building the right product?
15.	Draw V Model diagram and explain what arrows going to Validation Testing indicate?
16.	Functional specification/design is input to system testing. True or False?
17.	In the overall system development life cycle, which team are involved in which type or level of testing, why?
18.	Considering V Model, explain what are the basis (Inputs) for each testing phase
19.	What are the testing levels? How do they relate to development phases in waterfall model?
20.	Integration test cases are based on program specifications True/False?

3 Verification of Development Deliverables – Quality Assurance

3.1 Introduction

As discussed in the previous section, SW verification in general would mean verification of all the processes and phases to assure that whatever done till now and during the phase is good enough to build (develop) a quality application. This would typically mean, review of requirements, design and code such that the code which is constructed will meet the expectations. Thorough review of requirements and design are also important because the cost of fixing defects related to requirements and design is very high if not detected and fixed in time.

3.2 Requirement Analysis and Ambiguity Reviews

Let us first understand what we mean by requirement

Requirement is a **capability needed** by a user to solve a problem or **achieve an objective** that must be met or possessed by a system or system component. It could be to satisfy a contract, standard, specification, or other formally imposed document.

Having complete and clear understanding of requirements is very important. Incomplete and wrong understanding of requirements can lead to an erroneous system.

All the requirements are described in Requirement Specification Document. In general the specification document can be defined as below.

Specification: A document that specifies, ideally in a complete, precise and in verifiable manner, the requirements, design, behaviour, or other characteristics of a component or system, and, often, the procedures for determining whether these provisions have been satisfied. [After IEEE 610].

Note that, the requirements need to be understood by both developers and independent testers (who will be involved in Validation and System testing). Clear understanding of requirements will be useful to development team for developing correct application and will be useful for independent testing team to check that the application is as per requirements.

3.2.1 Challenges of Requirements

In reality, there are many issues/challenges in the requirements gathered, as described below, which can lead to incomplete or wrong understanding.

- **Requirements not clearly (explicitly) defined** – It is practically impossible to describe each requirements in detail. Business users also expect that people involved in development and testing have some level of understanding of the domain (E.g. Insurance, Finance etc) and standard operating practices within the industry.

- **Communication issues** – There are three basic communication issues that can result into incomplete / wrong understanding of the requirements
  - **Omissions** – Generally, system under development has **many users** and requirements are to be gathered from many of them. Many requirements either are missed out, because some of the users **do not have enough time or simply forget**.

    Requirements **not commonly used** are generally missed out.

    Focus is generally given on **what happens** and **what is not supposed to happen** is missed out.

    Omissions occur on the receiver side also. No human being can grasp 100% requirements.

  - **Untold assumptions** – The provider of the requirements and the receiver of the requirements both take some assumptions. These assumptions if not right, may result into bugs.
  - **Misunderstanding** – Everyone has different level of knowledge and background and likely to misunderstand what is provided. Misunderstanding also happens if the requirements are ambiguous.
- **Criticality, Priority not provided** – Most projects get into quality and timeline issues. Clear understanding of criticality or priority of the requirement help in such situations. However this information is not generally available.

Let us take one small example to understand these issues

User: I want a small vehicle to travel in the city

Developer: assumes a bicycle would best suit and conveys that it will be ready in a month's time and starts building bicycle

After 2 weeks, User says – 'By the way, it should be able to transport 4-5 people even in the rains' – (He assumes a kind of a car)

Developer has already started building a bicycle so he just modifies the designs to extend the middle rod to accommodate 4 seats between two wheels.

The example does not appear to be realistic but in software industry, something similar is very likely to happen.

3.2.2 Requirement verification, Ambiguity Reviews

In the current industry scenario of high outsourcing and offshorization, possibilities of incompleteness and misunderstanding of requirements, are even higher as there are language barriers and differences in terminologies. Many times, multiple vendors / teams are involved resulting into different understanding of requirements by different teams.

The primary objective of the **Requirement review** process is to **evaluate correctness, completeness, accuracy, consistency, testability and clarity** of requirements.

Requirement Ambiguities: A requirement is considered **ambiguous**, if it can create misunderstanding or different understanding to different people.

In order to avoid any opportunity of requirement related issues mentioned above, it is important to analyse the requirements for Ambiguities and report as defects of requirements.

Refer to following Problem statement for a Web based application requirement

---

The application allows user/members to book travel ticket online. The home page will have a provision to either create a new account or to login with existing account. All valid members (registered users) should be able to view various options for booking the tickets. However, even if you are not a member, you can see schedule between two locations. There are three membership categories Silver Gold and Platinum. Such card members do not have to pay any reservation fees.

Any adult can create a new account by providing user ID and Password. Registration form should input personal information – Name, Gender, Marital status, Birth date and Contact details such as full address, phone number, and mobile number. Once registered, user can book ticket online. The eTicket will be emailed to user. Gold card members get sms in addition to email.

If booking is done for return journey or number of seats booked are four or more and gold card member, you get 10% discount.

Company should have travel service from the locations specified. System should propose and passenger can book tickets to nearby locations if there is no travel service between the specified locations

Application/system should be user friendly and have a provision to provide help wherever you feel important.

Read the above requirement thoroughly and **note down ambiguous requirements** (requirements not clearly understood or may result in different understanding). We will discuss various ambiguities in the above requirements after understanding different types of ambiguities.

Following are various reasons because of which ambiguities arise. We may also refer them as different **ambiguity types**.

- **Sloppiness:** absence of due or proper care or attention

    Example: Following paragraph is written in an airline safety booklet (found in the seat pocket)

    "If you are sitting in an exit row and you cannot read this card or cannot see well enough to follow these instructions, please tell a crew member".

    If this is the only mode of communication to the passengers then there is an issue because if the passenger cannot read properly, then he/she cannot read the instructions provided in the booklet. So how can he/she tell crew member? Such instruction hence should be provided verbally.

- **Linguistic Ambiguity**

    One half of two and four = ??

    One may consider the answer to be 3 if you assume **One half of (two and four)** or

    One may consider the answer to be 5 if you assume it to be **(one half of two) and four.**

    The answer can be even different if meaning of 'and' is assumed to be multiplication instead of addition.

- **Dangling Else**

    The requirements which uses any of **MUST BE, WILL BE, IS ONE OF, SHOULD BE, COULD BE, CAN BE, SHALL** will result in ambiguity as there is no clarity what should be done if this is not true (Else part is not clear)

    Example:

    "The loan type should be first or second."

    Question: What should be done if the loan type is different? Should an error message be displayed and allow for correction or the processing should be stopped? The requirement is incomplete if this question is not answered.

- **Ambiguity of Reference**

    Many times some statements are used which refer to some details provided earlier in the document. If the reference is not explicit, the understanding can be wrong.

    Example: "Add Amount to Account-Balance. This number must be positive."

    Question: Which number must be positive? Amount or Account-Balance or both?

    Example:

    "Transaction 1 displays the customer's name and address.

    Transaction 2 displays the customer's account numbers.

    Transaction 3 displays the customer's account balances.

    Such transactions require the security code."

    Question: Which transactions require security code - only transaction 3 or all the above transactions?

- **Omissions**

    Applications generally produces some output (effects) based on some type of inputs (causes). However it is likely that one of the causes or effects may be missing.

    Causes without effects: Sometimes requirements are described such that effect is given for some causes but not for all. In other words, impact of certain inputs are not provided

    Example. "Code could be 1,2,3,4 or 5. Codes 1 through 4 produce the message."

    Question: Should the message be produce when code = 5 or not? If not, what should be done?

    Effects without causes: Sometime effects are given but which cause is resulting into the effect is not provided

    Example. "This message sometimes appears." —

    Question What exactly you mean by sometimes – 10%/50%/80% times? And under which specific situation the message should appear?

    Example "It is sometimes necessary for the operator to re-initialize the field."

    Question: It is given that operator should re-initialize but not clear when exactly it should be done

Complete omissions

Example: A Blank Line/Para/Page

Certain paragraphs may be missing or the page is completely blank

Question: Are there any details really missing or the page is intentionally kept blank?

Missing causes: Sometimes real cause is missing

Example - "If you drive through a red light you may get a ticket."

Missing - you must be caught doing it to get a ticket

Example- "If the number is 1, 3, 5, 7, 11, 13, 19, 23, or 29 it is a prime number."

Missing - 2, 17. They are also prime numbers.

Missing effects: A cause can have multiple effects. Not all are provided.

Example - "If the account is overdrawn reject the check."

Missing - notify the customer.

- **Ambiguous Logical Operators**

    What people write **"A and B produce C."** :This is confusing and may be interpreted as

    A and B each produce C -> If (A or B) then C

    Or "A and B together are required to produce C ->If (A and B) then C.

- **Confusing Compound operators**

    "If A or B and C produce D."

    This is also confusing. If [A or B] and C produce D? **OR** If A or [B and C] produce D?

- **Ambiguous Statements**

    Ambiguous verbs: Calculate, update, produce, modify:

    Example: "If it is month end calculate the interest earned."

    Question: What is the exact formula to calculate or what exactly to be updated?

    Ambiguous variables:

    Example: "If the interest amount is greater than $100, send notice to the customer."

    Question: Which Interest - Interest accrued? Or Interest earned? Or Interest paid? Or Interest anticipated?

Ambiguous adjectives:

   Example: "It is against the law to ride down the street on an *ugly* horse." *Law in Wilbur, Washington*

   Question: How to decide which horse is ugly? What is the actual meaning of ugly.

Ambiguous adverbs:

   Example: "The delete transaction must be processed *quickly*."

   Question: What is meaning of quickly? 5 seconds/ 5 minutes/ one hour?

   Example: "Field A is *usually* positive."

   Question: What is meaning of usually?

So, there are multiple reasons and challenges because of which requirements may be interpreted differently than expected and such ambiguities should be immediately clarified. This process is called Ambiguity Review process. Many organizations consider this as a very critical process and all ambiguities are sometimes termed as **defects in requirements** and reported similar to defects.

Ambiguity review **enables Timely feedback -** early in development life cycle and hence leads to **defect avoidance**

If you are expected to write requirements after gathering verbal requirements, then it is suggested to use some **tips** as provided below

o   Be sensitive to the language issue and use **simple, straightforward** words.
o   **Eliminate instances of careless writing** so that requirements are not ambiguous
o   Ask non-domain experts to do ambiguity reviews so that you eliminate assumed functional knowledge.
o   Avoid **Jargons** or define various terminologies in the glossary.
o   **Define Acronyms** in the data dictionary.

After having detailed understanding of how requirements could remain incomplete or can be misunderstood, let us revisit the problem statement defined earlier in the section and find out ambiguities

---

The application allows user/members to book travel ticket online. The home page will have a provision to either create a new account or to login with existing account. All valid members (registered users) should be able to view various options for booking the tickets. However even if you are not a member, you can see schedule between two locations. There are three membership categories Silver, Gold and Platinum. Such card members do not have to pay any reservation fees.

Any adult can create a new account by providing user ID and Password. Registration form should input personal information – Name, Gender, Marital status, Birth date and Contact details such as full address, phone number, and mobile number. Once registered, user can book ticket online. The eTicket will be emailed to user. Gold card members get sms in addition to email.

If booking is done for return journey or number of seats booked are four or more and gold card member, you get 10% discount.

Company should have travel service from the locations specified. System should propose and passenger can book tickets to nearby locations if there is no travel service between the specified locations

Application/system should be user friendly and have a provision to provide help wherever you feel important.

Following are the ambiguities in the above requirement document

- There are three membership categories Silver, Gold and Platinum. Such card members do not have to pay any reservation fees. – **Question:** Which card members do not have to pay reservation fees – Platinum or all the three?
- Any adult can create a new account – **Question:** Which age to be considered for considering adult? Note that different countries may have different rules. There could be difference for Male and Female.
- Registration form should input personal information – Name…… **Question:** What if some information not provided? Which are mandatory and which are not mandatory?

    Gold card members get sms in addition to email. **Question1:** Why only Gold Card members? Why not Platinum? From our general understanding platinum category is higher than gold category. So, if some benefit is given to gold card members at least that much benefit should be given to platinum card members also. **Question2:** eMail is sent to all types of members or only Gold Card members? **Question3:** Email ID is not taken as input- Should it be added?

- for return journey or number of seats booked are four or more and gold card member, you get 10% discount.
  Question: Which of the following to be considered?

    (return journey or number of seats booked are four or more) and gold card member
    OR
    (Return journey) or (number of seats booked are four or more and gold card member)?
- Passenger can book tickets to nearby locations. **Question:** How much distance is considered as nearby?

You may also need to clarify some missing processing rules as provided below.

- What is the process of becoming member? What are the criteria for each membership type?
- What is the cancelation process? Modification process?
- …..
- …..

You will now understand that some requirements which look almost fully understood may have many ambiguities and if not clarified in the initial stage itself, can result in to incorrect functionality.

3.2.3 Requirement Analysis Guidelines

Many a times it may not be easy to ensure coverage and find all ambiguities. Following guidelines can help for the same

1) Ensure Requirement coverage by understanding following aspects. You may need to ask many questions to get complete clarity.

   Functional areas / Departments: Sales, Distribution, Support departments

   Data Types: Eg Types of members, orders, categories, regions

   Rules applied on each type

         Eg. Urgent order needs to be completed in 24 hours

   Tracks / Paths / routs through which the specific data is received or functionality can be achieved. Eg. Order received directly online or through dealers

   States: Life Cycle of specific order may have multiple states such as in-process, completed, cancelled…. The application will respond based on the state of the order.

   Exceptional situations: Eg. VIPs may be given preference. Staff may be given additional discounts.

   Additional focus: Legal requirements, technically challenging requirements, Stakeholder mandated requirements, Security and Performance aspects

2) Itemize the requirements

   Divide complex requirement in to multiple simple requirements. This will not only help in identifying and clarifying ambiguities but will also help in translating into solution and test cases.

3) Verify the gathered requirements with the customer
- through review meetings
- Summarize and present the requirements as understood by you to the user/stakeholder
- Carry out Reverse walk through to eliminate bad or wrong understanding
- Clarify any unclear requirements or conflicts

3.3 Design Reviews

Reviews of Functional and Architectural Design, Component design, Database design, User Interface design and any other such design documents should be conducted once they are created. Architectural integrity, Component completeness, Interface complexity etc are some of the key aspects covered in design reviews. It helps identifying design related issues so that defects can be prevented in development and implementation

In general design is reviewed to ensure that it

- implements all the explicit and Implicit requirements
- Provides complete picture of the software addressing data, functional, and behavioural domain from implementation perspective
- Is logically partitioned in to sub systems and modules
- Contains distinct representation of data, architecture, interfaces and components that
  - leads to appropriate data structures
  - leads to components that exhibit independent functional characteristics
  - leads to interfaces that reduces the complexity of between components and external subsystems
- is readable, understandable, is represented using notations that effectively communicates its meaning

We will discuss two important design aspects – Database Design and User Interface design.

3.3.1 Database Design Reviews

Most applications will input, manage, process and show data. The quality of data entered and stored in the system plays an important role in quality of system. Most business applications use relational databases and hence we will discuss some important aspects related to relational database. It is assumed that you have conceptual understanding of Relational database design such as table, Primary key, foreign key, relationship between tables etc. It is suggested to quickly refresh your concepts if you do not have it.

Data Quality can be classified in to

Data consistency: ensuring that data is represented "semantically the same way" within and across tables in a database system.

Data completeness: Ensuring that there is no missing or inaccessible data because of inadvertently storing nulls, blanks and there are no partial data due to truncations.

Data correctness: Ensuring that corrupt or wrong data not stored; as well as, dirty data not being shown to the user.

Let discuss each of them in details

Data consistency Issues

Factor	*Description of possible issue*	*Example*
Data Definitions	The data **type and length** for a particular attribute may vary in tables though the semantic definition is the same.	Meal Code may be defined as: Number (10) in one table and Varchar2(15) in another table.
Varying Data Codes & Values	The data representation of the same attribute may vary within and across tables.	A flag representing Gender may be defined in many ways. **(M/F or 1/0 or Male/female)**
Misuse of Integrity Constraints	When referential integrity constraints are misused, **foreign key values** may be **left "dangling"** or inadvertently deleted.	A Passenger record is deleted but his/her flight records are not deleted. So, foreign key of a flight record does not link to passenger record
Partial composite key used	Partial composite key used while joining or while accessing the record	Flight number, Date and seat number makes composite primary key but while accessing the record, if only flight number and seat number used, multiple records may be fetched
Nulls	**Nulls may be ignored** when joining tables or doing searches on the column.	The **Agent** has been entered as **a null** value **for a given ticket** as ticket was booked without agent. The report would not list details for this ticker if inner join used for joining tables

Data Completeness Issues

Factor	Description	Example
Missing data	Data elements are missing because of a lack of integrity constraints or nulls, are inadvertently not updated.	**Passenger Email address is null** because of which email notification cannot be sent Estimated arrival of a flight is null thus impacting an assessment of variances in estimated/actual arrival data.
Inaccessible Data	Inaccessible record due to missing or redundant unique identifier value.	Customer numbers are used to identify a customer record. **The customer ID (45656) identifies more than one customer.**
Missing Integrity Constraints	Missing constraints can cause data errors due to nulls, non-uniqueness, or missing relationships.	Flight records with a Pilot identifier exist in the database but cannot be matched to existing Pilots.

Data Correctness Issues.

Factor	Description	Example
Loss Projection	Tables that are joined over non-key attributes will produce non-existent data that is shown to the user.	Manish Patel works in the Mumbai office in the Accounting department. When a report is generated, it shows him working in Marketing and Accounting.
Incorrect Data Values	Data that is misspelled or inaccurately recorded.	100 ft ananad Nagar Rd is recorded with 1) a spelling mistake Anand spelled as Ananad and 2) feet and road is abbreviated as ft and rd.
Disabled Integrity Constraints	Null, non-unique, or out of range data may be stored when the integrity constraints are disabled.	The primary key constraint is disabled during an import function. Data is entered into the existing data with null unique identifiers or wrong values
Misuse of Integrity Constraints	Check, not null, or foreign key constraints are inappropriate or too restrictive.	Check constraint only allows hardcoded values of "Economy", "First" But a new code "Business" cannot be entered even though valid.

Database Design Reviews focus on ensuring consistency, completeness through checking referential integrity and constraints implemented in Database design.

As part of the database design reviews, one need to ensure that the database design, the relationship established between the tables and the constraints applied on the various tables are such that the potential issues mentioned above are either absent or at minimum level.

3.3.2 User Interface Design Reviews

Every user of the application should feel good while using the application and hence User Interface of the application should be

- Simple, readable and easy to understand,
- easy to navigate
- aesthetically rich
- Make optimal use of screen size and resolution

While using different functionalities of the application, user should get same satisfactory feeling. The user interface will include Pull down menus, Links, Panels and controls to input various details from user, buttons and icons, images, pop ups and error messages.

All the programs should use above interface objects in consistent manner. The User Interface should be consistent across all the programs of the application. The User Interface design and guidelines need to be completed before coding starts. Some important aspects of the user interface designs include

- Position of Title, Menu options and standard buttons
- Alignment of fields
- Height and width of text boxes or any other control
- Font color and size of all labels, entered text, error messages
- Provision to distinguish frequently used options
- Mandatory input fields can be distinguished

Every program specification should contain screen design specific to the functionality and should follow the guidelines for all the aspects described above and should be reviewed to ensure that those guidelines are followed for each screen design consistently.

Note that these aspects are also tested once coding is done to ensure that the programs do implement these guidelines. User Interface and Usability Testing has been described in detail in section 8.2.1.

3.4 Code Reviews

Primary Objective of code review is to ensure correctness, understandability and maintainability of the code developed. Developers make some general mistakes resulting in some standard errors as described below. The code review process emphasis on checking that such issues are identified and corrected.

- Data Declaration Errors
  - Have all variables been explicitly declared? Meaningful? Case Sensitive?
  - Are variables/Pointers properly initialized in declaration sections?
  - Are variables assigned with correct length, type and storage class? Eg. Should a variable be declared as string instead of array of characters?
  - Are there variables declared which are never used in the program?
- Data Reference Errors
  - Is a variable referenced whose value is unset or uninitialized? (eg. Two variables with similar names and wrong variable is used)
  - Usage of array subscripts – Are they integers and values within the boundary? Some languages, it starts from 0 and in others it starts from 1
  - Is there any variable where constant can be used?
  - Is there any variable that is assigned a value of different type? Eg. Assigning floating point number to integer variable can cause issue
  - Is data structure defined identically in all functions where same data structure is referenced?
  - Is the usage of similar looking operators (=/==, &/&&) proper?
- Computation errors
  - Is there any computation using variables having inconsistent data types?
  - Is the target variable (on the left side of the = sign of an expression) of smaller size than right hand side expression?
  - Is there any possibility of division by 0?
  - Is there any possibility of loss of precision – eg in integer arithmetic.
  - Is there a possibility where computed variable assume value outside the range? Eg. If the variable represents % ensure it remains between 0% and 100%
  - In a compound/complex expression, check whether the order of evaluation and operator precedence is correct
- Comparison errors
  - Are there any comparisons between variables having inconsistent data types?
  - Ensure comparison operators are used correctly - </<=
  - Ensure that there is no precision problem when fractional or floating point values are compared.
- Control Flow errors
  - Are the statement blocks within a control structure proper? (Begin and End or blocks correctly used / Parenthesis correctly used)

- o Will every loop eventually terminate?
- o Is loop executed at least once? If not, is it really correct?
- o If the program contains multi-way branch statement (eg Switch .. Case), can the index variable exceed total possible numbers? If, so, is it handled properly?
- o Delimitation of parts in if then else
- Interface errors
- o Does the number of parameters received by the module equal the number of arguments sent by calling modules?
- o Also is the order correct?
- o Are the size and type matching
- Input/output errors
- o All I/O conditions handled correctly?
- **Standards-** Are all standards followed for Naming, Indentation, Comments
- Is there any unreachable or dead code (which will never be executed)?
- Has Go To or any other such statements used (which is not a good practice)?

Please note that code reviews are done without executing the code and hence it is also considered **Static Testing**. Static testing approach is explained in detail in the next section.

3.5 Static Testing Techniques

In previous sections of this chapter, we discussed about various aspects we need to consider while reviewing requirements, designs and code. We will now cover how we do those reviews to derive maximum benefits. The approach is known as Static Testing.

Static Testing is a process of **reviewing** the work product or code without execution. The fundamental objective of static testing is to improve the quality of software work products by identifying and fixing defects early in the software development process. Static testing is done not only on code but on specification documents, Design documents or even test plans and user manual.

It has been observed that, effective static testing can find 30-70% of defects. It is also important because it can find some types of errors which cannot be found by dynamic testing by executing the program such as

- Wrong understanding / Missing Requirements
- Design Defects
- Non-maintainability of code
- Inconsistent interface specifications
- Dead codes
- Unused variables
- Uninitialized variables
- Standard violations
- Infinite loops

We have already covered many different types of errors we can find using reviews in previous sections.

There are many other **advantages** of static testing

It can discover many problems at once – In dynamic testing when you find one defect, you tend to first solve the defect before you proceed with further testing (many times show stopper kind of defects do not allow you to proceed further even if you want). However in case of stating you can find multiple issues at a time.

It can discover root causes at an early stage – If you find a defect during black box functional testing at a later stage, you may not realize what the root cause for the defect was. Developers may have to spend lot of time to really get into the root cause and resolve the issues. Since Static testing is generally done as soon as the design/code for specific functionality is developed, many dependent defects can be avoided at a later stage.

It is Quality Assurance Oriented / Defect Prevention Oriented. Early feedback on quality issues can be established. Since the issues are resolved in the beginning at root causes level, many other defects are prevented and hence it gives some kind of assurance for the quality of the final product.

It reduces overall effort: Since defects and issues are identified early in the life cycle, the rework cost is reduced.

It lays strict emphasis on conforming to specifications and standards. Application readability and maintainability, quick customization and enhancements are some of the key requirements of today's applications. So, application code should not only meet the functional and non-functional requirements but the design and the code logic should meet required standards established. These standards can be checked during static testing.

It enables multiple perspectives from different people. Code Walk through and Inspection techniques are group activities. Multiple people brings multiple perspective at the same time improving the quality further

It saves computer resources – Since static testing is done without executing software, there is no need to have complete environment (Hardware, OS, Database, Application server etc.) set for testing.

It is Part of Formal Process models such as ISO 9001 and CMMI (Capability Maturity Model Integrated). In order to provide assurance of quality to customers, many software vendors implement established processes as defined under CMMI / ISO models. Static testing is part of these processes as it provides confidence of good quality from the beginning.

Exchange of information between the participants happens when the evaluation is done by a team. Static testing is also **educational/informational** or communicational as participants learn about the software work products which can help in understanding their role and future plan of activities.

Reviews vary from very informal to formal (i.e. well-structured and regulated). Initially informal reviews take place. In later stages these reviews become more formal often involving more people and a meeting.

Note that in contrast to dynamic testing, static testing finds defects rather than failures.

3.5.1 Informal Reviews

There may be different types of informal reviews where no documentation is done as an outcome of the review. In the early stage of life cycle, generally informal reviews are applied where a single person may review the work product (document or code).

There are two types of Informal reviews

Self-Review

Review is done by the person who is the author or who is responsible for a particular program code

The author or responsible person is assumed to have better understanding of the code and hence it is easy for him/her to review. It helps in eliminating some basic issues and saves time of others during other testing

However self-review cannot find some errors, if the understanding itself is wrong

Self-review is an informal process and can be done while the development work is still going on or immediately after developing the code

Independent Review

Review is done by the person other than the author of the program – may be colleague or senior programmer or a lead.

It helps detecting human errors that can be missed during self-review.

Since independent perspective is brought, independent review is also viewed as a one person inspection or walkthrough

Informal review is perhaps the most common type of review in practice.

Since it does not require large number of people it is often done on the desk and hence sometimes also called **Desk Checking**

As part of this process a person reads a program or a document and checks it with respect to standard error list and/or walks test data through it to find any errors. Corrections if required can be made, there itself. There is no need to maintain any log for the issues found. Since this is an individual activity, there is no need to prepare any schedule or arrange for logistics. Since this is person dependent, it is less effective as it depends on the experience of the single person involved in review.

3.5.2 Formal Review

The formality of a review process is related to factors such as the maturity of the development process, any legal or regulatory requirements or the need for an audit trail.

Different **roles** are assigned to participants to improve the effectiveness of the review

A moderator or Inspection leader – leads the process, plans, schedule the meeting and controls the meeting

A programmer/Author – is expected to explain during the process and capture defects identified and resolve those issues.

Reviewers/Checkers/Inspectors: The program designer and/or test specialist or representatives from QA organization who need to identify defects/issues/gaps

Recorder: has to record / log each defect/issue in a specified format

Manager – May or may not get directly involved in the process but need to allocate time, effort and provide training as necessary

Moderator takes responsibility of Distributing Material, Scheduling meetings, Leading sessions, and Ensure corrections

Phases of formal reviews: A defined process is followed as described below

Planning: The meeting is planned by the moderator. Planning involves date and time, participants and logistics requirement, role distribution

Distribution: Moderator distributes material in advance to all the participants

Overview meeting / Kick-off meeting: An Overview meeting is arranged before the actual review/inspection meeting during which the author describes the background of the work product, and objectives for the review (What is expected to achieve based on the review). This helps participants/inspectors to prepare before the actual inspection meeting. Plan is discussed and time / effort commitment is taken from the participants.

Preparation: Each reviewer/inspector individually examines the work product given to them to identify possible defects using the related documents, procedures, rules and checklists provided. The individual participants identify defects, questions and comments, according to their understanding. This process saves lot of time during meeting and the meeting becomes very effective

Review meeting: This is also known as discussion phase, decision phase and logging phase.

- The reader reads through the work product or visually displays the work product, part by part.
- The reviewers/inspectors analyse the program or a document against a check list (of historically common programming errors or any other such checklist). If the reviewers/inspectors have already found the issues earlier during preparation phase then they discuss and finalize here. If required, they raise questions& if errors exist and finalize their findings
- Recorder records/logs all findings.
- The moderator prevents discussions from getting too personal, rephrases remarks if necessary

Rework: The author makes changes to the work product according to findings derived from the inspection meeting.

Follow-up: Moderator follows up with the author for the revised program/work product and ensures that the changes done by the author are correct

3.5.2.1 Walkthrough (Presentation Review)

This is generally useful for higher level documents such as requirement specification or architectural documents but is also used for complex programs.

This is a **group activity**. Generally 3-5 people get involved but large number of people can participate with an objective to get as many suggestions as possible. Team generally comprises of one or more of following

- A highly experienced programmer / designer.
- A programming language expert
- A new programmer
- The person who maintains the program
- Some person from a different project
- Someone from the same team as a programmer.

This is a less formal or partially formal activity in which reviewers can raise questions and solutions are also suggested but there is no need to use review checklist or log the findings. The author does most of the preparation.

The primary objective of walkthrough is

- to present the document to stakeholders both within and outside the software discipline, in order to gather information regarding the topic under documentation;
- to explain (knowledge transfer) and evaluate the contents of the document;
- to establish a common understanding of the document;
- to examine and discuss the validity of proposed solutions and the viability of alternatives, establishing consensus.

In walkthroughs

> The meeting is led by author. A separate recorder may or may not be present
>
> Separate pre-meeting preparation for reviewers is optional.
>
> Scenarios and dry runs may be used to validate the content.

As part of the **walkthrough process**

> Author of the document under review guiding the participants through the document and his or her thought processes, to achieve a common understanding and to gather feedback.
>
> For code review, the designer simulates the program and explains the content / shows the program step by step what the program will do with the test data supplied by the reviewers.
>
> The simulation also shows how different pieces of the system interact and can expose awkwardness, redundancy and many missed details.

Participants are not expected to do detailed study of the document in advance

Due to involvement of expert review team members, the walkthrough process helps not only in finding omissions of requirements, style or concepts issues, but also helps providing approach to solution of the issues.

Sometimes, a new team member is also involved in the meeting. The walkthrough process helps him/her getting relevant information of the requirement, design and solution. Walkthroughs also helps understanding the product in absence of the documentation. This knowledge can be useful to the new resources for enhancements and maintenance or extract some approaches that could be useful in his/her own development.

3.5.2.2 Inspection

Inspection is considered to be one of the most documented and formal review techniques. Inspection is also a group activity.

The document under inspection is prepared and checked thoroughly by the reviewers before the meeting, comparing the work product with its sources and other referenced documents, and using rules and checklists. In the inspection meeting the defects found are logged and any discussion is postponed until the discussion phase.

It is usually led by a trained moderator (certainly not by the author). It uses defined roles during the process. It involves peers to examine the product. Rules and checklists are used during the preparation phase. A separate preparation is carried out during which the product is examined and the defects are found. The defects found are documented in a logging list or issue log. A formal follow-up is carried out by the moderator applying exit criteria. Optionally, a causal analysis step is introduced to address process improvement issues and learn from the defects found. Metrics are gathered and analysed to optimize the process.

The generally accepted goals of inspection are to:

- help the author to improve the quality of the document under inspection;
- remove defects efficiently, as early as possible;
- improve product quality, by producing documents with a higher level of quality;
- create a common understanding by exchanging information among the inspection participants;
- learn from defects found and improve processes in order to prevent recurrence of similar defects;
- Sample a few pages or sections from a larger document in order to measure the typical quality of the document, leading to improved work by individuals in the future, and to process improvements.

Note that the objective of this process is primarily to find errors but not to provide solutions to the errors. It helps in ensuring that the standards and specifications are followed, requirements are correctly transformed to the product and there are no side effects apart from finding some other defects.

3.5.3 Comparison:

Following table provides comparison of the techniques

Parameter	Informal	Walkthrough	Inspection
Level of formality / Process followed	Low / No	Medium / Partially	High / Fully
Checklist used?	No	Generally not	Yes
Logs maintained?	No	May be	Yes
Number of Reviewers	1	Group of 3 to 5	Group
Solution suggested	Yes	Yes	No
Effectiveness	Low	High (for better solution)	High (to find errors)
Material distributed in advance	No	May be	Yes
Time Required	Less	Medium	More

3.6 Summary

In this chapter we discussed verification activities for all the deliverables of the development phases in detail starting from Requirement Analysis to coding.

Requirement Reviews.

Requirement Analysis and Ambiguity review is very critical / important as the output is certainly going to be wrong if the requirements are not correctly and completely understood. Unfortunately there are multiple challenges in receiving requirements and hence there are lot of chances that requirements are either incomplete or ambiguous. We saw various ambiguity types such as Sloppiness, Linguistic ambiguities, Dangling Else, Ambiguity of Reference, Omissions (cause without effects or effects without cause or completely omitted), Ambiguity of Logical Operators or Confusing Compound Operators or even ambiguous variables, adjectives, adverbs etc.

In almost every project you will find many ambiguous requirements which are to be thoroughly reviewed and removed (clarified). The process of using a checklist, writing itemized requirements (small & simple) in our own language and verifying our understanding of those requirements from the user is extremely critical.

Design Reviews

As part of this, we should do database design reviews for consistency, completeness and correctness, User Interface design reviews for readability, easy navigation, aesthetics, and appearance.

Code Reviews

We discussed various types of common mistakes we make during coding such as data declaration errors, Data Reference Errors, Computation errors, Comparison errors, Control Flow errors, Interface errors, Input / Output Errors and Errors related to standards. Many of these errors would be difficult to find just by executing the code. So, we need to do code review to identify such errors.

Process:

Subsequently we discussed that **Static Testing technique** are used which involves **Informal Reviews** and **Formal Reviews**. **Desk checking** by **self or independent** person or **Walk-Through** in a team or **Inspection** by experts/auditors are the important approaches used as part of static testing. Desk checking is totally informal, whereas walk-throughs are partially formal and Inspections are fully formal approaches where a defined process is followed by team playing different roles of moderator, author/presenter, recorder, auditors, manager etc. The process includes planning, distribution, preparation, review meeting, recording feedback, rework and follow-up.

There are many advantages of static testing before any further testing is done such as ability to discover many problems at once, find root causes at an early stage, prevent further failures, meet the standards and hence reduce effort, time and cost of finding defects at a later stage.

3.7 Exercise

Sr.	Question
1.	Understanding of requirement correctly and completely is much more important than writing code very efficient manner (T/F?)
2.	Why should testing be done at an early stage?
3.	Provide main difference between Static vs Dynamic testing techniques
4.	Name static testing techniques
5.	For which kind of errors, Static testing is better?
6.	Name 5 important aspects to be covered in Code review checklist
7.	Who all could participate in code walk through?
8.	Briefly describe code inspection process
9.	Standard violation can be found using _____ Testing
10.	Differentiate between Desk checking, walk through and inspection (at least 4 differences)
11.	Provide at least five advantages of static testing techniques
12.	Static testing is quality assurance oriented (T/F)? Why?
13.	_____ and _____ are the two types of informal reviews
14.	Using static testing, you can discover many problems at once (T/F)?
15.	What are the disadvantages of Desk checking?
16.	Two third of 6 and 6 = _____ Options: a) 8, b) 10, c) Other, d) Cant' say
17.	Describe how ambiguities occur and what care as a developer/tester we should take?
18.	Splitting complex requirement into smaller requirements to understand the system is known as _____ Options: a) Requirement Analyses, b) Ambiguity Review, c) Test Design, d)Requirement Itemization
19.	What do you mean by ambiguities? Explain any 4 different types of ambiguities with examples
20.	List four different types of challenges in requirements and explain briefly
21.	Requirement says "There are three types of members- 1. Silver 2. Gold and 3. Platinum. Silver card members get 3% discount. Platinum card members get

Sr.	Question
	6% discount". Is there any ambiguity/omission in the requirement? If yes, what?
22.	Study the following requirement A student will be allowed to appear for the final exam if student has appeared in all the internal tests or his/her attendance is >= 70% and has submitted all the assignments Is this requirement Ambiguous? Why?

23.	Q.3 A file contains student's examination result for every test for every subject. There could be more than one tests conducted for each subject.
	
	Following routine reads each record of the file that contains student code, subject code, Test Code, and Test Marks. Then, it calculates and displays average marks for each subject of each student. Find out logical errors in the routine and rewrite the correct code.
	
	Int TestCount, TempStudentCode, TempSubjectCode, SubjectCode, TestCode, TestMarks
	TestCount = 0
	While not EOF // Loop 1
	{
	   Read Studentcode, SubjectCode, TestCode, TestMarks
	   While (TempStudentCode = StudentCode) // Loop 2
	   {
	     TempSubjectCode = Subjectcode
	     While (TempSubjectCode = SubjectCode) // Loop 3
	     {
	       TotalSubjectMarks=TotalSubjectMarks + TestMarks
	       TestCount = TestCount + 1
	       Read Studentcode, SubjectCode, TestCode, TestMarks
	       TempStudentCode = StudentCode
	       TempsubjectCode = SubjectCode
	     }
	   }
	   AverageSubjectmarks = TotalSubjectMarks/TestCount
	   Display StudentCode, SubjectCode, AverageSubjectMarks
	}
	
	A) How many times Loop 2 will be executed? Why?
	B) How many times loop 3 will be executed? Why
	C) Will the average test marks for each subject for each student will be calculated correctly? Why?

24.	Study the following requirement

Sr.	Question
	There are three types of members for a club -Silver, Gold and Platinum. All Gold card members are informed through email for any event that takes place in the club Is there any ambiguity in this requirement? Why?
25.	Briefly Explain Database Design review
26.	Provide any 2 classifications of Data Quality
27.	Briefly explain any two possible Data Consistency issues with example
28.	Briefly explain any two possible Data Completeness issues with example
29.	What is the Primary objective of Code Review
30.	List down any 5 types of errors expected to be found during code review
31.	Give example of data reference errors one can find during code review

4 Unit and Integration Testing with Structural based Test design

4.1 Introduction

Recollect Pen testing we discussed in chapter 2 where we discussed that instead of waiting for the entire pen to be assembled and then we start testing, we should do unit testing for individual pen components such as Ball Point, Refil, Pen body, Spring etc. Then we do integration testing to check Refill fits properly in pen body, cap fits properly on both sides etc and then only we do testing of entire pen assembled based on all the components to see that it functions properly, provides required performance etc. Similarly software testing is also done in levels.

Study following diagram providing how reservation module is decomposed in to various business functionalities which are visible to the users and some technical components (highlighted boxes which are not seen by the users (refer section 2.3).

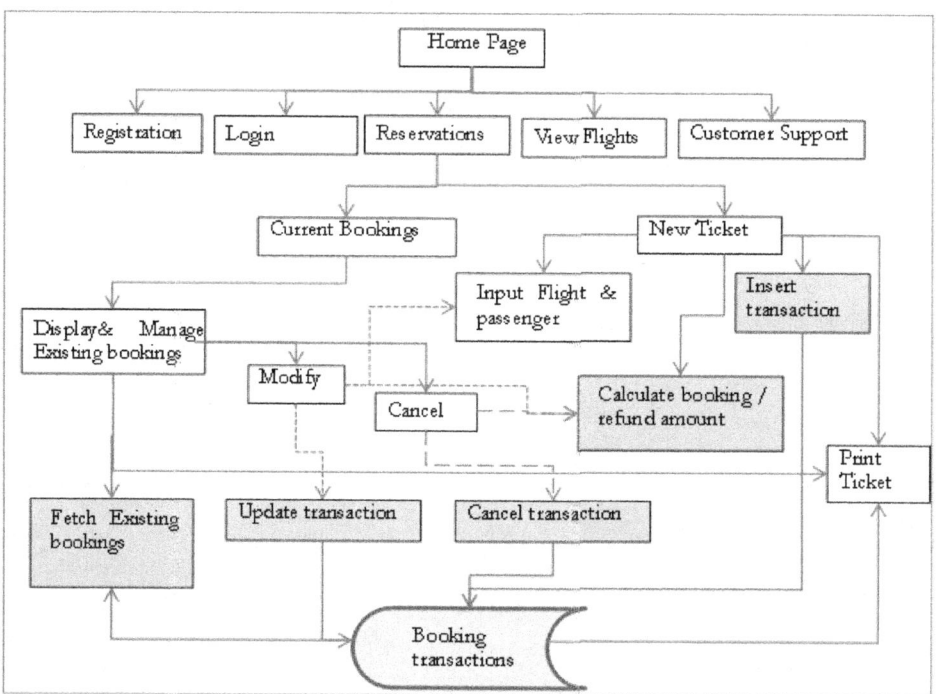

You can notice that some components (boxes to which there are two or more arrows) are reused in more than one functionalities. These individual components are developed first and hence each component should be tested as soon as it is developed to ensure that it accurately servers its purpose for which it is developed. Once other related components are developed and unit tested, they can be integrated as per architecture design and integration testing takes place to check that they work together also correctly by ensuring that the interface between them is proper. Once that is done, the full functionality such as New Ticket booking or cancelling existing reservation are tested to ensure that they are working as expected.

So, these are four levels of software testing. Unit Testing, Integration Testing, Validation and System Testing and Acceptance Testing. In practice, there may be more, fewer or different levels of development and testing, depending on the project and the software product. For example, there may be component integration testing after component testing and system integration testing after system testing. However the levels we will discuss here are most general.

Unit and Integration testing is primarily done by development team themselves. We will discuss details of both these levels of testing along with various test design techniques used to carry out these testing levels in this chapter.

We had already discussed code review in section 3.4 which is done using static testing technique. We will now discuss testing using **Dynamic Testing** technique (by executing the program or a component)

4.2 Unit Testing

Unit testing / Component Testing: The testing of individual software components (smallest testable part of an application) to demonstrate that their smallest pieces of executable code function suitably

It is the most **'micro'** scale of testing generally done by Developer himself.

From technical perspective a unit can be at a level of program, subprogram, subroutine, procedures, function or code modules, a class, or a stored procedure. Unit constitute of various statements, loops, IF-THEN-ELSE control structures, functions / procedure calls, assignments and related data – records, variables, constants etc

From a business perspective a unit can be at a level of specific menu option – Input form, viewing details etc. We will call them functional components.

Unit testing focuses on

- **Local data structures**: Data useful to the program logic are stored in variables which are then used at some places (on the right side of expression) or changed at some places (used on the left side of expressions) and removed at some places of code. For example, a variable will be used to store reservation amount. It will initially contain 0 and subsequently will contain calculated amount based on price fetched from the system, multiply with number of passengers. It will then be modified by reducing discount if any and then increased by taxes as applicable.

    Local data structures related issues include **Improper or inconsistent data types, incorrect variable names, overflow, underflow and exceptions**.
    For example,

a) The values of **enumerated data types used without indexing an array** (may cause errors).
b) **Initialization of variable with wrong value or Incorrect default value** (eg outside valid range) or buffer overflow can occur when we try to use/modify data in buffer without care.
c) Incorrect string handling or failure of other string function due to **parameter/operand occupying null value** due to some reason.
d) Using Public and not using Private or protected data due to which private **data could be exposed to un-trusted components**
e) Possibility of **null referencing due to non-initialization** before using a variable in some formula or in conditions.

So as part of unit testing, it is ensured that data structures used to store data maintains consistency and integrity as required.

- **All independent paths**: Every program will have some control structures such as If...Then...Else or Multi decision structures like Switch/Case or Loops such as For, While, Do Until. Execution of various statements would be done or not done or would be repeated based on control structures used. So as part of unit testing all independent paths through the control structure are checked to ensure that each statement is executed at least once during testing.

  The paths may not be executed correctly due to various issues as listed below.
  a) Usage of **wrong condition or logical operators in IF or SWITCH** statements due to which flow of control in program may not happen as expected.
  b) **SWITCH statement with no default case** (can result in unpredictable result).
  c) **Mistaken statement termination** or unintentional termination of loop.

- **Computation, comparison and Control flows** are checked for correctness and appropriateness. The issues could be
  a) Loss of bits/bytes due to **truncation**.
  b) Use of **arithmetic exception such as divide by zero** or **floating point exceptions** (can result into issue).

- **Boundary conditions:** Errors are more likely at the boundaries. For example error may occur at the nth element of an n dimensional array or when the maximum or minimum allowable value is encountered. So, testing should be done to exercise data structure, control flow and data values just below at and just above the maxima and minima to ensure that component operate properly at the boundaries to limit or restrict processing.

- **Error handling paths:** The system should handle situations such as invalid data input by user or not system not able to insert data in table due to constraint imposed and display proper error messages to the user. So, as part of unit testing, it should ensure that error handling paths are executed when error is encountered to reroute or terminate the processing. It also needs to ensure that error condition is correctly processed; error messages are easy to understand and provide enough information to assists the user to understand reasons for error and what steps to be taken.

- The program actually is expected to validate that the inputs provided by the user are valid and acceptable as per design and as per business rules. Some typical implicit expectations as per design would be as given below
    o **Input Type Validation:** For example, user enters characters by mistake when only numbers are expected (such as in number of tickets or phone number etc.)
    o **Input Length Validation:** For example system expects only 30 characters for passenger name but user enters 40 characters
    o **Value Limit Validation:** For example, in a single booking you cannot book ticket for more than 6 passengers but user enters 10
    o **Dependent Field Validation:** For example your return journey date cannot be prior to your travel date.

Some other typical errors one may find includes

- **Change in global variable's value** due to one requirement but the variables are used for some other requirement/functionality also.
- **Inappropriate storage or use of Control data:** Control data contains business rules and tells application what to do and how to behave. For example, Government tax rates and rules could be stored in table that support business function of pay calculation.
- **Mistakes in embedded query** statements / **improper use of joins** (without considering full primary key)

Any of the above and many other such issues can lead to wrong/unexpected output/result.

We can find these errors only if all the statements of the program unit under all the paths are tested at least once. So, we need to check

o Independent paths (Loops, Control flow): Execution of all branch statements, Single Entry &single exit loops, embedded statements in blocks. Initialization and termination of loops.
o Calculations

- o Logic for the required process
- o Correct interaction of code to hardware used.
- o Interfaces – Number of parameters and type and order matching.

Unit Testing Procedure

Unit testing is done against the detailed design or program specification as discussed and shown in the V Model in section 2.4.

There are three ways in which Unit testing can be and should be done.

1) Review of the code of the unit (static testing). We have already discussed this approach.

2) White box testing (testing by executing the program but considering the code structure

3) Black box testing – from user's perspective.

We will be discussing White Box and Black Box test design techniques in subsequent sections and chapters.

A component is generally not working stand alone, it may have some dependency on other component (main program) which is calling it or subordinate which is called by this component – refer diagram in the introduction section of this chapter. So, it may be difficult to test a component if those calling and called components are not yet ready. You may have to develop dummy components namely driver which calls our component under test and stub which is called by our component under test.

Driver: A software component or test tool that can be temporarily used in place of a component that takes care of the control and/or the calling of a component or system. Driver passes data to the component under test

Stub: A skeleton or special-purpose implementation of a software component, used to test an upper level component that calls or is otherwise dependent on it. It is used in place of a called component.

Stub receives data from the component under test and sends response back after some minimum manipulation.

Developing driver and stub requires effort and hence considered to be an overhead as they are not going to be part of the final product. So they should be very simple and less time consuming. If it is not possible test components effectively with simple drivers and stubs, then unit testing may be delayed till actual components are ready. That is also the reason because of which component addressing only one function with high cohesion design is not only easy to develop but is easy to test.

Various methods and techniques are used to derive or identify test cases which are effective and not redundant. These techniques are discussed in next unit.

Benefits: Unit testing helps us to find and locate smaller issues/defects due to which debugging task becomes easy. Simultaneous testing can be done by different team members on different units at a time. It improves quality of code before integrated in the entire system. It reduces the time and effort as bugs are found and resolved early.

4.3 Integration Testing

We discussed that modular design allows one function/process to access the services provided by the other function/components with a mechanism for passing control and data between modules.

Each component should either receive or pass control/ data to and from calling / called function properly as expected. If a component is used by multiple calling functions, it needs to ensure that it services all the calling functions in an accurate manner.

Even though components individually work as desired, integrated modules may give many issues as given below

- Data can be lost across the interface.
- One component can have in advertent, adverse effect on the other,
- Sub functions may not produce desired result as expected by major function,
- Individually accepted imprecision may be magnified to unacceptable levels,
- Global data structure can present problems.
- …

The **interface of the software with the database** may also be incorrect.

The issues could be due to Wrong protocols, Synchronization; Inappropriate formats of input and output data, restricted or no access.

Let us see some typical issues with examples.

Inclusion of wrong / inappropriate header or other files: If you are using file providing interface specification and by mistake include wrong file providing different specification, there could be issues. Eg. One may use a connection object to connect to test database and then forget to change before moving to live database. The live application will connect to test database and not the live database.

Incorrect parameter passing: wrong parameter type, wrong parameter order, or wrong number of parameters passed. For example, ticket booking process in an airline reservation system uses one form for basic travel information. Once basic information is given the system will pass control to Passenger information screen. If number of tickets entered in the first screen not passed to the passenger information screen and it assumes single ticket, it will input passenger details for only one passenger.

Inadequate Functionality / wrong location of functionality: Such issues are caused by implicit wrong assumptions by one part of the system (developed by one programmer) that the other part (developed by other programmer) will provide certain functionality but it actually does not.

For example, Active ticket view screen displays all active tickets and allows the user to cancel ticket. On clicking the 'Cancel' button for a specific ticket, control is passed to cancel ticket program. Cancel Ticket program assumes the required validation for eligibility of cancellation is done by calling program where as it was actually to be done by the Cancel ticket program.

For example the term-exam module is expected to pass whether the student has passed in the term exam or not but term exam module assumes it will be checked in the main module.

Misunderstanding of Interface: For example, for search functionality, a module calls a component to search and return the index of an element in an array of integers. The called module uses binary search with wrong assumption that the calling module gives a sorted array but the actually calling module assumes sorting will be done by called module. 2. A module passes a temperature value in Celsius to a module which interprets the value in Fahrenheit.

Data Structure limitation:

Sometimes, the field's width is different in table and what is assumed in the other tables or in the UI/Report, resulting into truncation of the value. For example Passenger information screen allows 40 characters for the passenger names but the database table column for storing passenger name has only 35 characters, the ticket will print only 35 characters for the passenger name. Truncation will take place.

If the data structure is defined for 100 records, it will fail, if records grow beyond 100.

Inadequate Error Processing: the calling module may fail to handle the error properly even if the called module may return an error code to the calling module.

Inadequate Post processing: These errors are caused by a general failure to release resources (eg. Memory) no longer required (failure to de-allocate memory)

Initialization/Value Errors: Initialization / proper assignment to variable or data structure is required every time before calling the function but not done. For example, the value of a pointer can change; it might point to the first character in a string, then to the second character, after that to the third character, and so on. The programmer may forget to reinitialize the pointer before using that function once again; the pointer may eventually point to code.

Reasons: All the issues above and many other such issues come in almost all the systems because there are multiple team members involved in designing and coding of various components. Every individual developer's understanding and programming logic may differ from other programmers.

These issues could be there in the original application developed or may be introduced when some changes are done in one part of application but without making corresponding changes / adjustments in the other parts

The expected number of errors found in integration testing are much less than from unit testing but it takes more time to find and fix the integration defects

Integration Testing: Testing performed to expose defects in the interfaces and interaction between integrated components. It verifies inter-component interfaces, external interfaces and user and business workflows to identify issues associated with inputs and outputs from one program to other. It is to ensure that components of a module or modules of an application are integrated properly and **function together** correctly.

Integration testing is generally performed by Development Team using static or white-box testing techniques in development environment.

During integration testing, focus is solely on the integration itself. For example, if components A and B are integrated, testing is done for the communication between the components, not the functionality of either one.

Sample Integration Test Cases

Sr	Interface	Requirement	Action	Expected Result	OK?
1	Main Page and 'Flight Schedule' Page	Flight Schedule page is displayed when 'Flights' button is pressed	Enter Travel Date, From Location, To location and Click on 'Flights' button	A new pop up page should be displayed showing all the flights on a specific date for selected location	
2	'Ticket Booking' and 'Passenger Detail' screen	Number of Tickets, Travel dates and Flight details correctly passed	Enter details in Ticket booking screen and press 'Submit' button	Travel date, Flight name correctly displayed. Number of rows for getting passenger detail are as per number of tickets	
		...			
3	'Current Tickets' And 'Cancel Ticket' Program	Cancellation is not allowed if not eligible	Press the Cancel button	'Cancellation' button should not be available / enabled for the ticket which is not eligible	
4	'Passenger Information' screen and 'Ticket Printing' program	All information entered in the screen should all correctly and completely appear in the printed ticket	Enter information for all passengers travelling. Submit ticket booking process and confirm ticket printing	There is no truncation of any data.	

As you can see, the above sample test cases aim to ensure

o   Required page is displayed on clicking a button or a link
o   The displayed details should be based on the inputs provided in the previous page

- o Specific validation should have been implemented in either calling page or called page
- o There is no truncation of data

Methodology

One may need to deploy different methodologies for different types of interfaces.

For example, one may need to trap messages and copy them to log file for real time systems.

It may also be useful to use **debugging tools** and set break points at interfaces. When control or data flow traverses an interface where a break point is set, control is passed to the debugger, enabling inspection and logging of the flow.

Black-box integration tests may be used to fully exercise the functions specified in design document. They are also used to verify that data exchanged across an interface comply with the data structure specification

Approach for Integration Testing

Integration testing can be done once all the components of the entire software product are integrated. This approach, commonly known as **Big bang** approach can create a chaotic situation not only for testing but also because isolation of root causes may not be easy and hence fixing also may not be easy.

So, generally an **incremental approach** is used so that the integration testing between two components are carried out as soon as they are integrated. The main advantage is that the testing can be started early (no need to wait for the whole system to be ready). This approach has some disadvantage of requiring additional effort for developing dummy code called stub/driver in absence of actual code and once again testing needs to be done when actual code is available. Let us understand incremental approach in little more detail. Integration can be either top-down or bottom-up as described below.

Top down Approach: An incremental approach for integration testing where the component at the top of the component hierarchy is tested first, with lower level components being simulated by stubs.

Under this approach development of modules and integration of modules happen from top (main control module) to bottom.

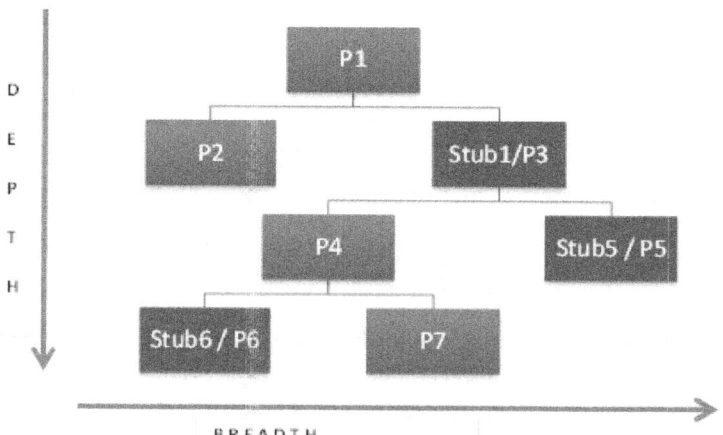

So P1 and P2 are integrated first and then when P3 is ready, it replaces stub and integration testing is done between P1 and P3. The process continues till last module P7 is ready and integrated with P4. As you can see in the diagram, stubs may be used initially when actual module is not ready.

Note that, Integration approach can be done **Depth-first or Breadth-first** depending on the development approach.

Depth-First: First component at all levels are developed and integrated first and then 2nd component of all levels are completed. So here P3-P4. P4--P6 are done first and then P3-P5 is done and then P4-P6 is done.

Breadth-First: All components of 2nd level are completed first and integrated, then 3rd level components are completed and integrated and the process is completed till last level components are completed. So, here P3-P4, P3-P5, P4-6, P4-P7 done.

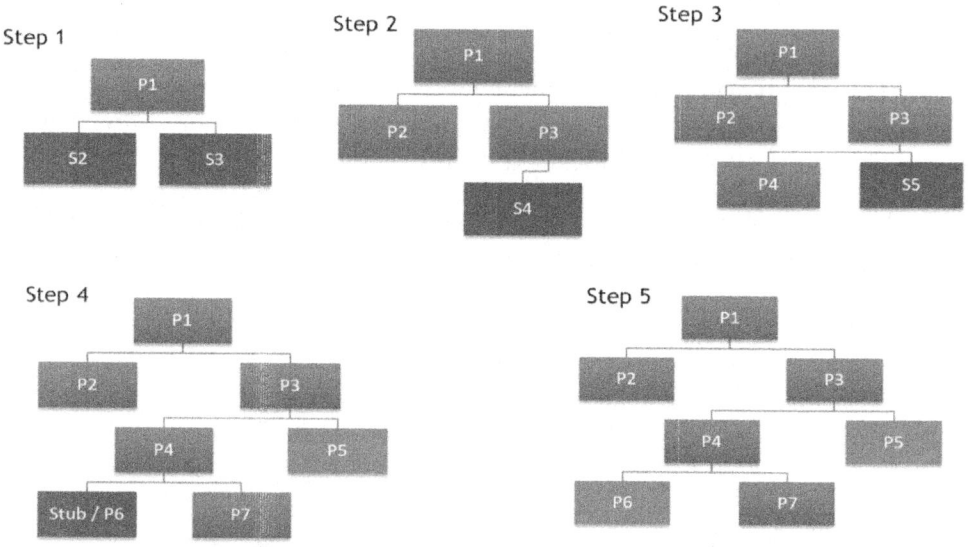

Bottom up Approach: An incremental approach for integration testing where the lowest level components are tested first, and then used to facilitate the testing of higher level components. This process is repeated until the component at the top of the hierarchy is tested.

Under this approach development of modules and integration of modules happen from top (main control module) to bottom. Here stubs are not required but dummy code at upper level known as Drivers are required. These drivers are replaced when actual upper level component is ready with which the integration takes place and testing is done at upper level. The process continues till top most level component is integrated and tested.

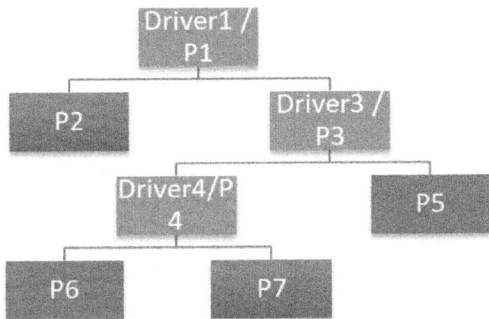

Below are the possible steps followed depending on the readiness of the modules. Box in Green indicates a Driver which is temporarily used to do integration testing with the lower level modules and is replaced with the actual module once ready.

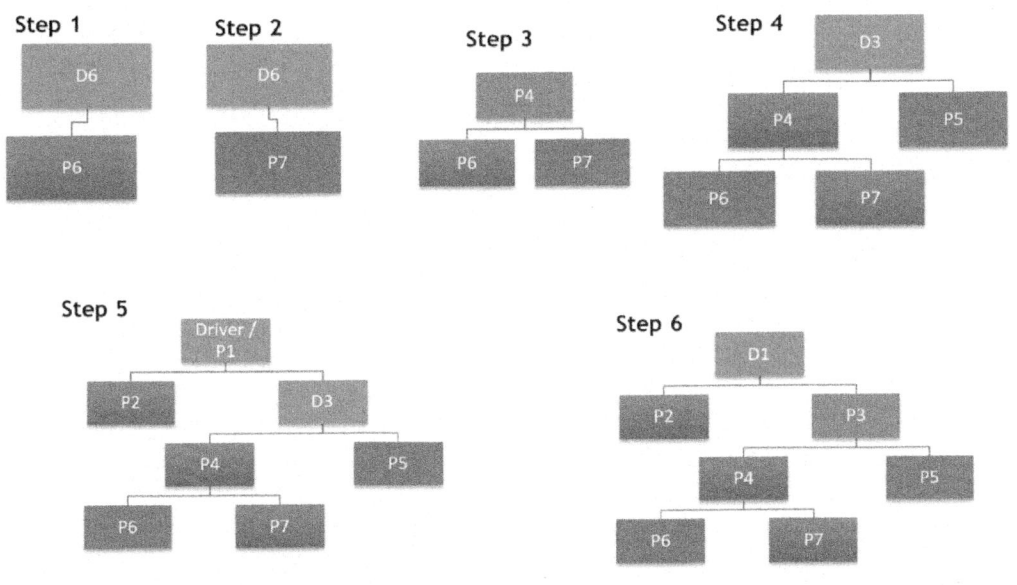

4.4 Structure Based / White Box Testing

Refer section 1.2 in which we discussed hat exhaustive testing is not possible and in section 2.1 we briefly saw that in order to find maximum defects from the application, we need to design test cases from both internal program structure and logic perspective and from external business perspective. We will discuss in detail White Box test design techniques in this section which is primarily used by developers for Unit and integration testing.

White-box test design technique is a **Procedure** to derive and/or select test cases based on an analysis of the internal structure of a component or system.

This is also known as **Clear-box** or **Glass-box** testing technique as the engineer examines the internal structure of the program - code, database tables and the logic applied, to implement all the rules / constraints with the use of specific programming language.

White-box testing is a way of checking functionality of code by testing the program code that realizes the functionality. The **test cases are designed** generally **based on control structure** and internal design flow of the code.

Let us try to understand the concept with small and simple example.

Requirement: A multiplex theatre has come up with a discounting scheme: 5% discount is given to everyone irrespective of the booking amount and 10% discount is given to students if the booking amount is > Rs 500.

Consider following code (please ignore syntax errors)

If (Visitor_type = "Student")

  If (Booking_amount >=500)

    Discount = Booking_amount*.10;

  Else

    Discount = Booking_amount*.05;

  Booking_amount = Booking_amount – Discount;

Is the above code correct? What data you will take to test the code?

Based on the static testing techniques you learned in the earlier section, you may be able to find an error of the assignment statement used in the first if condition. The first condition actually should be if (Visitor_Type == "Student"). Notice that == is comparison operator and = is an assignment operator.

Are there any other problems? If not, please try to run this code after adding few valid variable declaration statements and input statements to input Visitor_Type and Booking_Amount.

Typically as a student you will try this program with Visitor_type = "Student" and Booking_amount == 600 (or any such amount) and see the result. Having found the result OK, you will conclude that the program is correct. However that is not true. If you try with Visitor_type other than "Student" you will find that the discount calculated as 0 as against 5% as per requirement.

This is because the else statement is associated with the inner if and hence there is no alternate path given for the first If. So, no discount will be calculated if the visitor is not a student. The program hence is not correct

It is not easy to find such errors particularly with static testing techniques and also with just one data set. You may test the program with some other data sets but if that data set is also resulting in 'True' for both the conditions, it will give correct result. This means unless you test the program by providing values such that the first condition is falls, you will not be able find error in the program. So, for the given program, you need to take at least 4 test cases (data sets) as given below. Notice that apart from the input values for Visitor_type and Booking_amount, the table also shows two additional rows, one for expected result for the given data set and other is the actual result you get when you run the program with the given data set. If your expected result matches with the actual result, the test case is considered to be passed and otherwise the test case is considered to be failed and hence the program has an error.

Parameter/Variable	Value	Value	Value	Value
Visitor_type	Student	Student	Other	Other
Booking_amount	400	600	400	600
Expected Discount	20	60	20	30
Actual Discount	20	60	0	0

Understand that we have derived these 4 data sets because we have two if conditions and we considered all situations of each condition pass and each condition fails.

Let us say the code is now changed as below

    If (Visitor_type == "Student")
    If (Booking_amount >=500)
      {
    Discount = Booking_amount*.10;
      }
    else
      Discount = Booking_amount*.05;
    Booking_amount = Booking_amount – Discount

Let us test the code again with same test data

Parameter/Variable	Value	Value	Value	Value
Visitor_type	Student	Student	Other	Other
Booking_amount	400	600	400	600
Expected Discount	20	60	20	30
Actual Discount	0	60	20	30

In this case, the else is associated with the outer if condition. So, if the visitor is student but booking amount is less than 500, no discount will be calculated.

This and some such similar aspects have resulted in to some rules/guidelines which are known as test design techniques.

Concept:

Every **program uses sequential statements, control statements** (If-then-else or Switch) and **loop structures**. Various business actions are performed or calculations are done or data variables and objects, changes their values based on these control structures.

Typically **control statements breaks the normal sequence** of the statement execution as even simple if-then-else statement will result into two possible paths, one with true value and other with false value. In general we need to ensure during testing that actions taken or data input by the user force the execution of different paths based on the control statements. Each input action or input data set is considered a test case.

So, the primary **objective of white box** testing technique is to ensure that all the statements of the code, all the paths of the decision statement and all the results (true & false) of each condition used are covered at least once during testing. This is in general known as coverage testing.

The coverage goal is to ensure that

- Every statement is executed at least once.
- All independent paths/decisions within a module are traversed at least once
- All logical conditions are exercised on their true and false sides
- All loops at their boundaries and within operational bounds are executed

This can be achieved by using following techniques

- Statement Coverage
- Path / Decision Coverage
  - Two way
  - Multi way
- Condition Coverage
- Loop Testing

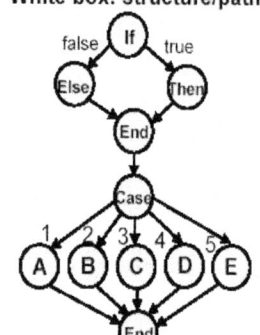

White box: structure/path

Coverage is a measure of the degree to which the test cases exercise or cover the logic (source code) of the program - % of code covered

Please note that we are not designing test cases based on business rules but based on Control statements – such as If statement and are not just considering one aspect (eg discount calculation as discussed in the example) but for checking effect on various aspects due to control flow.

There are many tools available in the market that can automatically analyse and track coverage by executing the code. However explanation of such tools and their operations are out of current scope

The example we are discussing is a very simple portion of code but in real life the code portions may be much bigger and complex. Also, programs may actually perform multiple actions, calculation in each path.

Let us see how a typical program can look with the help of one pseudo code as shown below. This pseudo code is for updating batch wise item stock for each transaction based on transaction type under different conditions / situations as per business requirement.

```
Read records from table
While (you get a fetched record)
{
   Statements
   if (a variable's value is 'PD' or 'IR' or 'AD')
   {
      if (tax >0)
      {
         calculate price inclusive of tax
      }
      statements
      Update stock and price in the stock table
   }
      else
```

```
{
Statements..
  calculate revised balance
  set flag to 'Y' ,set counter to 0 , set baseflag to 'N'
  while(revised balance is -ve and flag is 'Y')
    {
      {
        Set revised stock to 0
        if (counter == 0)
          {
            Update transaction with revised quantity
            Set baseflag = 'Y';
          else
          {
            Insert transaction into transaction table
          }
          Update stock table
      }
      if (pending quantity > 0)
      {
            Read record with stock > pending quantity.
            if (record avialable)
            {
              store record details in temporary variables
              increment counter by 1
            }
            else
            {
              Read record with stock > 0
                if (record available )
              {
                store record details in temporary variables
                increment counter by 1
              }
              else
              {
                set flag = 'N'
              }
            }
      }
      if (flag == 'Y' && baseflag == 'N')
        {
              Delete the transaction with original batch
        }
    }
    if (flag == 'Y')
```

```
            {
                statements
                if (counter > 0)
                {
                        Insert transaction in transaction table with new batch
                }
                else
                {
                   Update the transaction in transaction table with new price
                }
                Update stock with new batch
            } // end of Flag = Y check
        } // End of trn Type
        } // end while
}
```

Note that the actual program (with actual syntax and various other statements) is much longer.

So, for larger programs, it may be difficult to analyse the code from top to bottom and identifying various paths and derive test cases. Hence it is suggested to use flow graph depicting the control of the program or portion of the program. Let us understand flow graph in detail.

Now let us understand each of the above technique in detail.

4.4.1 Statement Coverage

As part of this technique one need to use test cases (or data inputs) such that all statements of the program are executed at least once. In other words each line of the code is tested. It helps in identifying faulty code.

If the program or a component uses only simple sequential statements without any control structure (condition branches), all the statements will get executed once first statement is executed. However if there are asynchronous exceptions in the code such as divide by zero, the test case may not cover all the statements.

Similarly section of code may be entered from multiple points due to which a test may not cover all the statements.

Statement Coverage = (Total number of statements exercised / Total number of executable statements in the program section under test) x 100.

So if there are total 200 statements of which 160 statements exercised, the statement coverage would be (160/200) x 100 = 80%.

Let us consider revised requirement as given below

Unit and Integration Testing with Structural based Test design

A multiplex theatre has come up with a discounting scheme: 10% discount is given to students if the booking amount if >= Rs 500. 5% discount is given if the visitors are other than 'FR' category or it is a morning show. This could be an additional discount for students

The portion of the main code is as given below

1. { If (vtype=='S'&& amt>=500)
2.   {discount=amt*.10;   }
3. If (vtype!='FR' || show=='M')
4.   { discount2=amt*.05; }
5. }

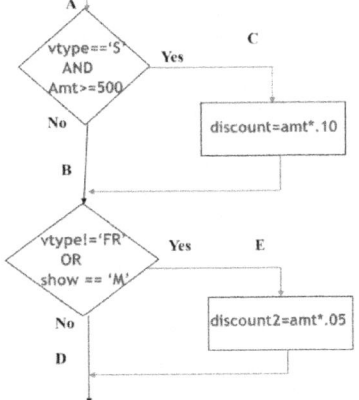

As you can see there are 5 statements in the code. For testing this function, you need to provide values of vtype, amount and show. Each combination of values vtype, amount and show can be considered as one test case. Let us use different test cases to understand how the code is covered

Test Case 1: vtype='S', amt=600, show='M'.

With these values, all the 5 statements will be executed at least once as both the If statements will result in to 'TRUE'. So, in this case we can say that statement coverage is 100%.

So, with this test case that covers path ACE, we will be able to cover all the statements. There may be some siuations where we may require one or more additional paths to cover all the statements, However if we stop at this stage, we may miss out some bugs as we are not testing whether function works properly when the If condition is not true. It may be easy to understand this using a flow chart

4.4.2 Decision / Path/ Branch Coverage

Every decision has two paths – one with TRUE value and other with FALSE value. So, we need to have additional test cases. We need to define test cases based on decisions and cover all the paths of the decision

As discussed earlier, statement coverage may miss out some defects and hence we need to apply technique called Decision Coverage or Path Coverage. With this we will need additional test cases.

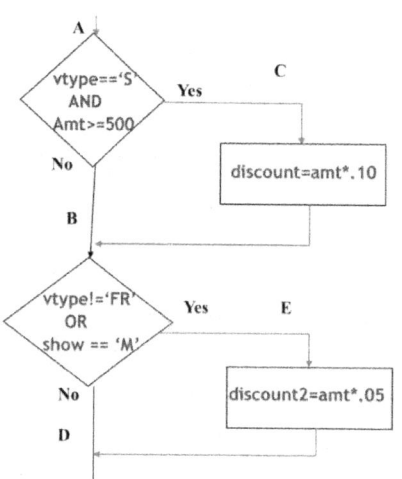

Test Case 1: vtype='S', amt=600, show='M'.- Both decision 1 and 2 are true and hence will take path ACE

Test Case 2: vtype='GN', amt=600, show='E'– Both decision 1 and 2 are false and will take path ABD.

Path Coverage = (Total Paths exercised / Total number of paths in the program) x 100.

Please note that there is a single statement in the two process blocks provided in the example for calculating discount depending on the compound condition specified in decision box. In some other example there may be multiple statements in the process blocks and some statements may set or change value of the variable used in the next decision box.

Let us assume that branch B and Branch C has some process blocks and both the process blocks have some statement that can change value of variable used in the next decision box. In that case we need to consider both the paths resulting in 4 end to end paths. ABD, ABE, ACD, ACE.

It is likely that the execution may not take intended path because of some mistake in constructing the structure. So the basis is to select test paths by studying the structure of the program and provide appropriate inputs so that every statement in every branch is executed at least once. The thoroughness of testing can be measured by checking how many such paths are executed successfully.

Control Flow Graph

For complex programs the graphs are further simplified by using nodes (drawn as circles) and Links (drawn as arrows). Node represents process block and also decision. Nodes are generally numbered. Links indicate direction of flow. If node also includes decision than it will have more than one links leaving it.

Node can be called a junction if more than one links enter it.

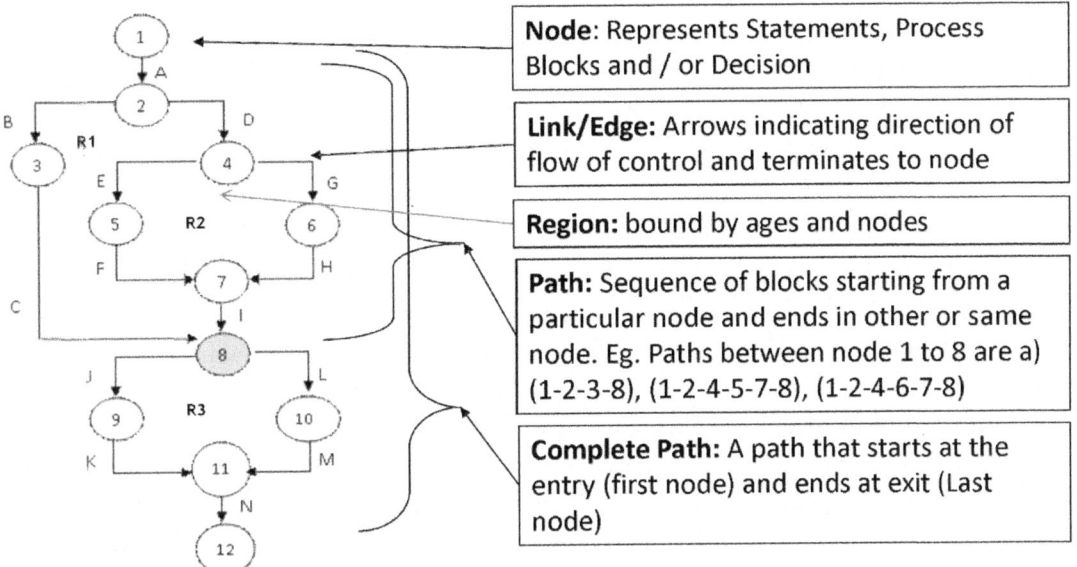

Node: Represents Statements, Process Blocks and / or Decision

Link/Edge: Arrows indicating direction of flow of control and terminates to node

Region: bound by ages and nodes

Path: Sequence of blocks starting from a particular node and ends in other or same node. Eg. Paths between node 1 to 8 are a) (1-2-3-8), (1-2-4-5-7-8), (1-2-4-6-7-8)

Complete Path: A path that starts at the entry (first node) and ends at exit (Last node)

Area outside the graph is also considered one region and hence there are four regions.

Paths can be either represented using sequence of nodes or using sequence of links as given below. Length of the path is is measured by number of links in that path

Complete Paths

Path No	Path using nodes	Path using links	Length of Path
a.	1-2-3-8-9-11-12	A-B-C-J-K-N	6
b.	1-2-3-8-10-11-12	A-B-C-L-M-N	6
c.	1-2-4-5-7-8-9-11-12	A-D-E-F-I-J-K-N	8
d.	1-2-4-6-7-8-10-11-12	A-D-G-H-I-L-M-N	8
e.	1-2-4-5-7-8-9-11-12	A-D-E-F-I-J-K-N	8
f.	1-2-4-6-7-8-10-11-12	A-D-G-H-I-L-M-N	8

Note:

a) Create separate node, if compound condition is used in IF statement
b) Above 6 paths constitute basis set of the flow graph. So, if test cases are designed to cover all the paths, every statement in the program will be executed at least once and every condition will have been executed on its true and false sides.
c) Some Branches are covered multiple times
d) All process blocks need to be covered at least once
e) If node has 'n' entry points then, same node should be covered n times (may have different impact)
f) If concatenated decision points, there could be duplicate paths. (eg. nodes 7 & 8 considered 4 times – last 4 paths). Last 2 paths could be ignored
g) Single entry single exit paths should be considered only once
h) Similarly combination of two paths also should not be considered

Reduce Redundancy: You will notice that some branches are covered multiple times. We need to keep following aspects in mind that all process blocks (or edges represented using arrow) should be covered at least once and hence if there is a decision node with two exit points, both exit points should be covered. Now if the node has two entry points then same node should be covered two times as different entry points may impact differently. However if you have concatenated decision points such as decision node 8 follows decision node 7. The entry point 7-8 is hence considered 4 times. Refer paths c) d) e) and f). This is duplication and last two paths e) and f) can be removed. Single entry single exit paths should be considered only once for reducing redundancy and unnecessary effort

Cyclomatic Complexity (CC):

As you can notice, the complexity increases as the number of independent paths in the program are increasing. Number of independent paths in the program is known as Cyclomatic Complexity. It can be computed with following formula

CC (Independent Paths) = Numer of edges (Arrows) – Number of Nodes (Circles) + 2.

In the example above we have

Number of edges = 14, Number of nodes = 12

So Cycomatic Complexity or Independent paths are = 14 – 12 + 2 = 4. And we have 4 independent paths as mentioned above.

Or CC = Number of regions = 4.

Cyclomatic complexity provides quantitative measure of logical complexity of the program. It also tells number of independent paths in the basis set and hence represents number of tests to be conducted to ensure coverage of all statements, paths and conditions.

Ideally a program should not have more than 10 independent paths. Otherwise it will become very complex to understand, maintain and test. The programs with higher than Cyclomatic Complexity of more than 10 are advised to be restructured make is simpler.

In order to execute all paths identified for testing, one has to see that the variables used in the condition determining paths should be accordingly assigned before the control enters the decision node.

Also note that it takes more time to test a path if the length of the path is longer.

4.4.3 Condition coverage

As part of decision coverage or path coverage all paths are being considered but note that each decision has two conditions. So there are actually 4 conditions. We need to use test cases such that each of these 4 conditions results in to TRUE and FALSE at least once. We will hence need to have additional test cases

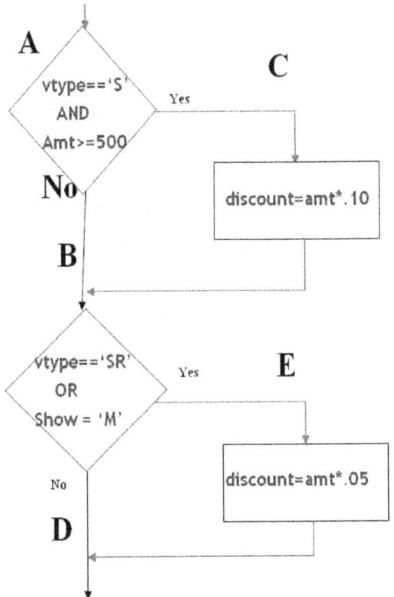

Test Case	Vtype == 'S'	Amt >= 500	Vtype! = 'FR'	Show = 'M'	Path
1. vtype='S', amt=600, show='M'.	TRUE	TRUE	TRUE	TRUE	ACE
2. vtype = 'FR', amt = 400, show = 'E'	FLASE	FALSE	FALSE	FALSE	ABD

3. vtype = 'FR', amt=600, show='M'.   FALSE   TRUE   FALSE   TRUE   ABE

4. vtype = 'S', amt=600, show='E'.   TRUE   TRUE   FASLE   FASLE   ACD

Now, in order to ensure that there are no issues in the program, should we not test the code with other values of these variables also – such as vtype='A','B',... amt= 200,250,300,320,550,600... and show= 'M','A','E','N'...

There can be infinite number of possibilities and the testing can take lot of time. We hence assume that if each path is covered once and each condition is tested for it's true and false path and if it works properly, the program will work for all other values if it take the same path.

Focus is given to ensure that the condition used in the program is correct. A condition will be incorrect if any one portion of the condition is incorrect – expression, Boolean or Logical operator, Parenthesis error

This is how we are limiting the number of test cases (or input data sets) and are able to do efficient testing with just four different sets.

Even if you test the code with 10 different data sets but if you miss out a specific path of each condition, you may leave the bug in the program.

So, the techniques help us to cover all possible aspects with minimum possible number of data sets.

Exercise: Identify the test cases (test data sets) and prepare a table providing expected and actual result for the following code

    Discount = Booking_amount * 0.05;

    If (visitor_type == "Student" && Booking_amount >= 500);

    {

      Discount = Booking_amount * 0.10;

    }

    Booking_amount = Booking_amount – Discount;

    Printf("Discount = %f", Discount);

You may also face issues with respect to syntax of a specific language and it may be difficult to execute the statements manually particularly for little complex if structure. Hence it may be a best idea to do white box testing and execute the code. One can use IDE environment providing debugging facility.

Condition Coverage = (Total Decisions Exercised / Total number of Decisions in the program) x 100.

Data Flow Testing (TutorialsPoint, ProfessionalQA.com)

Dataflow Testing focuses on the points at which variables receive values and the points at which these values are used.

So, the data flow testing method [fra93] selects test paths of the program according to locations of definitions and used of the variables in the program.

It aims to find out

- A variable that is declared but never used within the program.
- A variable that is used but never declared.
- A variable that is defined multiple times before it is used
- A variable is de-allocated before it is used.

4.4.4 Loop Testing

Loop testing focuses on validity of loop constructs. Loop is a commonly used construct required in most of the programs. Loops make path testing difficult due to the significantly increased number of possible paths, and they often contain bugs within the loop condition at the boundary values that specify the first iteration and the last iteration of the loop and are hard to find. So one has to consider initialization problems and termination problems. It is critical to ensure that

- Control does enter into the loop as per requirement
- Statements within the loop should be executed for the required number of times
- Control exits the loop as per requirement and execution does not end up into infinite loop

So, as part of testing we should design test cases that tests following condition for the correct results

Simple Loop Testing:

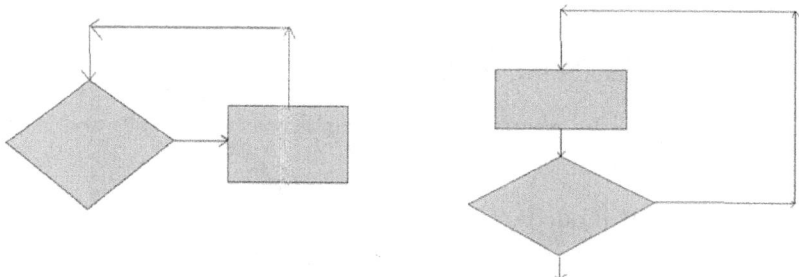

If there are maximum n number of allowable passes through the loop then following tests should be considered for testing

- Try to skip the entire loop (0 iteration). If it is successful then there can be a bug or zero may not be the initial value
- Assign –ve value to the loop control variable and look at the result.
- only one pass through the loop
- make 2 passes through loop
- m passes through loop where m<n
- n-1, n, n+1 passes through the loop

Example:

#!/usr/local/bin/perl -w

Open(DB, "filename");

$to_work_with = <DB>;

while (!eof(DB)) {

  print "$to_work_with";

  $to_work_with = <DB>;

}

close DB;

The program opens a certain file, reads it line by line, and processes this input. The problem is that the last line read is never used.

Example: Display Percentage obtained by students. Total marks for each subject is 100. Number of students and Number of subjects can be different for different course and hence take input

> Subtotal = 0;
>
> Input StudentCount
>
> Input SubjectCount
>
> While (I <StudentCount)
>
> {
>
> For (j=1; j< SubjectCount; j++)
>
> {Input Marks
>
> Subtotal = Subtotal + marks
>
> }
>
> Percent = Subtotal/j;
>
> Display Percent;
>
> Subtotal = 0;
>
> I = I+1;
>
> }

Find out the error in the above program.

Is the program correct? It may be difficult to find errors unless you follow the instructions of testing inner loop first and checking what is the outcome when loop is executed 0 times, 1 time, 2 times, n-1 time, n time and n+1 time. Also the data should be taken such that the at least for one case the subject marks are < 40.

Input					
Subject Count	0	1	2	5	6
Subject Marks	NA	30	50,60	40, 50,43, 65,86	45, 50,43, 65,86, 50

You will notice that if the SubjectCount = 0 it will still print the percent.

In Many programs you may not have only simple loops, but you may have nested loops, concatenated loop or Spaghetti loops. Let us understand what process we should follow for testing each of those types of loops

Nested Loop Testing Procedure:

Nested loops can result into impractical number of tests if the nesting increases. So, need to apply the approach suggested by Beizer [Bei90]

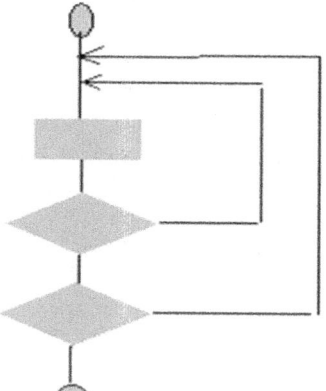

1) Start at the inner loop and set all the other loops to minimum values.
2) Conduct tests suggested above for simple loop while holding the outer loop at their minimum loop counter. Add other tests for out-of-range or excluded values
3) Work outwards, conducting tests for next loop but keeping all other outer loops at minimum values and other nested loops to typical values
4) Continue until all loops have been tested

Concatenated Loop Testing

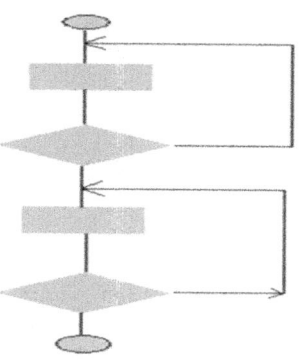

If each loop is independent of the other, test them as simple loops, else test them as nested loops

Spaghetti (Unstructured) loops Testing:

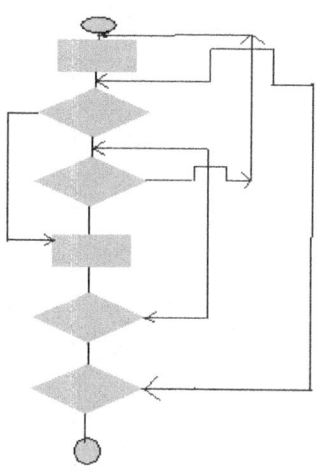

Such unstructured loops are not good for any design and should not be accepted. So, it should be reported as a defect and suggested to redesign using structured constructs

As per above discussions, you can notice that as the type of statement progresses from a simple sequential statement to if-then-else to Case/Switch to loops, the number of test cases required to achieve the statement coverage increases.

4.4.5 Approach, Advantages and limitations of White Box Testing

You may feel that black-box testing techniques can serve similar purpose but the advantage of white-box testing is that you need not execute the program from start to end for checking independent paths. Instead you can consider each portion of the code involving just one aspect / decision at a time. It is also best suited for reusable technical components. If the technical component has any error, all the business functions calling that component will give incorrect result. Finding and resolving errors from each technical component first can increase outcome quality of the business function.

There could be 2 approaches

1) Programmers may use diagnostic code – insert some print statements in between the code (to print values of variables) and to check whether program control passes through all statements of the controls structures (if then else, case / switch, loop structures). For example, one can include assignment statement with input values just before the decision starts and review the results immediately after the decision ends by including print/echo or similar statements. Programmer must remove these print statements after the defects are fixed.

2) Run the program under IDE (Interactive Development Environment) or debugging tools. These tools allow single stepping of statements and setting break points at any function or statement. Debugging tools also provide features to interrupt the execution (Breakpoint) just before the if condition statement and manually assign values of variables and also interrupt the execution again immediately after the decision completes and see the result before next set of statements are executed. Developers can observe contents of variables, buffers and memory more closely in the middle of the program execution. Developer can also step through the program one statement at a time or cause the program to continue running either till next breakpoint or till end.

This helps programmers/testers to view how the statements are getting executed and see values acquired by different variables in between or at the end and check whether the control flow works correctly or not.

The data objects gets created, used, modified, or destructed during the execution of programs. Use of IDE or debuggers, as discussed above can also help in identifying defects like referencing a variable with an undefined value and variables that are never used.

So, even if black-box testing has found some errors because of issues in the control flow, this technique helps **in locating where exactly the problem** is.

A **limitation** of white-box testing is its inability to show missing logic

Considering the approach, white box test design techniques and testing is best suited for unit testing and done by developers as it requires knowledge of programming and internal structure of the program.

4.5 Summary

In this chapter we primarily discussed what comes as part of **Unit and Integration** testing from technical perspective and also covered how **the white-box test design techniques** are used to do these.

We understood that various business functions could be realised by usage of one or more components. A component can be used by many other components. So, if there is any issue in the component, all the business functions using that component may give wrong result. Hence it **is important to first test all the components.**

Unit (a program / function / stored procedure / class) **testing** or component testing is a micro level testing done as soon as the unit is developed. It helps to identify some errors related to statement termination, wrong condition or logical operator usage, inappropriate / no initialization, null referencing or similar other such defects. These defects, if not found may surely result in some functionality error at a later stage.

In most cases these components / units are integrated to each other generally through function/procedure calls or direct inclusions with some parameter passing or using global variables. Typical integration errors include – inappropriate inclusion of header or other files, Misuse of interface, Inadequate/wrong functionality (both calling and called unit assume that other unit covers specific logic), misunderstanding of interface (by calling unit about the called unit), Inadequate error processing / post processing or initialization errors (Eg. Not releasing the memory allocated by other unit). **Integration testing** is done to identify such errors.

For both Unit and Integration testing, both white-box and black-box test design techniques are used but primarily white-box techniques are used.

There are two main approaches for Integration testing. In a **big-bang** approach in which integration testing is done after all the units/components are ready and in **incremental** approach where integration testing between two units/components done as soon as the components are developed and unit tested. Incremental integration testing may again be done **top-down or bottom-up** depending on corresponding development approach. Incremental approach may be difficult for some units if all the other units integrated to it are not ready and sometime dummy code may have to developed till the time actual unit code is developed. In top-down approach such dummy code is known as Stub and in bottom-up approach, it is known as Driver.

We then discussed **White-box test design techniques** in detail which is based on **internal structure** of the program and hence also known as **Structure based technique**. The objective is to ensure that our testing **coverage** is maximum (if possible 100% even if practically it may be difficult). Testing the program once would be good enough if the program is just a series of statements written in sequence. However the **control**

statements such as if-then-else, Swith / Case and Loop structure change the sequence or skips some code or repeats some code. So, coverage need to consider those aspects. Accordingly we discussed about **statement coverage -> path/decision coverage -> Condition coverage** (where compound conditions are used for a decision) and Loop testing.

So the objective would be to cover all the possible paths in testing with all possible conditions used in the control statement. We also discussed some approach to optimize our tests.

We discussed two approaches for white-box testing. 1) using diagnostic code (eg print statements) in between the code to display some messages or variable values and 2) run the program under IDE and use their debugging tools to interrupt the execution in between and check the values

White-box testing is best suited for unit and integration testing and requires knowledge of the code structure and hence done by developers. White box testing however cannot show missing logic.

4.6 Exercise

Sr.	Question
1.	Testing a module / Application to check if the components are integrated properly is example of _____ testing
2.	Explain Unit Testing with example
3.	_____ and _____ are the two approaches of Incremental Integration Testing
4.	Explain in short Top-Down incremental Integration Testing
5.	Initialization, Loops, Control flows etc are tested in _____ testing phase
6.	Under which situation you need to develop stub? Why?
7.	Describe approaches of integration testing
8.	One needs to create _____ for Top Down incremental integration testing
9.	One needs to create _____ for Bottom-Up incremental integration testing
10.	_____ is logic driven testing and permits Test Engineer to examine the internal structure of the program
11.	Explain Integration Testing with example
12.	White box testing is a static testing. (T/F)?
13.	Describe decision coverage in detail
14.	Name the type of testing to be done for testing a loop
15.	How should one test nested loops?
16.	It is possible easily to cover 75% of code coverage True/False?
17.	In white box testing, you do not need to execute the program (T/F)?
18.	Glass-box testing is same as _____ testing
19.	Draw flow chart for a program which determines whether the number is even or odd. Determine the paths which can be used for White Box testing
20.	Discuss limitations of structural testing
21.	What do you mean by Big Bang Integration strategy?
22.	What are Drivers and Stubs? Why are they required?
23.	Draw a flowchart for the following requirement and provide all possible paths

Sr.	Question
	to be covered as part of decision coverage
	In railway reservation system, there is a discount policy to be implemented as below
	All the people of age 60 or above gets 5% discount.
	If the reservation is done for return journey, then you get additional 10% discount.
	If the tickets are booked 20 days in advance, you get additional 10% discount.
	However the total discount should not be more than 18%.
24.	List down 4 names of all white box testing techniques
25.	Requirement: A multiplex theatre has come up with a discounting scheme: 5% discount is given to everyone irrespective of the booking amount and 10% discount is given to students if the booking amount if > Rs 500
	Study the following code and answer questions after the code
	If (Visitor_type == 'Student')
	If (Booking_amount >= 500)
	Discount = Booking_amount*.10;
	Else
	Discount = Booking_amount*.05;
	Booking_amount = Booking_amount – Discount
	Q1. Which of the white-box technique you will use to test the code?
	Q2. Minimum how many test cases (different test data sets) should be used to test this code?
	Q3. Why?
26.	Explain White box testing techniques with suitable example
27.	A vending machine dispenses either hot drinks (Tea or Coffee) or cold drinks. If you choose a hot drink, it asks if you want milk (and adds milk if required), then it asks if you want sugar (and adds sugar if required), then your drink is dispensed.
	a. Draw a control flow diagram for this example. (Hint: regard the selection of the type of drink as one statement.)
	b. Given the following tests, what is the statement coverage achieved? What is the decision coverage achieved?
	Test 1: Cold drink

Sr.	Question
	Test 2: Hot drink with milk and sugar c. What additional tests would be needed to achieve 100% statement coverage? What additional tests would be needed to achieve 100% decision coverage?
28.	Study following flow chart for date validation routine. Assumed that values are checked for numeric and also assumed that leapyear function is available and the array Daysofmonth contains days of month for each month 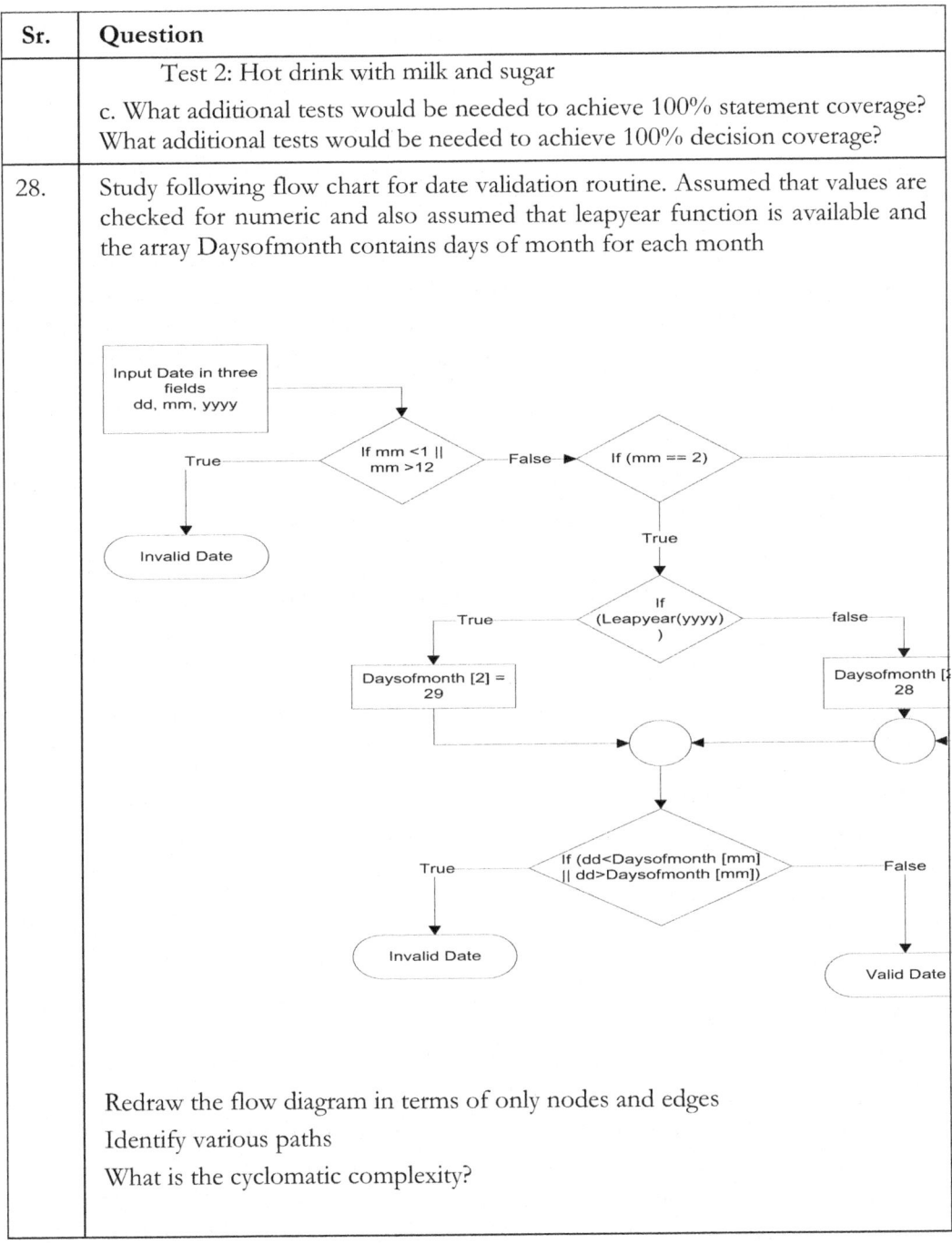 Redraw the flow diagram in terms of only nodes and edges Identify various paths What is the cyclomatic complexity?

5 Business Functionality Testing – Specification Based Test Design

5.1 Introduction

As discussed in chapter 2, Business functionality testing normally known as functional testing is done to ensure that the system works as per functional specifications and business rules.

Let us take example of Airline reservation system. The application may have much functionality such as Registration, Logging, New reservation, update/cancel reservation, Printing tickets, Maintenance of flights, preparing reservation charts and so on. Some of these modules/functionalities are useful for staff and some are used by the end users.

From a business perspective a Unit could be a business function/activity that represents a lowest level functionality. For example 'View Bookings', 'Book new ticket', 'Modify booking', 'Print ticket', 'Send mail' and so on. A business function can be realized (functionality can be achieved) by one or more of software programs / components.

Business functions can be tested by executing the program (Dynamic Testing) only from input – output perspective without worrying about internal logic in mind (Black-Box testing).

This again should be done at different levels – starting at lowest level of individual elements or fields in the input forms to full-fledged system. Let us understand all these levels in detail.

Business Unit / Function Testing

Field Level testing – Testing of individual field primarily for validating inputs

Form level testing – To ensure that the when all the field level inputs are entered accurately, system saves the data (once user presses submit button) and used for further processing.

System Testing

End-to-End functional testing – Ensure that all the business functions works well from start to end to achieve a specific goal. For example Login function, View flight function, ticket booking function, ticket printing function works well to complete a full ticket booking transaction. It focuses on correct implementation of interfaces. So, even if individual functions may work well, we may face issues, if the interfaces are not properly implemented. So, once I view flight options and select a flight and then click on 'Book Ticket' option, the selected flight details should correctly be transferred to the next module. Similarly once the ticket booking is done and then when I press 'Print Ticket; button, correct details should be transferred to printing program. Here our focus is primarily on a transaction or a business process comprising of one or more business units/components to be completed accurately at a given point of time.

Entity/Transaction Life cycle testing – This could be visualized as an extension to End-to-End function where all the transactions and processes are covered for the entire life of an entity. For example Reservation process, Update Process, Check-in process, travel confirmation process to be tested to cover full cycle of travelling on a specific ticket.

Techniques: Business functionality testing is done using black-box test design techniques where test cases are derived using business rules and functional specifications and is irrespective of the core technology of programming language used. These is also known as Input-output driven techniques as we consider software as a black-box with inputs and outputs for testing without having any knowledge of internal structure or logic used to meet the requirement.

5.2 Business Testing Levels

5.2.1 Business Unit / Function Testing

For our discussion, let us concentrate on online flight reservation module that is used by end user for booking any flight.

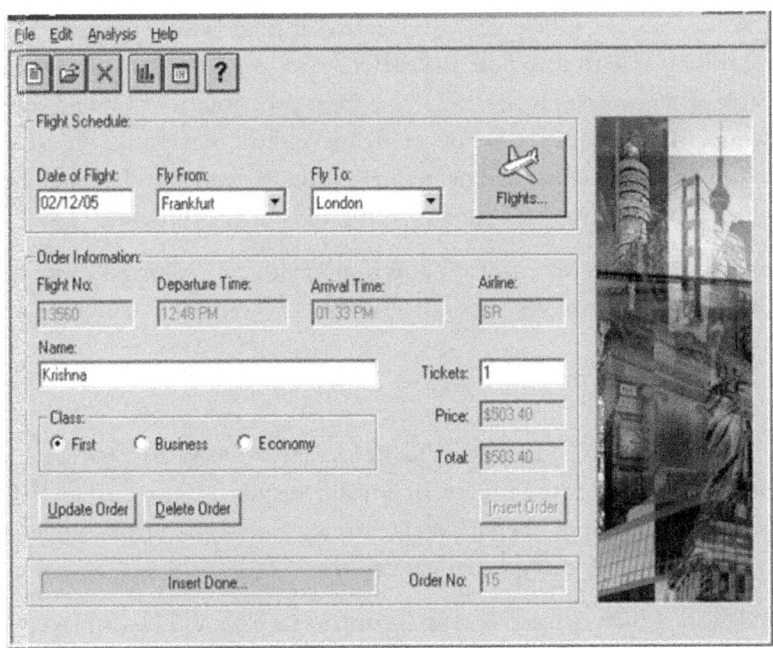

Figure 1: Flight Reservation Screen

Let us assume that it has some issues mentioned below

- It accepts past date for travel (if you already made payments, you may even lose money)

- It allows you to select Business Class even if flight does not have
- It accepts value of a location from where there are no flights.
- The Amount calculated is not correct.
  For example, you should have got 10% discount if you are a gold card member and booking more than 3 tickets in single order but you don't get

These issues or any other issues will make any customer furious and will probably move to competitor. We as a developer/tester need to ensure that we test the application properly to find all of above-mentioned issues so that they can be resolved before the application is moved to production.

In general, we do testing by entering some values for various fields as we feel appropriate for testing and check whether output is as expected or not.

For example, we may enter couple of different travel dates (one week from now and one month from now) and book tickets. We may miss out entering past date and checking that system should not accept it or we may miss out testing with date that is 3 months later than today's date when booking beyond 3 months not allowed. If we have to do exhaustive testing by checking each and every date, say for past one month and next 4 months, it would be very time consuming.

Similar will be the case for all the other fields and for all the other business rules. We need to hence see how we can do efficient and effective testing with optimum number of possible dates and still be able to find potential defects. So, we need to select a small subset from all the possible dates and yet it has to have a high probability of finding most of the defects. **Test Design Techniques** provide guidelines/ideas that guide our selection of inputs. Each individual technique is good at finding particular types of defect and relatively poor at finding other types. So, we may need to apply all of the techniques.

First important aspect of testing to ensure that wrong data is not allowed to be entered in the system. If the inputs themselves are not correct, the output is surely going to be incorrect.

1) Input Field validations

    The **Objective** is to ensure that data is valid before attempting to process it, thereby avoiding the generation of a run time error or invalid results. Almost every field on the screen requires some type of input validation else it may give some errors while storing in the database or may give wrong/unexpected results

    Field level validation should happen and an error message should be displayed when
    - the user attempts to leave the field.
    - the content of the field changes for any reason.

There are two basic types of fields:

a) **Independent field**: Fields that do not depend on other fields. So, each field is validated individually.

Inputs to the field can have **possible set of valid values and possible set of invalid values**. Possible values could be discrete values or may be continuous range of values.

Standard validations – Generally these rules are not provided by customer but are based on the design and as a developer we need to ensure.

Mandatory field – input **must** be provided for these fields

Length of the field: The length of the input data cannot be more than or less than specified length. For example, age cannot be of more than 3 digits or mobile number has to be exactly 10 digits or Passenger name cannot be more than 35 characters (as per column width provided in database).

Type of the field: Only specific type of characters are allowed as input. For example, some fields (Number of passengers) can contain only numeric data. Only specific characters are valid for some fields (eg only alphabetic and space for Name) or some specific characters should not be allowed for some fields.

Range: For numeric fields there could be **valid range**. For Integer Type field, the minimum and maximum values will depend on the size of the field or even type of field. For example integer / float / double may have different range of values that can be stored and accordingly input also need to be validated.

Note: You may not get above requirements explicitly from the customer. You may have to ask or may have to study database design to get some information such as type, length.

Validations Based on Business Rules

Only 'Economy', 'First' or 'Business' Classes are allowed. Other classes like 'VIP, 'Staff' should not be allowed

Travel date could be between tomorrow (next day of the system date) to 30th day from tomorrow assuming that as per rule, you can book tickets for next one month only). All the dates prior to system date and later than 1 month of the system date should not be allowed

Similarly number of passengers could be between 1 and 10.

b) **Dependent Fields** – the validation rule of a field depends on one or more other fields. For example, return journey date has dependency on travel date as return journey date has to be greater or equal to travel date. Similarly seat selection will depend on the class selected.

c) **Calculation / Derived Field Validation - Decisions based on multiple inputs.** There are businesses rules applied on one or more combination of fields to produce an output / derived field.

E.g: When you select or enter a flight number – Flight name and other fixed details appear automatically based on the input provided. One needs to ensure that they appear correctly.

E.g: Total travel cost is derived based on number of tickets booked, class selected, travel rate on the travel date for a given flight and any other additions (taxes) or deductions (discounts). One needs to ensure that this calculation is done correctly under different situations.

Flight Duration gets calculated based on **Departure Time** and **Arrival time** at a destination.

Similarly, in an HR system of a company, **Years of Service** gets calculated based on the **Date of Joining** and **Date of Retirement** entered.

2) Form (transaction) Level validation

After validating input and output fields (or derived fields), it is important to ensure that the Business transaction is completed successfully as expected once user provides input to all the fields and presses 'Submit' button. Primary objective of form level testing is to ensure that the details entered are accurately stored and be able to use it in generating any report or further processing.

This is primarily done by View or Print option for the same transaction. For example View booking should display all the details entered completely and accurately. If in some cases, there is no option to view the details, tester may have to look at relevant database tables and check the content.

There are three major options generally provided and to be tested

View – system displays the transaction details with all the data input and derived

Edit/Modify – System should allow modifying content. Business rules may or may not allow changing some information. This should not only make the changes in the transaction but also update other details. For example, if we change the travel date, system is also expected to release seat/ticket from old flight date and reserve for the new date

Delete – Delete the transaction. Most applications do not physically delete the data from the system but should put a flag as inactive or cancelled so that in future one can refer all cancelled transactions. Similar to update, one needs to ensure that all the related entities are updated accordingly.

Additionally one need to ensure that **duplicate entry** of the same transaction is restricted.

One may make use of decision table for testing above requirements where we consider Edit/Modify as cause and list down various effects. However Use case based technique is considered more relevant for transaction testing which we will discuss in the next section.

5.2.2 Validation and System testing

Validation Testing is the process of testing an integrated system to ensure that it meets specified requirements.

It demonstrates that the system works end-to-end in a production-like environment for all business functions specified in high level function design. Primary focus is on checking that various functions / transactions expected to be performed by different users are working as required.

Typically System level controls and sequencing related errors may come.

- Activation and execution of event does not happen at the right time or in required sequence. In an online /real time or embedded applications, it is important that various events are activated at a right time and in right sequence.

- Execution of a process even if pre-requisites are not fulfilled or Process is not initiated even if pre-requisites are fulfilled. There will be many processes which are to be executed only if specific pre-requisites are fulfilled. For example, Cancelation process to be initiated only if criteria for the same is met (eg. Before 24 hours of travel etc)

- Deadlock situation – In multi-processing /parallel computing and distributed systems, software and hardware locks are applied and it is possible that one or more threads mutually lock each other. One needs to ensure that such deadlocks do not occur.

- Missing functionality, Wrong functionality or Extra functionality. In large projects, when different functionalities are developed by different team members, miscommunication / misunderstanding is very likely resulting into such situation.

So, it is likely that business work-flow not appropriately followed or data not appropriately transferred from one business operation to other business operation resulting into errors. Validation and System Testing aims to find all such defects.

While Technical Unit and Integration testing and even business function testing is generally done by development team themselves, Validation and system testing is primarily done by independent testing team mostly using Black-box testing techniques. This is primarily User Interface driven in which various inputs are provided to the system and results are matched with the expected results.

End-to-End Testing (many times this is referred to be same as system testing but I consider it as an approach for system testing). This covers actual flow through a system in an end-user scenario. It is an approach used to **test** whether the flow of an application is performed as designed from start to finish and to identify system dependencies or interface issues and to ensure that the right information is passed between various system functions and systems. It also includes Integration with external interfaces.

For example, we test ticket booking process from start to end with following steps with an assumption that individual functionalities are tested separately.

    Login to the application

    View Flight options

Book a ticket – Select a flight, select date of travel, Provide passenger information, make payment etc

    Print a ticket

    Check the availability for updates

    Check the account for updates

    Check Passenger list for the flight

    Check Agent Commission details

Note that each of the above steps is an independent business function and we would have tested each of them as part of Business Function/Business Unit testing. So, the focus here is on how they are communicating with the other business functions, interfaces, database, network, and other applications and ensure that the transition from one business function to other business function happens properly.

Note that there could be multiple end-to-end scenarios involving different business functions / different sequence in which the business functions are used. Let us see some examples

    Login->View Booked Ticket->Reprint specific ticket

    Login->View Booked Tickets->Update details-> Print updated ticket

    Login->View booked Tickets->Cancel one ticket

    ……

    …….

In order to find out real interface issues, we need to consider each possible combination at least once.

Life Cycle Testing – This refers to the testing all functions required under different situation or at different point of time for the life of a specific entity or a transaction – from birth (initiation) to death (completion/deactivation).

For example, an entity 'Ticket' comes into existence by booking and cease to die (become inactive) once the passenger has travelled on the ticket or cancelled it. There can be multiple functions in between for a given ticket such as Update, Print, Email, Upgrade, Check-in and so on.

In a way, this could be an extension to cover business functions and processes which may also happen at a different point of time on the same entity. For example ticket booking and printing would happen at a given point of time, update at a different point of time, check-in at a different point of time and closure (travel completion) at a different point of time. So, the objective is to cover full life of the entity involving all the possible functions to ensure that all the processes happen as expected.

For both the testing explained above, we would primarily use Use-case based testing with normal and alternate scenarios. There could be multiple alternate scenarios as given below

    Booking, Check-In, Travel

    Booking, Update, Travel

    Booking, Update, Cancel

    Booking, Upgrade, Check-in, Travel

There could be some negative scenarios (which system should not allow). For example

    Booking, Cancel, Check-in

    Booking, Check-in on different date

    Booking, Cancel after travel date has passed

We will discuss Use Case based testing in details in the next section.

Note that **non-functional** testing is also done as part of System Testing as this is the final testing from IT/service provider, and hence should be very thoroughly done. We will discuss non-functional testing in chapter 8.

5.2.3 Acceptance Testing

Acceptance testing: Formal testing with respect to user needs, requirements, and business processes conducted to determine whether or not a system satisfies the acceptance criteria and to enable the user, customers or other authorized entity to determine whether or not to accept the system.

The main objective of Acceptance Testing may be to confirm that the system works as expected in business environment and to gain confidence that it has met the requirements.

Acceptance testing is done after the Validation and system testing is completed and almost all the defects found up to this stage are fixed. It verifies whether development team has met all the obligations and whether the system can be released to production or not. It also checks specific non-functional characteristics, e.g. usability, of the system.

It helps the user to

- Decide whether or not the right system has been created.
- Demonstrate that the developed system meets the functional and quality requirements from end user perspective

Acceptance testing is usually carried out **by the actual users (or representatives)** using environment simulating the operational environment to the greatest possible extent

Operational acceptance testing: Operational testing in the acceptance test phase, typically performed in a (simulated) operational environment by operations and/or systems administration staff focusing on operational aspects, e.g. recoverability, resource-behaviour, install ability and technical compliance

Software Application Products / COTS (Commercial Off-The-Shelf) Testing:

Product companies may have multiple levels of Acceptance Testing for COTS (Commercial Off-The-Shelf) software products depending on requirement as the companies themselves will not have the end-users within their companies. These companies have some domain or Subject Matter Experts (SMEs) within their companies who understands potential end users requirement from the market and documents the specification. However even if the product developed meets the requirement they have specified, it is critical to get feedback from the end users. Two levels of testing is done in for such products.

ALPHA TESTING: Simulated or actual operational testing by potential users/customers or an independent test team at the developers' site.

Alpha testing is termed as internal acceptance testing.

It is generally done **in the presence of the developer** at the developers site.

BETA TESTING / FIELD TESTING: Operational testing by potential and/or existing users/customers at an external site not otherwise involved with the developers, to determine whether or not a component or system satisfies the user/customer needs and fits within the business processes.

Beta testing is often employed as a form of external acceptance testing for off-the-shelf software in order to acquire feedback from the market. Many companies like Google / Amazon pre-release application for Beta testing and make changes after getting feedback.

It is done at the customer's site with no developer in site.

Some organization term, Alpha testing as **Factory Acceptance** testing and Beta testing as **Site Acceptance** testing

5.3 Specification Based/Black-Box Test Design Techniques.

As discussed earlier, techniques help identify tests that are most likely to find defects with limited test cases. We already discussed Structure based test design techniques in previous chapter where the tests are derived based on internal structure. We will now discuss, Specification based test design techniques where the tests are designed based on function specifications or business rules for the application.

Following techniques are used for input validations done as part of field validation as described earlier.

1) Equivalence Partitioning
2) Boundary Value Analysis

Following technique is primarily used to see how the system is processing different input combinations

3) Cause & Effect Graphing / Decision Table

Following techniques are used to do overall functional testing and verify system's behaviour

4) State Transition
5) Use Case Based

In addition to applying various techniques based on input types, one can guess possibility of defects based on **experience** and intuition on various other aspects or explore the functionality of new application and evaluating those functionalities based on experience. These techniques are known as

6) Error Guessing
7) Exploratory Testing

Before we discuss these techniques, let us understand some assumptions

Single Fault Assumption Theory: It is assumed that failures are only rarely the result of the simultaneous occurrence of two (or more) faults. In other words, even if there is a single fault, system failure will occur. In a very rare case more than one fault is required for system to fail. So while deriving different testing scenarios we will consider single data input, disregarding the combination effect of multiple inputs.

5.3.1 Equivalence partitioning

It is a **common sense approach** to testing, as most developers/testers use it informally without realizing it.

As per this technique, the input data of a software unit is divided into partitions/classes/sets of equivalent data from which test cases can be derived. All the data within the class or partition are equivalent means the system is expected to behave in the same manner for all the data of the partition. In other words, system is expected to produce equivalent output for each data within the partition. If the system behaviour changes for some values of the partition / set, then they are to be separated in a different partition / set. Hence test cases are designed to cover each partition at least once.

Let us understand some basic terminologies and how to derive these classes with examples.

Equivalence class: equivalence partition: A portion of an input or output domain for which the behaviour of a component or system is assumed to be the same, based on the specification.

For example

> For every **mandatory** field, you will have two classes, 1) Null value 2) Some value
>
> For **Length** checking you will have two classes, 1) All values whose length is less than the maximum length allowed and 2) All values whose length is more than the maximum length allowed.
>
> For every **Type** checking, you will have two classes, 1) All values with valid type, 2) All values with invalid type.
>
> Range checking. You can have 3 or more classes. 1) All values less than minimum allowable value. 2) All allowable values between minimum and maximum value. 3) All values more than maximum allowable value.
>
> **Equivalence partitioning technique:** A black box test design technique in which test cases are designed to execute representatives from all equivalence partitions. In principle, test cases are designed to cover each partition at least once. Since the system is assumed to handle all the values of the same class equivalently, testing with more than one data element from same class may not give different result and could be waste of time.

Business Functionality Testing – Specification Based Test Design

If we derive test cases based on 'Single Fault assumption theory, we consider it Weak and if we derive test cases based on Multi fault Assumption Theory, We consider strong.

Similarly if we consider only valid input values, we consider Normal and if we consider Invalid input values also, we consider Robust.

There are four types of equivalence partition testing

1) Weak Normal Equivalence Class Testing
2) Weak Robust Equivalence Class Testing
3) Strong Normal Equivalence Class Testing
4) Strong Robust Equivalence Class Testing

As part of our discussion, we will focus on most commonly used type – Weak Robust Equivalence class Testing – Which means single fault assumption and both valid and invalid classes of input values because in most cases we will apply this technique on variables which are independent and we would need to assure that application throws proper error messages when invalid inputs are entered.

Since the objective is to test what application is supposed to do (positive testing) and test what it is not supposed to do (negative testing), it is important that at least one value from each positive class / Partition (valid values) and one value from each negative class (invalid value set) is used as inputs for testing.

You may test the application with more than one value from same class but the expected result will be same or equivalent for all those values. However if you have some doubts on the classes identified or the system is modified which results in to change in the classes, you may decide to test with multiple values from the same class.

Please note that there can be multiple valid classes and multiple invalid classes.

Example 1: Travel Date condition: Travel date could be next day till one month from next day (Ticket can be booked only upto one month in advance)

Assume that today (System Date) is 15-Nov-18 and booking can be done for upto one month.

- Valid class: {16-Nov-18, 17-Nov-18……….. 15-Dec-18} –System allows booking

- Invalid classes: {…….. 14-Dec-18, 15-Nov-18}, {16-Dec-18, 17-Dec-18,……..} System should not allow booking and display error message.

If the today's date is 15-Nov-18 and we test application with 20-Nov-18, 25-Nov-18 or 30-Nov-18, expected outcome is same – to allow booking. So, it may not be necessary to test with all or many values from the same class. Rather, it would be better to test with date: 10-Nov-18 (from invalid class of date prior to system date) and 20-Dec-18 (from invalid class after one month) for which the system is expected to display an error message and say 25-Nov (from valid class) for which system should not display any error message and allow booking.

Considering the assumption we have taken, there is no need to waste time in testing with other values until the bug is fixed. You can notice that we will require only three tests (two from two invalid classes and one from valid class) and we will still have probability of identifying defect. In contrast you may test for 5 different dates but all from one class, you may miss a potential bug.

Example 2. The travel class must be either 'Economy', 'First' or 'Business'. So

Valid class/partition: {Economy, First, Business}

Invalid Class: (Elite, Employee,...., anything else}

Since radio buttons are used in the current application for the travel class, the user will be able to select only one of the valid values. However in this case, travel class is hard coded. For system to be flexible, drop-down may be provided but in some application, if input is expected from user, then this needs to be tested properly.

It is also possible that the application allows the three valid values in general but specific airline does not have flights with Business class. The valid class for that specific airline will be different.

Example 3: The Club membership applicant must be a person.

- Valid class: {person}

- Invalid class :{ corporation, ...anything else...}

As you can see the classes mentioned above are discrete classes or classes with discrete values. It may be practically required to take more input values from each of the class depending on how important it is for other processing

Example 4: Passenger name can accept only characters. Note that checking of field type can be done using this technique. For example, Passenger name can have following classes

- Valid class: All alphabets {A, B, C ……. Z. a. b. c…… z}

- Invalid classes: All numbers {0,1,……9},

All special characters {@,#,z,......}

Example 5: The input variable is an applicant's income. The valid range is Rs. 1000 to Rs. 75,000

- Valid class: {1000 > = income < = 75,000}

- Invalid classes: {income < 1000}, {income > 75,000}

Example 6: A test function int Max(int a)

The Equivalence Classes for the arguments of the functions will be

Arguments	Valid Values	Invalid Values
A	{-32768 <= Value <= 32767}	{< - 32768) , {>32767}

If an input condition specifies a continuous range of values, there is one valid class and two invalid classes

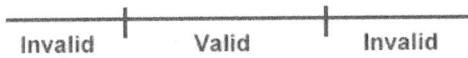

Equivalence classes are not only based on input domain (valid and invalid) but could also be based on **output domain.**

Example 7: In an examination result processing, Student's grade depends on %marks obtained as given below

    <40%   Fail

    40% to 50%   Pass Class

    50% to 60% Second Class

    60% to 70% First Class

    >=70%   Distinction

As you can see, there are

two invalid classes {.......-1%}, {101%,102%.....} and

valid class {0%,1%,......99%,100%}

However the output is different for different valid percentages and hence we have to have multiple valid classes

    Valid Class 1: {0%, 1%.......39%}

    Valid Class 2: {40%,41%....49%}

    Valid Class 3: {50%,51%....59%}

    Valid Class 4: {60%,61%....69%}

    Valid Class 5: {70%,71%....100%}

We will hence have totally 7 equivalence partitions and testing should be done with at least one value from each partition.

Note:

1) When you are analysing the test basis (e.g. a requirements specification), equivalence partitioning can help to identify where a drop-down list would be appropriate
2) Deriving correct partitions is very important for any requirement and sometimes derived based on assumptions. In such case, it is better to try several values in a partition. If this results in different behaviour where you expected it to be the same, then there may be two (or more) partitions where you initially thought there was only one

It may be a good idea to verify the partitions with the customers

We can apply equivalence partitioning to

a. **Numeric value**: If an input condition specifies a specific value then one valid class (with only one value) and two invalid classes defined
b. **Boolean condition**: If input condition specifies Boolean condition then one valid class with only True value and one invalid class with only false value
c. **Set of related values**: If input condition specifies member of a set then one valid class of all valid values and one invalid class for all the other values not in the set.

For all the tests to be performed should be documented in advance so that

o Important tests are not missed out
o It is easy to plan and track actual testing activities
o Evidences can be provided after testing

So let us see some sample unit test cases based on Equivalence Partitioning technique

Name of Unit/Program: Ticket Booking

Field	Requirement	Input	Expected Result	OK?
Passenger Name	Mandatory	Blank/Null	Display Error	
	Max 40 Characters	45 Character Name	Display Error	
	Between 1 to 40 characters	30 Character	Allow	
	Only Character Type	Enter few numeric characters	Display Error	
From Date	Mandatory	Blank/Null	Display Error	
	Only Current or future date	Past Date	Display Error	
		Current Date	Allow?? Only for future flights?	

Business Functionality Testing – Specification Based Test Design

Field	Requirement	Input	Expected Result	OK?
		Future Date within one month	Allow	
		Future Date beyond one month	Display Error Message	
Return Date	Should be >= From Date	Earlier than travel date	Display error	
	...	After travel date but after one month	Display error	
	...	After Travel Date within one month	Allow	
....	....			

5.3.2 Boundary value Analysis

For all continuous classes/partitions, even if you consider one value from each class, you may miss errors as errors may occur at the boundaries. For example, if today is 15-Nov-18 and business rule says that travel booking can be done from tomorrow till 30th day from tomorrow. Which means, travel booking can be done till 15-Dec-18. It is most likely that system may not allow booking for date exactly on 15-Dec-18 due to erroneous condition.

So, instead of considering any value from the class, this technique suggests that you take values from the boundary and improve chances of finding errors. This technique hence is **an extension to Equivalence Partitioning technique**

Boundary value: An input value or output value which is on the edge of an equivalence partition or at the smallest incremental distance on either side of an edge. For a range of values there will be lower boundary and upper boundary (for example the minimum or maximum value of a range).

Note that smallest incremental distance could 1 or a fraction value as per precision required. For Integer range, it will be 1. For fraction value such as amount with 2 decimal points, it would be .01.

Lower Boundary could be termed as Start / first / Smallest / Minimum / Lowest

Upper Boundary could be termed as Finish / Last / Largest / Maximum / Highest

Boundary value analysis: A black box test design technique in which test cases are designed based on boundary values.

Test cases or values at the boundary of each input Includes the values at the boundary, just below the boundary and just above the boundary

So if we refer to example 3 mentioned above

Example 1: The input variable is an applicant's income. The valid range is Rs. 1000 to Rs. 75,000

- Valid class: {1000 >= income <= 75,000}

- Invalid classes: {income < 1000}, {income > 75,000}

So, for testing take values 999, 1000, 1001, 74999, 75000, 75001

Values 999 and 75001 should not be accepted by application and through an error message whereas other values 1000, 1001, 74999, 75000 should be accepted by application as valid values

All values within the boundaries are known as **nominal values**.

Example 2: Similarly if for a given application, count can take values between 1 and 999.

Valid class is (1>= Count <=999).

Testing should be done with values 0, 1, 2 and 998, 999, 1000 where values 0 and 1000 are invalid values for which system should throw error message and other values are valid values and system should accept them.

Example 3: Boundary value analysis can be applied to the whole of a string of characters. Eg. Passenger Name.

The number of characters in the string is a partition,

Valid Partition: {e.g. between 1 and 30 characters} with boundaries 1 and 30

Invalid Partition: {0 character} {31,32,32...... characters} with boundaries 0, 31..

The invalid boundaries should produce an error message.

Boundary Approaches:

The approach we have considered is a **three-value approach** where we consider value exactly on the boundary, one below the boundary and one above the boundary.

However if we think boundary as a dividing line between two things then there will not be any value exactly on the boundary. And hence each boundary will have only two-values. Let us understand example 1 again with this approach

Example 1: The input variable is an applicant's income. The valid range is Rs. 1000 to Rs. 75,000

- Valid class: {1000,1001.... 74000, 75000}

- Invalid classes: {0,1,.....999}, {75,001,75002.........}

So, for testing take values 999, 1000, 75000, 75001

Values 999 and 75001 should not be accepted by application and through an error message

Many theories propose this **two-value approach** also.

There are also theories which consider only valid inputs on the boundary as part of the basic BVA technique and when we consider invalid value also that is min- and max+ then it is called Robustness **BVA Technique**. We propose to use Robustness technique with two value approach in most cases unless strongly typed languages result into run-time errors aborting the execution of the program for any invalid inputs.

Let us see how the sample test cases discussed earlier are refined using BVA technique. You should derive similar test cases for all the individual fields where user is going to enter some inputs.

So, let us refine our test cases

Field	Requirement	Input	Expected Result	OK?
Passenger Name	Mandatory	Blank/Null	Display Error	
	Between 1 to 40 characters	Name with 0 characters	Display error	
		With 1 character	Allow	
		30 Character	Allow	
		40 Character Name	Allow	
		41 characters	Display Error	
	Only Character Type	Enter few numeric characters	Display Error	
From Date	Mandatory	Blank/Null	Display Error	
	Only Current or future date	14-Nov-18	Display Error	
		15-Nov-18	Allow?? Only for future flights?	
		20-Nov-18	Allow	
		15-Dec-18	Allow	
		16-Dec-18	Display Error Message	
Return Date	Should be >= From Date	Earlier than travel date	Display error	
	...	After travel date but	Display error	

		after one month		
	...	After Travel Date within one month	Allow	
....	....			

Note that for Name field validation first two test cases are same. Mandatory means 0 character length not allowed and hence one of them can be removed.

We are also assuming that date control is used for date field and hence type of the input will always be correct.

Note:

We can apply equivalence partitioning and boundary value analysis more than once to the same specification item. Let us understand this with an example.

Example: An internal telephone system for a company with 200 telephones has 3-digit extension numbers from 101 to 500,

We can identify the following partitions and boundaries:

• Input type

Valid Partition: {digits 0 to 9}. **Invalid partition:** non-digits {a,b,....., Z, .,;.....}

• Input length - number of digits,

Valid partition {3}. invalid partition length {0, 1, 2, 4, 5,...}

• range of extension numbers, 101 to 500

Valid Partition: {101,102......,499,500}, **Invalid Partitions:** {1,2,....99}, {501,502....}

One test case could test more than one of these partitions/boundaries. For example, Extension 409 would test all three valid partitions: digits, the number of digits, the valid range.

EP and **BVA** techniques are generally used for Unit testing. However they can also be used for integration testing where system receive data from other sources such as other system/modules via some interface as value of an interface parameter may also fall into Valid and Invalid equivalence partitions. For example, if there is a separate component for providing grade based on marks / %marks passed as parameter from different calling programs such as Assignment grading, semester exam grading etc, we can apply these techniques during integration testing for result.

5.3.3 Decision Table

As you saw in various examples discussed earlier, Equivalence partitioning and Boundary Value Analysis techniques are important when you need to select value for validating a **single input field**. These techniques are primarily used to validate whether application is really accepting only valid values or is processing only for valid number of items and also to ensure that it displays proper error messages for invalid inputs. Many times, these techniques are also used to check if there are business rules generating different output for different valid inputs (eg Examination result) based on single variable.

However many times, business decisions are taken based on different combination of inputs given in more than one fields. The processing, calculation or output could be different for different valid values entered in those fields. Such rules cannot be tested based on equivalence partitioning or Boundary Values Analysis. You need a different technique.

Let us take few examples suitable function or subsystem that has a behaviour which reacts according to a combination of inputs or events.

Example 1: In airline reservation system, there is a discount policy to be implemented as below

o If the tickets are booked 20 days in advance, you get 5% discount
o If more than 3 passengers are booked in a single ticket/order, you get additional 5% discount.

> As you can see in this example, discount depends on two variables – a) Number of days in advance the booking is done and b) number of passengers in single ticket. So, EP and BVA can be used for both the individual input fields to ensure only valid inputs are taken for each one, but will not help validating whether discount is calculated correctly for different combination of the two fields and hence we need to apply Decision table technique.

> Note that inputs in these variables are **causes** and the discount % applied is an **effect**. For complex situations, it is suggested to draw graph indicating how combination of inputs effect output. So, this technique is also known as Cause-Effect graphing Technique.

For applying this technique, we need to follow **steps** mentioned below

1) Identify the causes and effects from the specification

Causes	Effects	Final Discount
• Number of days in advance the ticket is booked (Difference between Travel Date and Booking Date)	• Discount due to advance booking	0%
	• Discount due to higher number of passengers	5%
• Booking for three or more passengers in single ticker/order		10%

Note that you may first identify various causes or conditions and then identify the outcomes or effects or sometimes you identify various possible outcomes and work back to understand which caused / conditions will result into these outcomes.

2) Prepare Decision table
   a) Write down the conditions (or causes) in the table

C1: Tickets booked 20 days in advance				
C2: Number of Passengers > 3				

   b) Identify all the combinations of true and false for these conditions and write as rules

Rules:- →	1	2	3	4
C1: Tickets booked 20 days in advance	F	F	T	T
C2: Number of Passengers > 3	F	T	F	T

As you can see that there are two conditions. Each condition can have two possible values 'True' or 'False' (we shortly consider 'T' or 'F'). As a next step, we will have to write down each unique combination of values for these two conditions. These combinations are also known as rules. Each combination / rule may result in different effect. So we then write effect for each combination/rule.

Please note that the number of rules depends on number of conditions. If there are 2 conditions, you have $2^2 = 2 \times 2 = 4$ combinations. If there are 3 conditions then you have $2^3 = 2 \times 2 \times 2 = 8$ rules.

3) Identify the correct outcome for each combination (rule) and write

Rules:- →	1	2	3	4
C1: Tickets booked 20 days in advance	F	F	T	T
C2: Number of Passengers > 3	F	T	F	T
E1: 5% Discount for booking in advance of 20 days	N	N	Y	Y
E2: 5% Discount for higher number of tickets	N	Y	N	Y
Final Discount	0%	5%	5%	10%

You may write each effect separately based on specification and then write the final outcome which may be combination of the all the above effects.

4) Combine the rules if the alternatives does not make any difference or remove any rules which are not going to be possible.

5) Prepare Test Cases based in Decision table

As per the decision table prepared above there will be 4 test cases or different combination as per 4 rules specified above with expected result specified for each in Final discount row. Please refer to the following table indicating how the program needs to be tested for 4 times with different data values given in each case.

Test Condition / Scenario	Test Case	Input /Test Data	Expected Result	Pass/ Fail?
None of two conditions True	Ticket not booked in advance of 20 days and Passengers < 4	Travel Date = 19 days after Number of tickets = 3	Discount = 0	
One of two conditions True	Ticket booked more than 20 days in advance but Passengers < 4	Travel Date = 20 days after Number of tickets = 3	Discount = 5%	
	Ticket booked less than 20 days in advance but Passengers > 3	Travel Date = 19 days after Number of tickets = 4	Discount = 5%	
Both conditions True	Ticket booked more than 20 days in advance and Passengers > 3	Travel Date = 20 days after Number of tickets = 4	Discount = 10%	

Notes:

1) Decision table in which all conditions are binary (takes only one of the two values T or F) is called **Limited entry decision Table**.
   For Limited entry decision tables if there are n conditions then there will be 2^n rules.
   So, if there are 3 conditions, there will $2^3 = 2*2*2 = 8$ rules.

2) Decision table with conditions allowing more than two values are called **Extended Entry Decision Table**. We will see example
   For Extended entry decision tables, number of rules will be multiplication of number of values for each condition. So, if there are 3 conditions, 1st condition can take 2 value, 2nd condition can take 3 values and 3rd condition can take 3 values then total number of rule will be $2*3*3 = 18$.

3) Rules in the entry section will be converted to test cases. So number of rules will be same as number of test cases.

4) The completeness and consistency of the decision table can be checked by ensuring that
   a) Number of rules cannot be more than number of rules calculated. Some rules can be removed due to redundancy or not possible cases or mutually exclusive situations. We will see example of the same later.
   b) Number of Yes's and No's in each row should be equal for limited entry table.

Example 2: For a movie ticket booking If (booking is done 5 days in advance or number of seats booked are four or more) and registered member, you get 10% discount.

Rules: →	1	2	3	4	5	6	7	8
C1: Registered Member	F	F	F	F	T	T	T	T
C2: Tickets booked 5 days in advance	F	F	T	T	F	F	T	T
C3: Number of seats booked >=4	F	T	F	T	F	T	F	T
E1: Get 10% Discount?	N	N	N	N	N	Y	Y	Y
Final Discount %	0%	0%	0%	0%	0%	10%	10%	10%

Since there are 3 conditions each with two possible values, there are $2^3 = 8$ possible combinations.

If you actually notice, the discount is given only to registered members. So, if the member is not registered, we need not check any other condition and accordingly we can reduce number of rules.

Rules: →	1-4	2	3	4	5
C1: Registered Member	F	T	T	T	T
C2: Tickets booked 5 days in advance	-	F	F	T	T
C3: Number of seats booked >=4	-	F	T	F	T
E1: Get 10% Discount?	N	N	Y	Y	Y
Final Discount %	0%	0%	10%	10%	10%

The "-" (Hyphen) represents any or don't care the value. It indicates that the condition is irrelevant. Since there are 2 hyphens for rule 1, this rule is equivalent to $2^2 = 4$ rules.

This process allows us to reduce number of rules and hence number of test cases. However, if there is any risk identified for a specific functionality, one may decide to actually consider all the 8 rules.

So, for testing this functionality, you should be providing inputs in such a manner that these combinations are covered and final discount displayed by the application should match with corresponding expected discount % provided

Note: Simplification of the decision table can be done by evaluating / analysing effects. If the effects for the two or more rules in a decision table are identical, there could be a condition that allows the rules to be combined with hyphen (Don't care entry).

Example 3: Discounting Policy for club members

Consider reservation function for an event that gives 10% discount to all but person with gold card membership gets additional 10% and with silver card membership gets 5% additional. However if the members have not paid membership renewal fees fully then only 3% discount is given

Rules: →	1	2	3	4	5	6	7	8
C1: Gold Card Member?	F	F	F	F	T	T	T	T
C2: Silver Card Member?	F	F	T	T	F	F	T	T
C3: Membership Fully Renewed?	F	T	F	T	F	T	F	T
E1: 10% Discount general	N	Y	N	Y	N	Y		
E2: 10% Discount for Gold Card members	N	N	N	N	N	Y		
E3: 5% Discount for Silver card members	N	N	N	Y	N	N		
E4: 3% Discount restriction for partial renewal fee payment	Y	N	Y	N	Y	N		
Final Discount in %	3	10	3	15	3	20		

Notice that last two rules are blank and final discount is not applicable as a specific person cannot have both Gold and Silver membership. These two conditions are mutually exclusive. Depending on requirement you may either ignore the cases or if you feel that validation may be required and such situation if practically occur should be identified by the system and display an error message then you can add one more effect 'Display Error message' and adding it for those two conditions.

The test cases derived based on the above 6 rules can be documented as given below

TC ID	Test Case	Test Steps	Input /Test Data	Expected Result	Pass / Fail?
T1	membership not fully renewed and not 'Gold' or 'Silver' type get 3% only		MemberType='Bronze', Fully_Renewed='No'	Discount = 3%	
T2	Membership fully paid but not 'Gold' or 'Silver' gets 10%		MemberType='Bronze', Fully_Renewed='Yes'	Discount = 10%	
T3	membership not fully renewed and 'Silver' type get 3% only		MemberType='Silver', Fully_Renewed='No'	Discount = 3%	
T4	Membership fully paid and 'Silver' Type gets 15%		MemberType='Silver', Fully_Renewed='Yes'	Discount = 15%	
T5	membership not fully renewed and 'Gold' type get 3% only		MemberType='Gold', Fully_Renewed='No'	Discount = 3%	
T6	Membership fully paid and 'Gold' Type gets 20%		MemberType='Gold', Fully_Renewed='Yes'	Discount = 20%	

Example 4: Library Usage charges policy

A college Library has the following norms for yearly charge increase

- Fee increase will be 100 If female student and no defaults in last year else 150
- Fee increase will be 200 For any age if number of defaults made is between 1 to 3
- Send warning letter if one or more defaults made.
- Cancel the membership if 4 or more defaults made

Identify the causes and effects from the specification

Note that Cause and Effect listed above are two separate lists without any relation.

Also note that even if there are 4 causes listed above there are actually two variables impacting the causes –

One for gender which can have two values impacting effect a) Male and b) Female

The other variable No of default can have 3 values a) 0 b) 1-3 c) >= 4

So, there will be 2*3 = 6 possible combinations / Rules

Rules: →	1	2	3	4	5	6
C1: Female?	F	F	F	T	T	T
C2: Number of defaults	0	1-3	>3	0	1-3	>3
E1: Fee Increase 100	N	N	N	Y	N	N
E2: Fee Increase 150	Y	N	N	N	N	N
E3: Fee Increase 200	N	Y	N	N	Y	N
E4: Warning Message	N	Y	N	N	Y	N
E5: Cancel Policy	N	N	Y	N	N	Y
E 1-3 Fee increase	150	200	NA	100	200	NA

As you can notice, effects E1 to E3 can also be combined into single line as per last row in the table. Also notice that when there were more than 3 defaults, the membership is cancelled and hence there is no question of increasing any fee (so it is mentioned as NA in the last row). Note that Rule 2 and 5 indicated number of defaults could be between 1 and 3. You can hence apply BVA technique also so the rule should be ideally tested with boundary values 1 and 3 both. Which means it can result into additional test cases and not just 6. Number of defaults 0 and > 3 are already covered.

Exercise: Write test cases in excel test case format for above rules.

In addition to identifying optimum test cases, this technique is also able to point out incompleteness and ambiguities in specifications

Example 5: Examination result rule for giving grade is as below

    <40%   'fail'

    >=40% but <50%   'Pass'

    >=50% but <60%   'Second Class'

    >=60% but <70%   'First Class

    >=70%   'Distinction'

However if the student's attendance is <60%, his grade is reduced to 'Pass' even if his percentage of marks obtained is >= 50%.

There are two variables 1) % of marks which could take any of the 5 ranges and 2) % of Attendance which could take any of the two ranges

Rules: →	1	2	3	4	5	6	7	8	9	10
C1: % of Marks	0-39	40-49	50-59	60-69	70-100	0-39	40-49	50-59	60-69	70-100
C2: % of Attendance >=60%	F	F	F	F	F	T	T	T	T	T
E1: Grade	Fail	Pass	Pass	Pass	Pass	Fail	Pass	Second	First	Distinction

Once again, you can apply BVA also for checking each rule and hence you may consider both the boundaries for each range resulting into actually 20 test cases and not just 10 test cases as shown above.

For example with attendance >=60% you should test with 0% - fail, 39% - Fail, 40%-Pass, 49%-Pass, 50%-Second Class, 59%-Second Class, 60%-First Class, 69%-First Class, 70%-Distinction, 100% - Distinction, 101% . We assume that separate test cases had already been prepared for invalid inputs such as -1% or 101%. Or if the percentages are calculated by the software based on marks obtained, we assume that % calculation logic is separately tested and it will be between 0% to 100% only. However if the % calculation is done by the system then our test cases should include marks for each test case so that a specific rule become true and testing is done as per each rule of the decision table.

One may also think that rules 4 and 5 may not be applicable and can be ignored since the outcome is same for all the 3 conditions as the business rule says if % of marks > 50 will also get 'Pass' class if the attendance is <60%. Whether to consider those rules or not may depend on various other risk factors. So, it is advisable to consider those rules unless there time/effort crunch.

Decision Table can also be used to design test cases for validating inputs which are based on more than one variable.

Example 6: A loan application where the user can enter one of the two things a) monthly repayment amount or b) loan period (number of years in which the amount will be repaid). If you enter both, the system will have to make compromise between the two if there is a conflict.

Rules:→	1	2	3	4
C1: Term of Loan is entered	F	F	T	T
C2: Repayment amount is entered	F	T	F	T

	1	2	3	4
E1: Process The Term			Y	Y
E2: Process the Repayment Amount		Y		Y
E3: Display Error Message	Y			

While preparing decision table, you may realize that we hadn't thought what should be done if user doesn't enter any of the two fields and assume that the system should display an error message. This is how this technique also helps in identifying any ambiguities in the specification. Ideally, all assumptions should be verified with the customer and if you discuss with customer, he mentions that the user should not be allowed to enter both the details. In that case the effect for rule 4 will change and 'Y' will need to be removed from E1 and E2 and to be written for E3 (Display error message).

Benefits:

Decision tables provide a systematic way of stating complex business rules, which is useful for developers as well as for testers in exploring various possible effects of combinations of different inputs and can be useful in finding ambiguities in specifications also.

In absence of this technique, one may use some random combination of inputs for testing resulting in some misses (of important combination) due to which you may not be able to identify some possible defects. OR you may end up testing same combinations with multiple data sets which could be waste of time.

5.3.4 Use Case Based Test design

A **use case** is a description of a particular use of the system by an actor. The actor may be something that the system interfaces to. Actors are generally users (people) but they may also be communication links or sub-system or other systems. Each use case provides sequence of steps that describes the interactions the actor has with the system in order to achieve a specific task or, at least, produce something of value to the actor.

For example

Use Case: Customer makes online reservation

Steps:

Actor - Selects Trip Type and enters travel dates, number of passengers

System – Available options matching the input are displayed.

Actor - Selects one option

System - Passenger information page appears

Actor - Fills Passenger details and submits

System - Payment Page appears

Actor - enters credit card details and presses 'Submit'

System – control is passed to accounting system and confirmation message displayed

Similar use case details will be there for following use cases

Agent Makes reservation

Agent Cancels Reservation

Supervisor Waives Penalty

….

Use cases are defined from the point of view of the actor, not the system, describing what the actor does and what the actor sees rather than what inputs the system expects and what the system 'outputs. They often use the language and terms of the business rather than technical terms, especially when the actor is a business user.

Use Case Model: The use case model involves various actors and various business actions that can be performed by those actors (users).

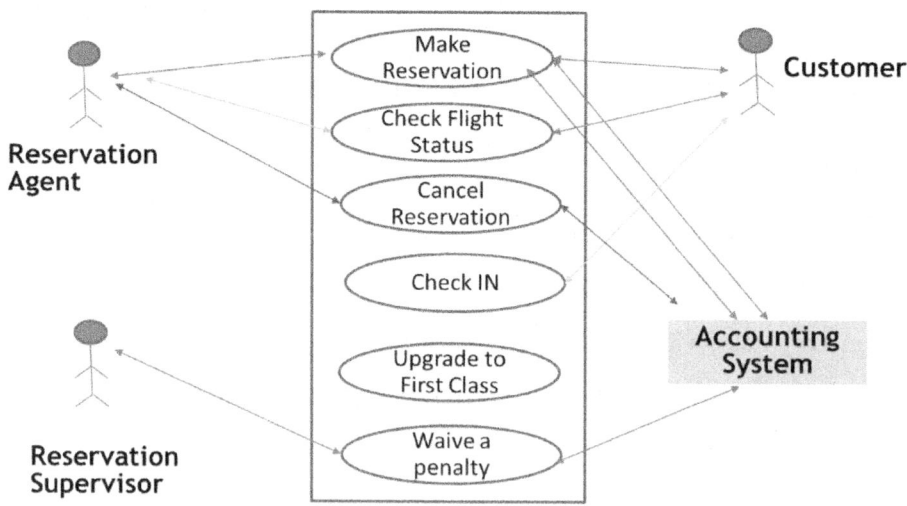

Each use case has two **types of scenarios** – a) Primary and b) Alternate

1) Primary / Basic Scenario

   It is the most common way for a use case to happen; as if everything goes as per normal process.

   It represents normal functionality described by the use case.

   For example, online reservation by passenger with all valid details using normal payment mode

2) Alternate Scenario

   This is a scenario where the precondition steps, actions or sequence of actions are different from the one described in the primary scenario. This includes special cases or exceptional conditions or even error conditions.

   For example, User enters all the details, but later on changes mind and modifies details before confirmation. User Cancel's in between or Flight gets full for a given date/slot or Invalid card is used.

Identifying alternate/error scenarios:

An alternate scenario can occur if

- Any other action can also be taken at this time

    Eg. Anytime before customer clicks 'Book', customer may click 'Cancel'. Post Condition: Customer still logged in. Pages initialized

- Any other event can happen that can cause the system to behave differently

    Eg. Accounting system can notify that the credit card has been declined. Post Condition: Allow to correct information

- Anything that can go wrong (by the system, by user or by other actor)?

    Eg. System crashes before system displays confirmation message. Post condition: system saves partially entered data, such as Ticket entry is done but actual reservation does not happen (seat allocation does not happen)

Developing Negative (Destructive) test cases based on Scenarios

There are two sources for deriving negative test cases

- Test Cases based on alternate scenarios with invalid data
- Test cases that violate items in pre-condition

    Example

    Cancel reservation that does not exist

    Cancel reservation where flight time is < 24 hours

    Cancel reservation for which boarding pass was already issued

Components of Scenario

Pre-Conditions

   Anything that must happen before the scenario can start

   It describes the state in which the system must be before the scenario start

Steps

   All interactions between the system and actors that is necessary to complete the scenario

Post-Conditions

   Anything that must be true after the scenario is completed

   What state the system acquires after the scenario has been completed successfully

Example 1 of Scenario: Customer makes flight reservation

Pre-Conditions	Steps	Post-Conditions
• Round trip is available • Customer has logged in successfully • Credit card is valid	• A - Select trip type • A - Enter travel details • A - Press 'search' button • S - Available options displayed • A - Select one option • S - Passenger information page displayed • A - Fill Passenger details • S - Payment page displayed • A - Fills credit card details and press 'Book Tickets' • S - Transaction is to Accounting system • S - Confirmation message is displayed	• Reservation has been made • Seats are assigned and removed from inventory • Credit card transaction is posted • Customer is still logged into the system • 'Update' and 'Cancel' buttons are enabled

In steps, **A-** Represents action taken by **Actor** and **S-** represents response by the **System**.

Use case testing: A black box test design technique in which test cases are designed to execute scenarios of use cases. It helps us identify test cases that exercise the whole system considering all use cases with every scenario from start to finish. They are used mostly at the system and acceptance testing levels & useful for finding defects in the real-world use of the system.

Use case based testing can uncover integration defects caused by the incorrect implementation of a solution by a component considering the inputs provided or processing done by the previous component. Please note that technical integration problems may be identified during integration testing but business rule based integration may be identified more accurately using this technique. For example cancelation of ticket may be technically possible but from a business rule perspective, the ticket can be cancelled and refund can be given only if the cancelation is done before 24 hours of travel time. Such defects can be uncovered by relevant primary and alternate scenarios.

So for online payment functionality, you may have tested different scenarios covering different payment modes such as Cash, Cheque, Credit Card, Debit Card, Net Banking with slight variation in steps or responses from the system.

We can derive multiple test cases from each scenario with different combination of data inputs. In this case, the pre-condition or steps followed may not change but the data used may change.

The system test cases for various transactions are derived based on these use cases as per the process described below.

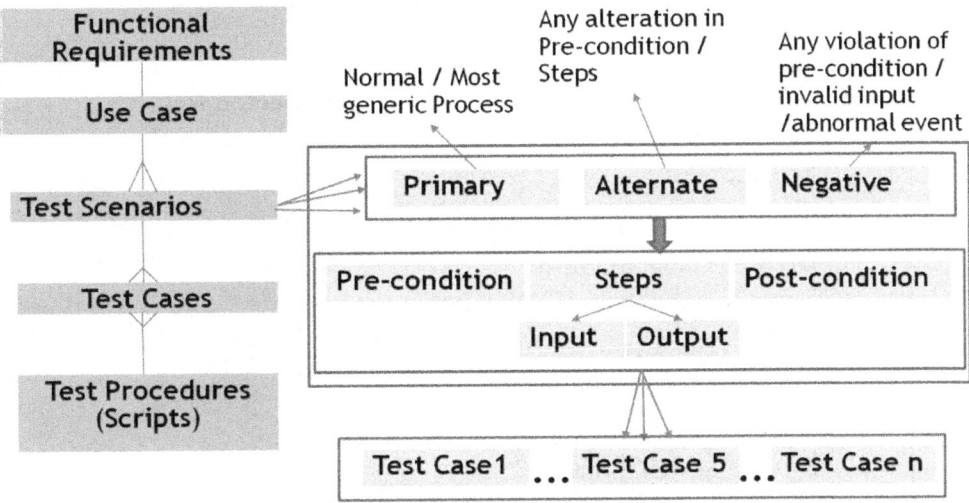

Each variant in the pre-condition and/or input becomes a test case.

We will discuss test procedures in next chapter.

If the use cases are written in detail, they can be directly used for testing. For example, if you directly use above use case, then at the time of testing you will first read the pre-condition and bring the system to the desired state (eg login with valid user ID and Password) and all the other relevant information ready (eg credit card). Then follow the steps, do what is provided against A- and ensure that system responds as provided against S-. Once all the steps are completed, ensure that all actions are taken by the system as provided in post-condition. If at any place the system response is not as expected or if any action not taken by the system correctly as provided in post-condition, there are bugs in the system and to be reported.

It is however advisable to derive and document test cases from each use case scenario instead of directly doing testing using Use case. This is because; you can provide actual input data to be used during testing so that if defect occurs, it is possible to reproduce the defect using same input data. It is also likely that you may have to use different input data where expected results don't just depend on the steps followed but also on the data entered. So, it is likely that there are more test cases for a single scenario.

The test cases derived from the above use case scenario is explained below.

Test Case ID: TC0001

Description: Verify that travel reservation is completed successfully by a passenger

Pre-Condition:

1) Passenger has valid credit card for booking 2) Round Trip is available between two cities – Ahmedabad and Mumbai. 3) A user is successfully logged in with User ID: passenger1 and Password: passenger1 and Home page is displayed which contains a button 'Reserve Ticket'.

Step #	Steps and Test Data	Expected Result
1	Enter Trip Type: Round From Location: Ahmedabad To Location: Mumbai Travel Date: 15-Nov-2019 Return Date: 18-Nov-2019 Number of passengers: 2 Select Class: Economy Press 'Search' Button	System displays various flight options with number of seats available and price/cost
2	User Selects a specific flight option by clicking 'book' button against that flight	System displays forms to input passenger details
3	Enter Passenger details (Name, Gender, Age) for both passengers 1 Manish Tripathi, M, 55 2 Mona Tripathi, F, 54 Press 'Submit' Button	System verifies and accepts the details and displays payment form
4	Provide Credit card details Credit card agency: ICICI Credit Card number: xxxxxxxxx Press 'Submit' button User confirms and Press Submit button	Control goes to Accounting system, credit card details are verified and then confirmation message is displayed. Payment if transferred. Ticket is generated and displayed

Post Condition: Verify that 1) Reservation is done, 2) Seats are removed from inventory, 3) Credit card transaction is posted, 4) Customer is still logged into the system, 5) 'Update' and 'Cancel' buttons are enabled (so that user can update or cancel the reservation if required).

Note:

1) You will notice that steps are at high level as compared to Unit testing because it is assumed that unit testing was already done and individual field level rules are assumed to be working fine.

2) If system is not in pre-condition state then we need to first take some steps to bring it in pre-condition state.

3) One need to Identify inputs in the pre-conditions and in steps and provide exact data to be used.

4) Output described in each step and post-conditions are expected results and to be verified. They are all to be considered as separate test cases and in some cases may have to be documented separately.

5) Each variant in the pre-condition or steps becomes separate test case. For example, user has valid debit card instead of credit card or does not confirm the details after entering details and changes the data in between or enters age such that passenger becomes a senior citizen

Example 2 of Scenario: Agent Cancels Reservation

Pre-Conditions	Steps	Post-Conditions
• Reservation Exists • Not cancelled before • Payment Made • Credit card is still valid • Flight time is at least 24 hours before cancellation time (business rule) • A boarding pass has not been issued	• Enter Reservation no. • System Displays Reservation details • Click 'Cancel' • System asks for confirmation • User provides confirmation • System sends credit transaction to accounting system • Confirmation is displayed	• Reservation will have been marked cancelled • Seat is made available • Credit transaction has been generated and confirmation number is displayed

Exercise:

a) Prepare test cases for above scenario.

b) Prepare alternate scenarios and negative scenarios

5.3.5 State Transition

Many times, application appearance/output for the same input/state is different depending on what has happened before.

For example, a word processing application has two states - Open and Close. The 'Close' button is available only if a document is open. After you select 'Close' once, you cannot select it again for the same document unless you open that document. In Windows Paint program, the screen and the cursor changes its shape based on the tool selected – Pencil, Brush, rubber etc

Similarly in a banking application, if you request to withdraw Rs 500 from your account, it disburses cash. Later you may make the same request again, but system may refuse (because you do not have enough balance in your account now). This is because the state of your bank account changes due to first withdrawal request.

Similarly an online reservation system may provide different output for unregistered users and registered users. It can provide different buttons if no tickets are booked and different buttons if some tickets are booked (means current state of the user or transactions of the user). So, 'Update' and 'Cancel' buttons should be disabled until any ticket is booked and is active (travel not yet happened).

Every system can be in different finite number of states. System may transition to other state if some action is taken. It is important to ensure that system behaves as expected due to changes in the state (situation / position / circumstances) of system/customer/any other entity such as account.

A **state transition model** has following components

1) Application can occupy various states – Identify unique states the application can be in.

   For reservation application

   - **Unregistered User/Start State**–You are accessing the application for the first time and have not yet registered
   - **Registered User State** – You have already registered to the application and have successfully logged in
   - **Active customer State** - You have done some travel booking and it is still active – you have not yet travelled

2) Application can move to only specific state from the current state

   Application can move from State 1 to state 2 but cannot move from state 1 directly to state 3.

Application moves from state 2 to state 3 when the booking is done and again moves back to state 2 when travel takes place

3) Only specific transaction or events are allowed in the particular state

Unregistered User/ Start State - will display options only for viewing various flight schedules but will not display any options to book any tickets. The application will also display option to register

Registered User State – In addition to displaying option for viewing various flight details, the application will also display options and buttons to be able to book the ticket

Active Customer State - Once a ticket is booked and active, the user becomes active customer. Under this state, application will display additional option for updating or cancelling the ticket. So corresponding buttons to Update or Cancel will now be enabled.

4) Only specific events results into a transition to other state

As an unregistered user, if you just view flights, the state does not change but if you register you can move to state 2. Similarly you can move from state 2 to state 3 only if you book ticket

The input or condition or event that takes the application from one state to other could be a key press, a menu selection, an input, or a telephone ring or any other such process. State cannot be exited without any reason / event. So, until some event takes place, application will remain in the same state.

5) The actions or effect that result from a transition (an error message, or success)

Once you move from state 2 to state 3, the buttons 'Update' and 'Cancel' will be enabled. In general, this includes a menu or buttons being displayed or hidden, a flag being set, calculation being performed or any other such thing happening due to transition.

State transition testing: It is a black box test design technique in which test cases are designed to execute valid and invalid state transitions. It helps to validate various states when a program moves from one visible state to another

To be thorough, we may want to make sure that we cover every state (i.e. at least one test goes through each state) and every transition from one state to other state using all possible transactions that result into those transition.

Current State		#	Action	New State
S1	Start/Unregistered user	1	View Schedule	S1
S1	Start/Unregistered user	2	Register	S1
S1	Start/Unregistered user	3	Login	S2
S2	Registered User	4	View Schedule	S2
S2	Registered User	5	Book Ticket	S3
S3	Active Customer	6	Print Ticket	S3
S3	Active Customer	7	Cancel Ticket	S2
S2	Registered User			

As you can notice, we have to test each of the above 7 situations and ensure that the system takes us to new state correctly. Some actions do not change the state but some other actions change the state. It is also possible, same action may result in state change under one situation and may not result into state change in some other situation. So, if we have two active travel tickets – If we cancel one ticket, state may not change but if we cancel 2nd (last) ticket, the state will change.

So, State transition technique can also be considered as technique to find **more scenarios** under use case based testing.

The test can be formally documented in standard format based on the State transition table

Pre-Condition	Test ID	Test Case	Test Steps	Input -Test Data/ Action	Expected Result	Pass/ Fail?
Unregistered User		Viewing Schedule does not change the state		View Schedule	Application shows schedule, State remains same S1	
Unregistered User		Behaviour changes after registration		Action: Register	Registration completes. State remains same S1.	
Registered User		Registered User tries to login (with valid UID, PWD)		Login	Application display User name and allows booking (State 2)	
-----		---				

Let us take other example

Example: Login to banking application for cash withdrawal

This being critical application impacting financial aspects, the application may have provision to lock the account if wrong user ID & Password given for four times. In this case Login screen is same, the inputs required are same but action required after 4th trial is different. After 4th trial the application has to move to locked state and should not allow user to access the application unless he/she gets it unlocked by providing necessary proofs to bank officials. Please also note that since application has to internally maintain count of the trial at each trial, each trial is treated as a separate state. Sometimes transition diagram looks better to easily understand relationship between each state and transition from one state to other state.

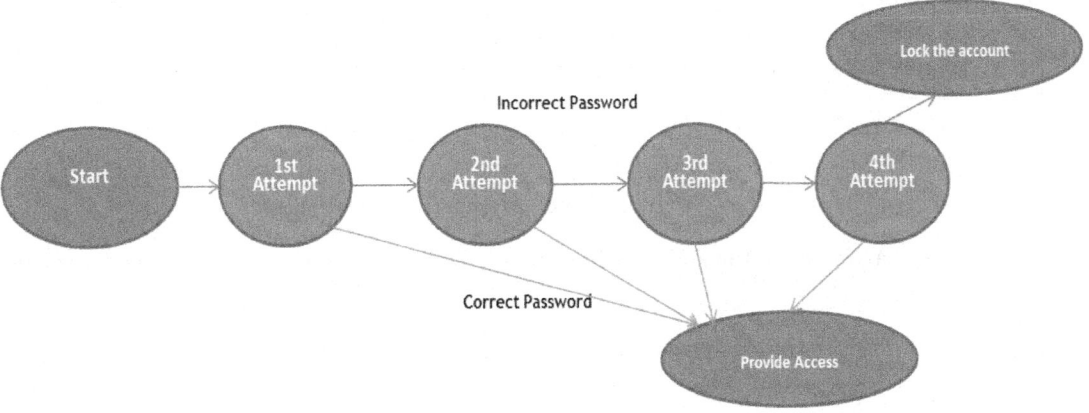

The test cases can be written in table format also.

States		New state if you Enter Correct Password	New state if you Enter Incorrect Password
S1	Start	S6	S2
S2	1st Try	S6	S3
S3	2nd Try	S6	S4
S4	3rd Try	S6	S5
S5	4th Try	S6	s7
S6	Access	?	?
S7	Close Application	-	-

As part of the testing, one may have to try correct password and incorrect password at all trials but entering correct password at all trials may not be required.

Example: Online Shopping Cart functionality.

It starts with an empty cart. As you select items for purchases, they are added to the shopping cart. You can add more items or remove Items from basket. Once you complete selection of all items to be purchased, you decide to check out. System will display a summary of the items in the cart with price and the total cost. Once you confirm, the system go to the payment Option. Otherwise you go back to shopping (so you can add or remove items if you want).

This functionality of any shopping site will generally have following states.

S1 – Empty Shopping cart

S2 – Potential purchase (when there are at least one item added to the cart). Even if more items are added to the cart the state remain same. Items can be removed also from the cart and the state remains same until last item is removed. When the last item is removed from the cart, it goes to S1.

S3 – Check Out (Completed item selections – no more items to be added or removed from the cart). Here the application displays summary of items selected (with prices and discounts if any) and expects the user to approve

S4 – Payment. Application comes to this state once the user makes approval on summary.

See the diagram below depicting various states and actions/events due to which application moves from one state to other.

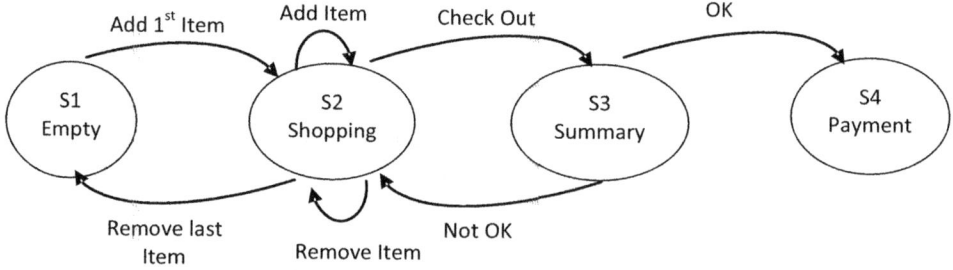

Below are the tests covering all the transitions. In this example end state is not mentioned for each action as it is the start of the next event. This is with an assumption that all the tests will be executed in the same set

STATE	Event (Action)
S1	Add Item
S2	Remove (Last) Item

S1	Add Item
S2	Add Item
S2	Remove Item
S2	Check out
S3	Not OK
S2	Check Out
S3	OK
S4	

Since we are limiting our scope to only shopping cart functionality, we are currently not interested in what happens from state 4 even though there will be some events and actions after payment is done. That can be treated as a separate functionality and hence part of other state diagram. (eg. Deduct the amount, send email etc.). Note that we have removed last column depicting expected end state because the start state of the next action represents the end state of the previous action. So, we can simplify our table with only two columns. However this could be possible only if you execute the tests in the same sequence. Each step to be treated as a test case.

We can also prepare a state table as given below

State-> Actions	S1 Empty	S2 Shopping	S3 Summary	S4 Payment
Add Item	S2	S2	-	-
Remove Item	-	S2	-	-
Remove Last Item	-	S1	-	-
Check Out	-	S3	-	-
Not OK	-	-	S2	-
OK	-	-	S4	-

Note that Top row represents starting state and first column represents action and the interaction represents, the ending state if you take the action mentioned on the left side when the application is in the state mentioned on the top. So, if you are in S1 state and if you add Item, you should move to S2 state. If you are in S2 state and if you add item, you still remain in S2 state. You can interpret all the intersections in this manner and derive test case for each intersection.

Some intersections may not be possible or could be treated as invalid. All of the boxes that contain '-' are invalid transitions in this example. This table can help us identify some negative tests such as

a. Attempt to add an item from summary state (S3)
b. Try to remove an item from empty state (S1)
c. Try to enter 'OK' while in shopping state.

System should not display buttons or provide any other options to take above invalid actions or display corresponding error messages if user takes any of these actions.

Other Examples

Microsoft Word: Let us say you have a word document opened. If you try to close the document without any changes it will close without prompting to save. But if you make some changes in the document and then try to close, the application displays a message asking whether you want to save changes or not.

Reducing number of Test cases (transitions)

The examples we discussed are relatively small and simple. In reality many applications and their functionalities will have large number of states, events and transitions making testing very complex and time consuming. Like we did for other techniques, we need to try to reduce the effort and time by reducing various state transition rules to optimum level. We need to follow guidelines provided below

- Visit each state at least once.
- Test the most common state to state transition
- Test the least common paths between states (as these paths could have been ignored and more likely to find defect)
- Test all the error states and returning from the error states. Improper error handling is also a common issue and more likely to get bugs. Error messages should be proper/relevant and software should recover properly once the error is fixed
- Test Random test transition. After following above steps, you can pick up some states and transitions randomly and test them. If you find errors, test more.

5.4 Experience Based Test Design

5.4.1 Error Guessing

As discussed, test design techniques will help us identify test cases for finding potential defects. Experience and intuition of a person can also find many errors and sometimes those errors which may not be even easily possible through various techniques discussed above.

Example: Suppose we have to test the login screen of an application. An experienced test engineer may immediately see if the password typed in the password field can be copied to a text field which may cause a breach in the security of the application. There are many people who have knack of "smelling out" errors.

Error guessing is based on number of aspects described below

- **Domain or Application experience** or testing experience of the person.
- **Defects History** – If someone is good in analysing the defects found in previous modules or some other applications, they may anticipate similar errors in the new module / application.
- **Understanding of possible errors** or error-prone situations primarily based on technical knowledge.

  Empty or null lists/strings,

  Blanks or null character in strings

  Zero occurrences

  Negative numbers

- Defects around **exception situations**. Requirements around exceptional situations are generally missed and some experience people with required domain knowledge can quickly point out those aspects.
- Defects around **changes in functionality** – business rules. When the functionality changes or business rules changes, the user knows what was earlier valid and now invalid or what is likely to get impacted because of change.

All the tests identified based on various aspects mentioned above should be documented and used during test execution.

5.4.2 Exploratory Testing

As its name implies, exploratory testing is about exploring, finding out about the software (it's functionality and features - what it does, what it doesn't do) and also testing to find what works and what doesn't work. It also involves learning about its strengths and its weaknesses

So, Exploratory testing is simultaneous learning, test design, and test execution.

It is an informal test design technique where the tester actively controls the design of the tests as those tests are performed and uses information gained while testing to design new and better tests. [After Bach]

In this hands-on approach, minimum planning and maximum test execution is done. The planning involves creation of a test charter, a short declaration of the scope of a short (1 to 2 hour) time-boxed test effort, the objectives and possible approaches to be used.

The test design and test execution activities are performed in parallel typically without formally documenting detailed test cases. Test cases are created and executed on the fly and decision regarding what to test next or where to spend time is being constantly decided.

This does not mean that other, more formal testing techniques will not be used. For example, the tester may decide to use boundary value analysis but will think through and test the most important boundary values without necessarily writing them down. Testers can also explore new opportunities or issues during the session.

Some notes should be written during the exploratory-testing session, so that a report can be produced afterwards.

Test logging is undertaken as test execution is performed, documenting the key aspects of what is tested, any defects found and any thoughts about possible further testing.

This approach is most useful when there are no or poor specifications available and/or when time is severely limited. It can also serve to complement other, more formal testing, helping to establish greater confidence in the software. This approach is also useful for evaluating off-the-shelf software products.

5.5 Gray / Grey Box Testing

Gray box testing is a testing performed with some limited information about the internal architecture / data structures and algorithms of the system but not very detailed control structures. So, the application is treated like a semi-transparent or gray box enable to use effective combination of Black Box and White Box testing.

Gray Box testing can be effectively used for integration testing where test cases are designed after getting some internal details of the units or modules which are interfaced. The actual tests may be executed based on Exposed interfaces. It is also suitable for Web Based applications where most validations are done on the client side and remaining processing and data access done on the server side. You want to test scenario for checking how system will behave if some negative inputs received (for example invalid eMail ID). If you know that currently the system is receiving only valid inputs as Javascript is validating the inputs on the client side, it may be difficult to test the required scenario. Tester may have to disable the Java script and then test the scenario. Such testing may be required because in reality Java Script may fail because of some unexpected reason or eMail ID is received directly from other system/sub-system.

It provides combined benefits of White-box and Black-box. Some complex test scenarios could be handled more intelligently if we have some internal information. White-box testing can be done by developers knowing complete understanding of internal structures but Gray-box testing can be done by even those testers who have access to design documents and have partial understanding of internals.

5.6 Summary

In this chapter we discussed in detail, Business Functionality testing (normally known as functional testing). Each **business function** or **transaction** can be termed as business unit and can be tested at two levels – **Field level** testing and **Form level** testing. Once individual business functions are tested, System testing is carried out which will cover **End-to End** Testing (where related business functions are executed one after other) and in some cases **Entity Life Cycle** Testing is also carried out to test all the business functions from start (birth of the entity or transaction) to end (death of the entity or transaction).

Business function testing is done using **Black-box test design** techniques where test cases are derived using function specifications irrespective of the language or the internal code structure.

The first and most important part of testing would be to ensure that user can **input only valid data** otherwise the results are bound to be wrong. Every input field can have set of possible valid values and set of possible invalid values. As part of standard field validation, we cover Null allowed or not (Mandatory), maximum length allowed, Type of characters allowed, a range of values allowed (particularly for numeric fields) or there are some set of possible valid values as per business rules.

We accordingly discussed three Black-box test design testing primarily used for Input validations

Equivalence Partitioning: Test cases are designed to execute at least one representative from each equivalence class/partition. There could be multiple classes with valid and in valid values. Each class may contain one or more possible values. Since the system is assumed to handle all the values of the class equivalently, if we test the system with one value from each class and find that it works fine, we can assume that system will work fine for other values of the class also. Similarly if the system is not working fine for one value, then there is no point in testing with other values of the same partition as we are likely to get similar error.

We discussed how requirements, such as mandatory field, maximum length or field type kind of requirements can also be tested using this technique. It is important to note that, deriving classes is very important. We can apply this technique to numeric value, Boolean condition, or discrete set of related values.

Boundary Value Analysis: This technique is an extension to Equivalence partitioning and suggests that instead of taking any value from the class, if we take values on the boundary/edge, our chances of finding errors increases. So, test cases are designed based on **boundary values minimum, minimum -1 , maximum, maximum + 1**. So, for example for the input field salary, if the specification says that salary amount between 10,000 to 75,000 allowed, testing should be done for salary 9,999, 10,000, 75,000, 75,001.

For salary input 9,999 and 75,001 the system should not accept the salary and display error message but for salary input 10,000 and 75,000, system should accept and proceed further.

EP and BVA techniques are generally used to validate whether the application is accepting only valid values or not. But sometimes, they are also used to check if there are business rules generating different output for different valid inputs (eg Examination result) based on single variable.

We can apply equivalence partitioning and boundary value analysis more than once to the same specification item – for example type of input, not null and specific input range all can be combined into single test.

Decision Table: Many business rules do not depend only on one variable but may depend on two or more than two variables. For example, discount may depend on total number of passengers, and in how much advance the booking is done. In such case, Decision table techniques is used in which table is prepared with a) conditions related to dependent variables, b) combinations of True, False for those conditions and c) corresponding outcome for each combination. Each combination is considered a rule based on which test cases are designed.

We studied **Limited Entry Decision** table where all conditions are binary (takes only one of the two values Y(T) or N(F)). The decision tables where conditions are allowed to take value other than binary or more than 2 values in general, then the decision table is known as **Extended Entry Decision** Table. In case of Limited Entry decision table, total number of rules would be 2^n where n represents number of conditions. For Extended entry decision tables, number of rules will be multiplication of number of possible values for each condition

We also discussed various guidelines using which we can reduce number of rules (eg. Removing rules which are not going to be possible or combining rules which are very similar or which are going to give same result). We also discussed that while using the data that can satisfy each rule, we can apply BVA technique to increase the probability of finding errors.

Decision tables provide systematic way of stating complex business rules and hence can be useful to developers as well as testers in exploring various possible effects of combinations of different inputs and can be useful in finding ambiguities in specifications also.

Use Case Based Test Design: Once Input field level validations are done using EP and BVA techniques and derived results are checked for multiple input combinations using Decision Table test design technique, one should move forward to do testing at a business function level or transaction level. Use Case is description of a particular use of the system by an actor (a user or a system) detailing interaction of an actor with the system in order to achieve specific task. So, Test cases are designed based on use cases to check whether business functions are really working as expected by use case.

As part of this testing we consider two types of scenarios, a) Primary scenario – which is most common way / approach used assuming everything goes well and b) alternate scenario – covering sequence of actions that are different from the one described in Primary scenario and also includes error conditions.

Customer making reservation, Agent cancelling reservation etc are example of use cases.

Each scenario includes Pre-conditions, Steps and Post-conditions. Once the scenario is prepared, test cases are derived.

State Transition Technique:

Many times the application is expected to appear / behave slightly differently depending on the state in which the application is for a given user or a given transaction. For example, some buttons need to disabled under some situation or menu options / links need to appear or disappear or some actions allowed / not allowed based on some situation. Testing for this behaviour of the application is known as State Transition Testing.

Four things to be remembered, 1) Application can occupy various states 2) Application can move to only specific states from current state, 3) Only specific transaction or events are allowed in the particular state, 4) Only specific events results into a transition to other state and 5) the effect that result from transition.

State Transition table or Graph can be prepared to demonstrate the states, possible actions in the state and new states due to the actions taken. Test cases are then documented for each row of the state transition table.

Error Guessing Technique: In addition to various techniques which are based on some concepts, Experience and Intuition of person can also find many errors including some, which cannot be found by other techniques. This technique is known as Error Guessing.

Exploratory Testing: It involves testing while exploring the application functionality. So, you try to understand functionality and features of the application and at the same time identify what works and what does not work. This technique best used when there are no or minimum specifications and also for the off-the-shelf software products.

Gray-Box Testing: Towards the end we discussed gray-box testing which can be applied where information about internal structures and algorithm is not fully available. It provides benefits of both white-box and black-box testing.

5.7 Exercise

Sr	Question
1.	Explain Field Level testing covering independent fields and dependent Fields
2.	Provide meaning of End-to-End System testing with example
3.	Alpha testing is generally done at _____ site
4.	Beta testing is done at _____ site
5.	Differentiate between Alpha and Beta Testing
6.	_____ testing is also known as Factory Acceptance Testing
7.	Provide assumptions of Equivalence Partitioning Technique.
8.	Black box tester must study and understand the code well for testing using black box testing techniques
9.	_____ Testing demonstrates that the system works end-to-end in a production-like environment
10.	_____ testing is about exploring, finding out about the software, what it does, what it doesn't do, what works and what doesn't work (simultaneous learning about application and testing)
11.	What is single fault assumption theory?
12.	Explain EP technique
13.	What is the general definition of equivalence class partitioning? Where is it used?
14.	What is the general definition of boundary value analysis?
15.	Closed box testing is same as _____ testing
16.	In a specific club there is a rule that only people of age 18 to 60 years can become member. What technique you will use to validate proper implementation of this rule. What kind of data you will use?
17.	Post office has decided their rates as given below. 25p up to 10g, 35p up to 50g plus an extra 10p for each additional 25g up to 100g. Which test inputs (in grams) would be selected using equivalence partitioning? a. 8,42,82,102 b. 4,15, 65, 92,159 c. 10,50,75,100 d. d. 5, 20, 40, 60, 80
18.	Consider reservation function for one event that gives 10% discount to all but

Sr	Question
	person with gold card membership gets additional 10% and silver card membership gets 5% additional. However if the members have not paid membership renewal fees fully then only 3% discount is given 1. Develop Decision table 2. Develop Test cases
19.	_____ Testing is data driven or Input / output driven testing
20.	There is a need to validate input for mobile number. Provide valid and invalid equivalence classes
21.	What are the basis for guessing errors as part of error guessing technique?
22.	What are assumptions for error guessing technique?
23.	What are the limitations of BVA (Boundary value Analysis). What technique should be used to overcome those limitations
24.	Explain state transition testing using example
25.	One of the important components (guideline) of state transition technique is that 'Application can move to only specific state from the current state'. True/False?
26.	_____ technique is based on experience and Intuition of the person
27.	What is the difference between white box testing and black box testing techniques
28.	_____ testing is simultaneous learning, test design, and test execution
29.	Consider the following techniques. Which are static and dynamic: - Equivalence partitioning - Use case testing - Data flow analysis - Exploratory testing - Decision testing - Inspections
30.	In a banking application, there is a rule that if someone tries to logging with wrong user ID or Password for 4 times then after 4th trial the application locks. However if the user enters correct user ID and Password on 1st, 2nd or 3rd trial the user is allowed to access the application. Prepare a state transition diagram OR State Transition Table that depicts the above rules.
31.	What are the key components of State Transition Technique, based on which

Sr	Question
	the test cases are prepared using
32.	There is a program to find largest number from a given set of n numbers. Design test cases for this program
33.	Salesmen in an organisation are evaluated on their performance based on points they earned during their probation period. There is a program that displays action to be taken by management as per below rules 0-20 Thank You 21-40 Extend Probation 41-60 Confirmation 61-80 Promotion 81-100 Promotion with letter of recommendation a) Which test design techniques you will use? b) Write down test cases using that technique
34.	Design Decision table for following program If student has (secured > 80% and Attendance is > 70%) or (secured > 75% marks and attendance > 80%) will get scholarship of Rs 1000
35.	White box testing is complementary to black box testing and not an alternative. Why? Give example to prove the statement
36.	Acceptance testing is done by _____
37.	What are the two types of User acceptance testing used for software product testing?
38.	Explain Exploratory testing
39.	Explain User Acceptance Testing by illustrating relevant case
40.	In a specific game zone, Entry ticket can be issued only to those children whose age is between 5 and 12 years. (a). What technique you will use to validate the input field 'AGE'? Why? (b). Which data you will use to test?
41.	State Transition Technique is generally used during _____ Testing Options: (a) Unit (b) Integration (c) System (d) Static

6 SW Testing Project Execution Process

As we have seen, SW Testing is very important and intense activity. Even if we consider only functional validation testing, it requires enormous amount of time to design the tests, document the tests and execute the tests. We have discussed all the important aspects such as work product reviews, static testing, testing levels with corresponding test design techniques using which we design tests at various levels.

Even validation and system testing involving independent team is also a huge effort. The entire effort requires large number of team members involving test manager and leads. So, Testing needs to be treated as a project involving planning and execution with milestones. Additionally effectiveness of testing activities also needs to be tracked. So, in this chapter, we will discuss how testing project is executed involving various phases and how quality of testing is measured.

6.1 SW Testing Quality – Testing Metrics

Like any other product, service or activity, the outcome of the SW testing activities needs to be of good quality. Like SW development, SW testing is also done by people and they are also likely to make mistakes. There are multiple reasons because of which they may miss some important aspects, they may miss some defects or may report defects which are not really defects. Some of the key reasons are listed below.

- Wrong interpretation of requirement and function specification resulting to wrong test cases
- Incorrect creation of dummy codes (Stubs and Drivers) for doing testing when all units are not yet developed (refer integration types)
- Complex scenarios
- Inadequate or inaccurate test data in database
- Lack of time
- Inexperience resources
- Incorrect automation scripts (required for automated test execution)

The testing activity should also be completed in specified time frame which requires progress tracking at every stage.

The performance of the SW testing project or SW testing team should hence be quantitatively measured and necessary actions to be taken to continuously improve.

Metric as per IEEE standard is a quantitative measure of the degree to which a system, component, or process possesses a given attribute

It measures a particular characteristic of a program / process / person / team's performance or efficiency. Metric relates the individual measure in some way to give some meaning

Eg. % of marks obtained in exam is a measure of performance of a student.

% of sessions attended is a measure of class attendance

% of topics covered in the process of preparation is a measure of study progress

% of components having defects.

Similarly Test metrics are an important indicator of the effectiveness of a software testing process. As such there may be many metrics generated, we will discuss only few important metrics here.

6.1.1 Coverage Metrics

Test Coverage determines how much testing planned & designed against requirements and how much testing done against planned

Test Design Coverage: (% of Requirements for which test cases prepared).

(Number of Requirements for which test cases designed * 100) / Total number of Requirements

Because of various constraints such as time, management decide not to cover some requirements in testing but sometime requirements are simply missed out. Please note that we should considered itemized requirements as discussed in next section.

So if there were 400 requirements of which 350 requirements were covered in test design then the Test Design Coverage would be (350 * 100) / 400 = 87.5%

Test Execution Coverage: (% of test cases Executed) :

(Number of Test scripts or Test cases executed * 100) /Total number of Test scripts or Test cases Planned for execution.

Apart from time or effort constraints, some tests may not be executed due to environmental issues, data non availability etc.

So, out of 350 test cases designed (and assume that all of them were to be executed), 300 test cases were executed then Test Execution coverage would be (300 * 100) / 350 = 86%.

Lower the coverage, higher the risk of missing some potential defects.

Automation Coverage (% of test cases automated): We will discuss automation in subsequent sections but generally, test automation is done for regression test cases because regression testing for all or selected regression test cases is done in every release of the product due to small or large enhancements or modifications in the software so that it does not take much time.

(Number of Test cases automated * 100) / Total number of Test cases planned for automation.

So if there are 150 regression test cases and all of them are planned to be automated but at a given point in time say 40 test cases are automated then automation coverage would be (40 * 100) / 150 = 27%.

Practically not all regression test cases are automated as it requires additional effort and cost. However higher automation helps in higher regression testing coverage and cost saving in long run.

6.1.2 Productivity Metrics

Productivity metrics determine unit of time (Eg hours) required to perform one unit of task (Eg Test case creation).

Productivity is measured once the task is completed.

Test Case Creation Productivity (Number of hours / minutes required for one test case creation):

Total number of Hours spent for test cases creation / Total number of test cases created

So, if 50 hours were spent for creating 300 test cases, test case creation productivity would be (50*60)/300 = 10 minutes. This means that on an average the 7 test cases are created per hour. Please also note that the productivity may be different for different levels and organizations may accordingly maintain separate productivity.

Test Case Execution Productivity (Average number of hours required to execute one test case):

Total number of Hours spent for test execution / Total number of test cases Executed

So, if 60 hours were required to execute 300 test cases, the test execution productivity would be (60*60)/300 = 12 minutes. This means average 12 minutes required to execute one test case.

Test Case Automation Productivity (Number of hours required to automate one test case):

Total number of Hours spent for creation of test scripts / Total number of test scripts created

This is similar to Test case creation productivity but it is used for automation. So, if 40 hours were required to automate 40 test cases, test case automation productivity would be 40 / 40 = 1. Average 1 hour required to automate one test case.

Productivity calculated for past project or past module is used to estimate and plan these activities for the future module or project. This is with an assumption that average productivity would be almost same.

So, in some other module, if there are 700 test cases, one can assume that it would require

700*10 = 7000 minutes = 7000/60 = 117 hours (approximately) for creating test cases and 700*12=8400 minutes = 140 hours for execution. The actual productivity may not be same for the next project or module but it certainly helps to estimate approximate how much effort will be required and planning can be done accordingly. Over a period of time the estimation accuracy would increase.

6.1.3 Process – Quality Metrics

We will now discuss few important metrics primarily used to monitor quality of testing effort.

Test Case Adequacy: This defines the number of actual test cases created vs estimated test cases at the end of test case preparation phase. It is calculated as

(No. of actual test cases * 100) / No of test cases estimated.

If it is much below 100%, one need to check if any requirements are missed out.

Test Effectiveness: It measures the bug finding ability and quality of test.

TE = (Total number of defects found during testing *100) / (Total defects found during testing and after testing)

For E.g. If defects found during testing = 5, No of defects found after testing = 5,

TE = (5*100)/(5+5) = 100*0.5=50%

Low Test Effectiveness means – Testing was not done properly.

This has to be as high as possible (100%). For many commercial projects it expected to be at least around 95%

Test Case Effectiveness: This defines the effectiveness of test cases which is measured in number of defects found in testing without using the test cases. It is calculated as

(No. of defects detected using test cases * 100) / Total no: of defects detected

It is practically possible that while executing some test cases, we find some defect for which there was no test case created though it should have been created. So, our test cases designed were not good.

Defect Acceptance Rate

It tells us for how much % of defects of the total defects were accepted. This indirectly measures level of knowledge the testing team has. The defects reported can be rejected by user or development team due to various reasons such as - (a) It is already reported (duplicate) (b) it is not a defect, it is as required (c) could not reproduce (d) it is a change request or any other such reasons.

DAR= (No. of accepted defects * 100) / Total No. of Defects

So, if 45 defects were accepted out of 50 reported defects,

$DAR = (45*100)/(50) = 90\%$

This has to be as high as possible because such defects could unnecessary take away lot of time.

6.1.4 Effort /Schedule Metrics

Effort related metrics determine effort spent in various phases and variance between actual and planned.

Schedule Variance:

((Actual number of days – Planned number of days) *100) / Planned number of days.

Where

Planned number of days = Planned end date – Planned start date

Actual number of days = Actual end date – actual start date

This metric determines delay in terms of schedule. Schedule variance is calculated and monitored for each phase so that the project manager can get an idea how much delay is likely for the overall project and take some measures such as adding resource or change priorities or postpone some functionality to next version or delay the schedule.

Effort Variance:

((Actual hours spent – Planned hours) *100) / Planned hours

This determines variance against planned effort in hours. Positive variance indicates additional cost. This metrics is measured for each phase or for the entire project

Effort distribution:

(Number of hour Spent in Phase * 100) / Total number of hours spent in all phases

This helps analysing where the effort goes more and is also useful for future planning. STLC phases are explained in detail in subsequent sections of this chapter.

6.1.5 Metrics – Summary and Benefits

Coverage	Productivity	Process / Quality	Project (Closure)
• Test Design Coverage • Test Execution coverage • Automation Coverage	• Test case design productivity • Test case execution productivity • Test Script Creation productivity	• Test Case Adequacy • Test Effectiveness • Test Case Effectiveness • Defect Acceptance Rate	• Schedule Variance • Effort Variance • Effort distribution

Various metrics we learnt in above sections are summarized below

Please note that there can many more metrics captured for a project. It depends on project and organization requirement.

Benefits

Measuring and tracking these metrics for various projects / team can provide many benefits as listed below to the organization

1. Effective and unbiased comparison of performance of project or team or a person.
2. Tracking Projects against plan and Getting early warnings
3. Take timely corrective/preventive actions
4. Use for Future estimates / project plan
5. Use for driving continuous improvements and tracking the same.

6.2 Software Testing Life Cycle Phases (STLC)

Software testing phases and processes are aligned to software development phases and processes. Validation and System testing is generally done by independent testing team in a large project and needs to follow detailed processes. So, like there are SDLC (Software Development Life Cycle) phases there are STLC (Software Testing Life Cycle) Phases.

Refer to following diagram that depict SDLC phases and STLC phases aligned to those phases

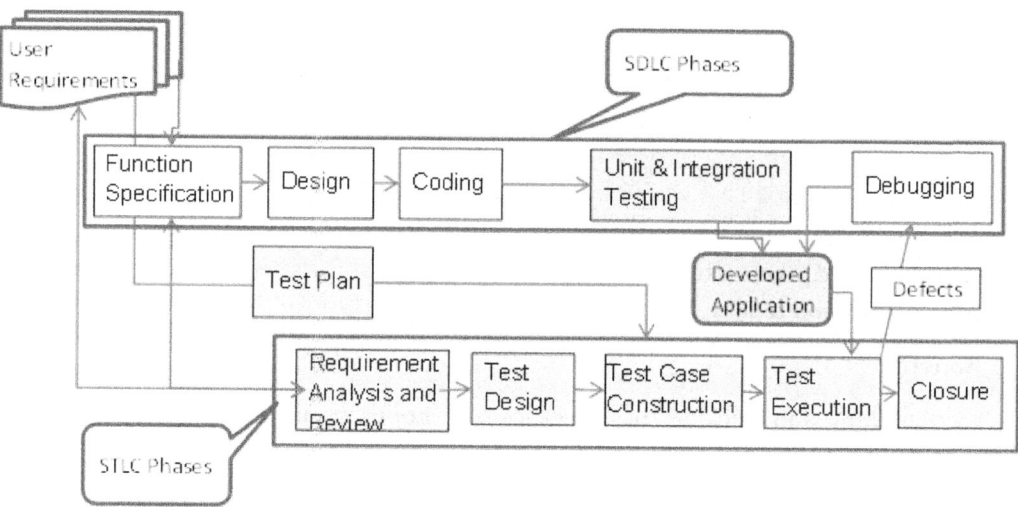

Business Requirements are the key inputs for both Development and Testing teams. Based on Business requirements, functional requirements or function specification documents are prepared generally by development team. These requirement documents become input to both development team and testing team and they proceed with their respective phases. Development team on one side will develop the code and carryout unit and integration testing. Testing team on the other side will analyse requirements and construct test cases.

At this point of time both the teams work together for Validation and system test execution phase during which testing team would execute the test cases and development team would fix the defect reported by testing team.

Objectives and detailed process for each of the STLC phase are described in subsequent sections.

6.2.1 Requirement Analysis and Ambiguity Reviews

As discussed in SW Verification, the first step would be to do requirement review.

Additionally, it is also important to identify testable and non-testable requirements and plan the testing activities accordingly.

Many a times it may not be easy to ensure coverage and find all ambiguities. Following guidelines can help for the same

1) Understand the requirements from all angles
2) Understand Functional Requirements of the Computerised application
3) Itemize the requirements – Convert long requirements provided in paragraphs into small single specific requirements. Requirement should be singular in a sense that each requirement must address only one thing.
   Consider all implicit requirements as well.
4) Identify testable and non-testable requirements
5) Identify Ambiguities in the requirements and gather clarifications from customer
6) Verify Requirement Understanding from Customer/Users

Let us understand each of the above points in more detail

1) **Ensure Business Requirement coverage** by understanding requirements from all angles such as

- **Functional areas / Departments**: Eg. Sales, Distribution, Management, Support departments
- **Data Types**: Eg Types of members, Types of orders, Travel categories, regions etc
- **Rules applied** on each type: Eg. Cancellation and refund policy, Upgrade (of travel class) policy.
- **Tracks/Paths/ routs** through which the specific data is received or functionality can be achieved. Eg. Booking done directly online or through agents.
- **States**: Life Cycle of specific order may have multiple states – initiated, active, fulfilled, cancelled etc.
- **Exceptional situations:** For example, Order can be cancelled only before 24 hours of travel time. However, if there is an approval from Branch manager, it can be done for specific cases
- **Additional focus**: Legal requirements, Technically Challenging requirements, Stakeholder mandated, Security and Performance aspects

   Practically full requirements with all business rules, exception situations are hardly conveyed. It is hence important to elicit details by conducting meetings, clarifying doubts, studying existing documents.

2) **Understand Functional Requirements of the Computerised application.**
   Business requirements provides how business works but may not provide how the

computerised application is expected to meet those requirements. It is important to understand those expectations also very clearly. Following aspects should be studied in detail.

Functionality	What you need to know
Features	It is made of Web based application having three forms – Login, Registration, Enquiry and Booking with facility to register, enquire (with or without registration and) reservation. Registration form also has provision select membership type.
Actions performed	1. Register. 2. Enquiry. 3. Reserve ticket. 4. Modify personal information 5. Modify/cancel booking information 6. View bookings 7. Print ticket
States	For Unregistered members – Will display options to login, register or enquiry For Registered members – Will have options to Login, Enquiry and Reservation For active customers – will have option to update or cancel the reservation
Inputs	Login: User ID, Password Registration – Personal information and membership information Enquiry – Source and destination locations Reservation – Source, destination locations, number of passengers, class, date, Service number (Flight Number, Train number, Bus number)
Expected outcome	Become member Get Schedule details, seat availability details Get reservation details Email to all users after booking Sms booking details for gold card members Print tickets

Note: We have to consider many other requirements which may not be specified in specification documents but related to Domain constraints, Real world rules, Industry specific functionalities, or standard rules with respect to technical requirements. Please refer section **8.1.1** for more details on these requirements.

3) Itemize the requirements

Convert long requirements provided in paragraphs into small single specific requirements. In other words, document complex requirement in to multiple simple requirements

Each requirement is assumed to be independent of other and at granular level with each separate condition

Requirement Id	Description	Category	Priority
BR-01	Registered users are able to access the application	Access	
BR-02	Unregistered users are able to access only schedule page	Access	

Requirement Itemization – Registration Form

Requirement Id	Description	Category	Priority
RF-01	Registration form is displayed once 'New Registration' button clicked on home page	Explicit	Medium
RF-02	Registration form has provision to input all personal information - Name, gender, marital status, Birth date and contact details such as full address, phone number, mobile number, and fax number, eMail ID	Explicit	Medium
RF-03	Name, Birthdate, Mobile Number and email ID are mandatory fields	Implicit	High
RF-04	Age should be >= 18 years	Explicit	High
RF-05	Email Id and mobile numbers should be in valid format	Implicit	High
RF-06	Registration form has provision to input membership type and it should be one of Silver, Gold, Platinum	Explicit	High

RF-07	Should have provision to enter valid user ID which is of between 6 to 10 characters and there should not be any other member with same user ID	Implicit	Medium
RF-08	Should have provision to accept valid password which is of between 6 to 10 characters	Implicit	Medium
RF-09	Confirmation message should be displayed after successful registration process but displays error message if any details entered are not valid	Confirmation	Medium

Requirement Itemization – Reservation (booking) Form

Requirement Id	Description	Category	Priority
BK-01	Reservation form is displayed once 'Reserve Tickets' button clicked on home page	Explicit	Medium
BK-02	Reservation form has provision to input all booking details - From Location, To Location, Date, Service Number, Class, number of tickets. From location and To locations are different. Date is a future date and number of tickets entered is > 0.	Explicit	Medium
BK-03	Once the class details entered, form should display ticket rate		
BK-04	Amount should be automatically calculated (Number of tickets*Rate) and displayed		
BK-05	Reservation charges as applicable (Rs 20 / ticket) should be displayed and added in amount except for Platinum card members (which is 0).		
BK-06	Calculate and display discount of 10% If (booking is done for return journey or number of seats booked are four or more) and Platinum card member and reduce discount amount from total amount		

BK-07	Once all details are entered, user should be asked for confirmation and once confirmed, form should accept Payment mode (Net Banking, Credit Card, Debit Card)		
BK-08	Application should connect to payment gateway of specific bank for further processing		
BK-09	The user should have option to change the details or cancel the booking till the payments are made		
BK-10	Once booking is done the seats should be reserved for the specified service on specified date		
BK-11	User should be able to modify/Cancel the booking before 24 hours of the Journey time.		

As you can observe in the table above, you

- Itemize each requirement and assign identification number
- Write specific requirement description
- Categorize the requirement. Categorization could be based on type of functionality, type of requirement or feature etc. E.g. Access, File Handling, error handling, system requirements, Security or Individual business rules

Here the requirements are also categorised into Explicit or Implicit requirements. Explicit requirements mean the requirement is explicitly provided by customer (and available in requirement document). Implicit means, requirement is not explicitly provided but we are assuming based on other inputs. Such requirements should be verified with the customer.

You can also

- Prioritize requirements in to High/Medium/Low. Priorities help deciding the priority in which the testing should be done or if not enough time is available for testing, which test cases can be skipped. High Priority requirements must be covered, Medium priority requirement may be tested but may be at high level and low priority requirements may not be covered if enough time is not available

There are two ways in which the requirements are documented for categories.

Option 1: Single sheet with Category as column

- Useful when requirements are for smaller projects
- Requirements can be filtered category wise for creating test cases
- Only one sheet needs to be maintained

Option 2: Multiple sheets – each for one category

- Used for larger project requirements

Benefits of requirement itemization: This process

- Simplifies the requirements and improves understanding
- Helps in identifying different Test Scenarios / Test Conditions
- Helps in identifying testable items for the application
- Helps in Identification of expected and unexpected error conditions
- Helps in identifying any ambiguities in the requirements

4) Identify testable and non-testable requirements

It is also important to check whether all the requirements are testable or not and communicate to client.

Testable requirements: Any requirement is considered to be testable if it is possible to design and execute the test under the given test environment so that one can determine whether the requirement has been met.

Most Requirements are testable such as data validation, form validation, field validation, & so on

Non-Testable Requirements: There could be some requirements which cannot be tested because of various reasons

a. **Requirements which changes dynamically on web applications.** For example if the session variable for the URL in web application is stored in some HTTP file and it is changing dynamically.

b. Some implicit requirements where **query needs to be raised** may be non-testable in the initial stage, but they may be testable items when the query is resolved.

For example: If it is not stated who are the users for the application and what are the access rights for those users in the requirements document then such items could not be tested unless the query is resolved. Once the query is resolved these non-testable items will be converted into testable items.

c. **Testing requires availability of specific Environment** – For example performance related requirements needing specific HW/SW is not available and hence out of scope. For online shopping application, the payment module can be tested only if there is connectivity to application of the bank (for payment through net-banking). Such connectivity may not be available during testing.

d. **'No Limit' expectations** – For example a requirement says that user should be able to enter any number of characters in 'Remark' field. Whatever number of characters with which you try to test, there is need to check whether it can accept even more characters. Hence, we cannot conclude that there is no limit to the field.

5) **Identify Ambiguities in the requirements and gather clarifications from customer**

We have discussed Ambiguity Reviews in greater detail in section on Verification. Review all the requirements against possible ambiguity and clarify from users.

6) **Ensure our understanding is correct.**

Last but not the least, review all the itemized requirements with customer through periodic review meetings or reverse walk through or by presenting your understanding of requirements in summarized form and clarify all the doubts. If required, rewrite the requirements.

Example

Let us see how we can implement the overall Test Design process for the exercise we had seen "Online Travel reservation" system. We had seen some ambiguities for the application. Let us assume that after getting all the clarifications from the business, the problem statement is revised as below.

Application allows user/members to book travel ticket online. The home page will have a provision to either create a new account or to login with existing account. All valid members should be able to view various options for booking the tickets. However even if you are not a member, you can see schedule between two locations. There are three membership categories 1.Silver 2. Gold 3. Platinum. Such (Platinum) card members do not have to pay any reservation fees.

Any adult (Age >=18 years) can create a new account by providing user ID and Password. Registration form should input personal information – Name, gender, marital status, Birth date and contact details such as full address, phone number, mobile number, and fax number. (Email ID)

Once registered, user can book ticket online. The eTicket will be emailed to user. ~~Gold~~Platinum card members get sms in addition to email.

If (booking is done for return journey or number of seats booked are four or more) and ~~gold~~ Platinum card member, you get 10% discount.

Company should have travel service from the locations specified. Passenger can book tickets to nearby (Distance less than distance between Source and Destination Specified) locations if there is no travel service between the specified locations

Application should be user friendly and have a provision to provide help wherever you feel important.

6.2.2 Test Design

Testing should not be carried out in ad-hoc manner or in random manner as per tester's mind but tests should be designed using structured approach applying various guidelines and techniques. We look at various things (we say **Test Basis**) to see what could be tested (derive **Test Conditions**).

Test Basis could include all Requirement specification, Functional specification, technical specification or even code itself (for test conditions related to structural aspects). **Test condition:** An item or event of a component or system that could be verified by one or more test cases.

The process of analysing test bases and deriving test conditions is known as **Test Analysis**. Test Analysis not only helps in identifying test conditions but also helps in identifying possible ambiguities and also identifying non-testable requirements. Subsequently detailed **Test Cases** are prepared based on test conditions and then test cases are organized in specific sequence to form **Test Procedures**.

Please note that apart from customer specific requirements there are some standard requirements one need to consider while designing the tests.

6.2.2.1 Standard rules

Apart from the business requirements specified in specification documents, we also have to consider some **standard rules** while testing. Such standard rules are generally not specified in any specification documents but are assumed to be covered in testing.

1) **Domain Constraints:**

   Domain Types: Attributes may have the same domain such as only characters, only Numeric, only Integers…

   e.g. passenger name, city name, Agency name, Agent name etc are only characters. Number of pasengers can contain only numeric data

   So, as part of Independent field Validations (Fields that do not depend on other fields), each field is Validated individually for it's valid type on inputs.

Same type–different values: At the conceptual level, we do not expect passenger name to have the same names as cities or agencies in general. However agent name of the airline service may have same name as passenger name

It is not feasible that computer application can differentiate this at the time of entry. However when names are displayed on the screen, observations can reveal that the application is picking up wrong names from internal database and displaying.

2) **Real World Rules (norms)** :

There are some norms / rules followed in general. For example,

- A Passenger has only one name, is in one department.
- An employee's salary should not be greater than that of the manager of the department.
- Commission value of agent cannot be greater than the total travel cost.

So, such rules need to be considered while doing testing even if they are not explicitly mentioned.

3) **Industry Domain Specific Functionalities.**

There may be many other standards, processes and rules generally prevailing in specific type of industry. There also could be some government norms under which all companies within the industry need to operate their businesses. Such requirements may not be defined explicitly in the project related functional specification documents. However, it is necessary that the application complies with those requirements and hence to be checked during functional testing. For example,

- Rate for Economy class cannot be higher than rate for Business class
- Standard taxes or charges to be applied as per government norms
- Senior citizens should be provided some discount as per government norms

You may find many such norms or processes in some other standard industry domains such as Insurance, Finance and Banking.

It is hence important to understand those requirements, get specific inputs on exact implementation for the given project and carry out testing accordingly

4) **Standard rules with respect to technical requirement (Implicit)**

Inter-Field & Inter-Form Dependencies– requires that a value referred to in some attribute actually exists in some entity. For example

- The Agent must exist as an Agent ID in agents list.
- Return journey date cannot be earlier to main journey date
- Null Checks

It might not be detrimental if a passenger's home phone number or address is not there. However, it might not be permitted to have a record of a passenger that does not have an passenger's name or email ID on which confirmation email needs to be sent

Fields for which input is required are known as mandatory fields. If user keeps it blank (null), the software should display error message.

Functionality Check - The Form must perform its intended functionality of **insertion, update and Delete** etc.

For example, the form for updating an employee profile must update it and not add a duplicate one

If you try to delete agent and there is an order which references that agent, you need to decide whether to delete any order associated with the agent and then delete the agent OR do not allow the deletion unless the order is deleted.

As part of functional testing all the above requirements are tested along with stated functionalities. We have discussed in detail how test cases can be prepared for functional testing using various test design techniques.

6.2.2.2 Test Design Process

This section describes all these terminologies and the process in detail with the help of simple Login requirements and also Registration and reservation process of Airline Reservation System.

Example: Requirement: A login form takes user name and password data as input in two text boxes and checks for valid username and password. Enters home page if user name and password is valid else it displays error message

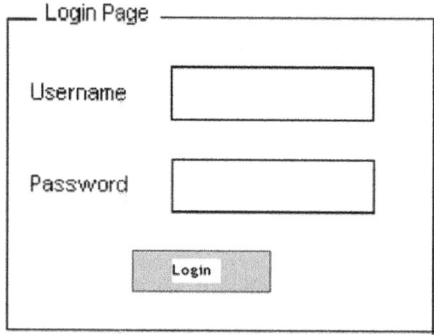

Based on this simple requirement, we can derive Test Conditions as given below.

    i. Check that Application displays error if login details entered are not valid
    ii. Check that Application displays home page after user logs in successfully

Since this is a very simple requirement, we have not itemized requirements and directly

wrote test conditions. However it is advisable to document itemized requirements and test conditions for more complex requirements.

The table provided below lists all the itemised requirements (as per previous section) for Registration Process along with test conditions for each requirement

Id	Itemized Requirement	Test Condition
RF-01	Registration form is displayed once 'New Registration' button clicked on home page	Ensure that system displays Registration form when user clicks on 'Registration' button
RF-02	Registration form has provision to input all personal information - Name, gender, marital status, Birth date and contact details such as full address, phone number, mobile number, and fax number, eMail ID	Ensure that various fields are available on the registration form and user is able to input details in these fields
RF-03	Name, Birth date, Mobile Number and email ID are mandatory fields	Ensure that system displays error if Name is kept blank Birth date is kept blank Email ID is kept blank Mobile number is Kept blank
RF-04	Age should be > 18 years	Ensure that System displays error if Age calculated based on Birth date is < 18 years Query: What if the age is exactly 18 years? Allow? Or not allow?
RF-05	Email ID is in valid format	Email ID should contain @ sign followed by valid website address
RF-06	Email Id and mobile numbers should be in valid format	Ensure that system displays error if Mobile number is not of 10 digit Mobile number contain non-numeric character
RF-07	Registration form has provision to input membership type and it should be one of Solver, Gold, Platinum	Check that Membership type field is displayed and allows input Check that user can select only one of the three options for membership type
RF-08	Should have provision to enter valid user ID which has between 6 to 10 characters and there	Ensure that system displays error if user ID is

		should not be any other member with same user ID	Less than 6 characters More than 10 characters Any other user already exists with same user ID
	RF-09	Should have provision to accept valid password which is of between 6 to 10 characters	Ensure that system displays error if password does not meet the criteria.
	RF-10	Confirmation message should be displayed after successful registration process but displays error message if any details entered are not valid	Ensure that when user presses submit button system - validates all fields and displays error message when not valid or - Displays confirmation message and inserts registration details in the database if details entered are valid

As you must have observed, Test Conditions are written to specify what exactly the condition to be checked in a computerized application. It is based on the specific itemized requirement

Note that as in case of requirement RF-04, we can come up with some questions / doubts which we may want to clarify before moving further.

It is not necessary to write test condition just aside the requirement and can be listed separately. However, it should be possible to link Test conditions back to their sources in the test basis (requirements here), so that it is possible to ensure that requirements are not missed out.

Different organizations / teams may use different template for documenting requirements and test conditions. The format, tool, content and level of detail etc could depend on project requirement and process standards used in an organization.

Test conditions can also be prioritised, and if required, low priority (not important) test conditions may be ignored for further detailing in test cases.

Test conditions can be rather vague (not very specific), covering quite a large range of possibilities.

Detailed test cases then developed based on test conditions which are very specific. We have already discussed various test design techniques in chapter 5 using which we can derive test cases.

6.2.3 Test Case creation

Test case: A set of input values, execution preconditions, expected results and execution post conditions, developed for a particular objective or test condition, such as to exercise a particular program path or to verify compliance with a specific requirement. [After IEEE 610]

As an example, test condition related to invalid login credentials can be converted to following specific test cases with actual specific input data

- Null User ID (User ID: "", Password: "prakash123")
- Null Password: (User ID: "Prakash71", Password: "")
- Invalid User ID (User ID: "ABC", Password: "abc123")
- Valid User ID, Invalid Password (User ID:"Prakash71:, Password: 'Pradash123")
- Valid User ID and valid Password (User ID: "Prakash71", Password: "Prakash123") where Prakash71 is a valid userID and is available in the database and Password is also matching with password stored in database.

There could be many other test cases with different possibilities as per business requirements such as

- Ensure that only *s are displayed in place of actual characters entered as password
- If wrong user ID, Password entered for 5 times, the user is locked
- And so on.

However for the time being we will restrict to only basic test cases for our discussion.

You may actually come up with many such test cases using different valid/invalid usernames and Passwords. However we can restrict to 3 test cases based on test design techniques we learned earlier.

First we apply Equivalence partitioning technique for User ID

    Valid Partition: All the valid User IDs in the database

    Invalid Partition: All the User IDs which are not available in the database including blank

Next we apply equivalence partitioning for Valid User ID

    Valid Partition: Password against the given User ID

    Invalid Partition: Any other word which does not match with the password for a given User ID.

Null User ID will be part of Invalid partition and we can ignore this test assuming that it will be treated in the same manner as other user Ids which are not blank but do not exist in database.

One may also think of using Decision Table assuming that the outcome depends on combination of two fields User ID and Password.

Similar will be the case for Null password. Checking of password is important only if User ID is valid. There is no need to check password if UserID itself is not valid.

Please note that to check this functionality you will have to have some valid users in the system. This cannot be possible until the system is ready and some registrations are done. However it would be too late to design test cases if we wait till the registration form is developed and some registrations are done. In practice, test cases need to be prepared before the system is ready and hence generally test cases may have to be prepared and documented without actual data assigned. Such test cases are known as **High Level Test Cases**.

High level test case: A test case without concrete (implementation level) values for input data and expected results. Logical operators are used; instances of the actual values are not yet defined and/or available.

Once the software development is completed, the test cases with specific input values are written for the test cases either in advance or at the time of execution.

Low level test case: A test case with concrete (implementation level) values for input data and expected results. Logical operators from high level test cases are replaced by actual values that correspond to the objectives of the logical operators

Traceability: The ability to identify related items in documentation and software, such as requirements with associated tests. Traceability helps assuring that no requirements are missed out.

Test cases can now be prioritized so that the most important test cases are executed first, and low priority test cases are executed later, or even not executed at all

Test case Documentation

In order to be able to read, review update and use effectively during actual testing (test execution) test cases are documented in much proper way, generally in tabular format as given below. Many organizations also use some tools in which requirements and or test cases are entered and maintained.

Test Case ID	Test Condition / Scenario	Preconditions (If any)	Test Steps	Input /Test Data	Expected Result	Pass / Fail
TC_01	To validate the login page with Invalid user name	The application is invoked and login page is displayed	Enter User Name	User Name= "prakash7"		
			Enter password	Password= "prakash123"		
			Press LOGIN Button		Display Error Message Box "Invalid User ID. Enter Again"	
TC_02	To validate the login page with valid user name but invalid password	The application is invoked and login page is displayed	Enter User Name	User name = :"Prakash71"		
			Enter password	Password= " Pralash123"		
			Press LOGIN Button		Should Display Message Box "Invalid Password "	
TC_03	To validate the login page with valid user name and password	The application is invoked and login page is displayed	Enter User Name	User name = "Prakash71"		
			Enter password	Password= "Prakash123"		
			Press LOGIN Button		Display Welcome message and display home page	
TC-04						
..						

Test Case ID: Each test case is given a unique identifier. There could be thousands of test cases for a given system under test. Giving unique identification to each test case helps in tracking the test cases.

Pre-Condition: Environmental and state which must be fulfilled before the component/unit can be executed with a particular input value. Before you execute a specific test, the system should be in the state mentioned here. Test Preconditions can also include availability of required test data in the database. For example in case of Login functionality there must be some valid users available in the system so that we can test whether system works fine (displays home page) if valid user ID and Password entered. If the precondition is same for all the test cases, precondition can also be described only once.

Test Steps: A detailed description of steps to execute the test. One may also include **Step Number** for each step.

Test Data/Input: Inputs & its combinations / variables used

Expected Result: include information displayed on a screen in response to an input, and also include changes to data and/or states, and any other action triggered (e.g. email to be sent etc)

Expected output and actual output are compared to determine Pass / Fail –

If the program works as given in the specification, it is said to pass otherwise Fail.

Additional columns: In addition to above columns, each test case may also include many other information such as

Test Condition ID, Requirement ID (for tracing back to Test condition or Requirement)

Step Number: Showing the sequence in which the steps are executed.

Actual Result: Indicating what was the actual outcome by the system. This may particularly help if the test case has failed.

Also note that one test scenario or condition may result into multiple test cases and can be based on any of the techniques learnt.

Test Procedure (Test Script):

Please observe that there are three test cases written in the same table in a specific sequence. As such all three test cases are independent of each other and can be executed in any sequence but if you execute test case 3 (TC-03) first and if the application worked properly then a home page will be displayed. Now in order to execute TC-01 and TC-02 you will have to first log out otherwise you will not see option to log in if you are already logged in. Similarly all test cases will have pre conditions. So, it is always advantageous to document and execute the test cases **in** such a way that after executing the current test case you are brought to the pre-condition of the next test case.

Note that whenever we do testing, we are providing some inputs, submit and then system will provide some output which we compare with expected result.

Some processing can be done immediately when you provide some input in one single field. For example basic validations are done immediately. So if you enter say some character in field for number of tickets, system may immediately respond with an error message or if you enter / select flight number, fight name, airline name time etc could be immediately displayed without waiting for 'Submit' button.

In some other case you have to provide inputs to all the fields and submit the form then only some processing will happen. For example, actual reservation happens only when all the details are provided and submitted. Sometimes validations are also done after submission of form.

It depends on implementation of the functionality.

So, the test cases are generally organized in a specific sequence for the entire form till submission step is executed.

This does not apply to only field level test cases but also applied and important for functionality level testing. So, if you execute the test cases for Registration functionality first, then Login functionality, then booking functionality, you will be able to save time as execution of previous functionality can put you to precondition of next functionality. The execution of previous functionality may also include inserting some data in the database which would be used for testing the next functionality.

If the test cases for different functionalities are documented separately then Test Procedure Specification document will specify sequence.

So, as part of the test procedure document, test cases are grouped in a sensible way along with sequence in which they are to be executed during execution phase.

So, **test procedure specification** is a document specifying a sequence of actions for the execution of a test. It is also known as test script or manual test script. [After IEEE 829]

Separating Input data to reduce / avoid redundancy

As you can notice the steps for all the above test cases will be same and under current format all the steps should be repeated. However a simplified format can be used where you write steps only once and data to be used are separately written in different table. While executing the test case, tester will need to follow same steps for all the data sets given in different table.

Test Case ID	Preconditions (If any)	Test Condition / Scenario	Test Steps	Input /Test Data	Expected Result	Pass / Fail
TC_01	The application is invoked and login page is displayed	To validate the login page with Invalid and valid User ID and Password combinations	Enter User Name	UserName = InputVar1		
			Enter password	Password= Input var2		
			Press LOGIN Button		ResultVar1	

Test datasheet for the above test cases.

ID	InputVar1	InputVar2	Resultvar1
TC-01	Prakash7	Prakash123	Error Message "Invalid User ID"
TC-02	Prakash71	Pradash123	Erro Message "Invalid Password"
TC-03	Prakash71	Prakash123	Home Page displayed
	....		

As you can notice, detailed test cases have parameters instead of actual data inputs to be provided. Same steps can be repeated using different data provided in the data sheet above. This reduces lot of preparation and maintenance effort (in case changes to be done in the tests or additional input values to be tested).

Test Cases **for Reservation form.** Only sample test cases are given for illustration purpose

TC Id	Test case Description	Pre-condition	Steps Description	Expected Result	Pass / Fail?
TC-01	Check that user reservation form displays on pressing 'Reserve Tickets' button	User has successfully logged in and home page is displayed	Click on 'Reserve Tickets' button	Reservation form is displayed	
TC-02	Check that all required information could be entered	Reservation form is displayed	Verify that From Location, To Location, Date, Service Number, Class, number of		

				tickets fields are available and enabled to be able to enter data		
TC-04	Check that inputs are valid	Reservation form is displayed	Input From location = 'Ahmedabad'	Accepts	
			Enter To Location = 'Mumbai	Accepts	
			Enter Date = '12-Dec-2010'	Display error1	
			Enter Date =0 '12-Dec-19'		
			Enter Number of tickets	Display error2	
			Enter Number of Tickets = 3		
			Class = 'Economy'	Display Rate	
			…		

We can have separate table for error and warning messages

Error1	"Bookings can be done only for future dates"
Error2	"Number of Tickets should be > 0"
Error3	"From Location and To location cannot be same"
Message3	"Are you sure you want to cancel?"
….	

Using Test Design Techniques to derive test conditions and test cases.

Please note that the test cases written above are not enough. We have to use all the test design techniques we discussed earlier for designing test case.

- **Equivalence Partitioning (EP) and Boundary Value Analysis (BVA)** for all individual field level testing
- **Decision Table** for all business rules dependent on more than one fields
- **State Transition Technique** to check transition from one state to other and corresponding valid/invalid functions or actions
- **Use Cases** for all variations of business functions and transactions.
- **Experience** for any other important aspects not covered by any technique but based on past experience and intuition of the tester.

I am reproducing some of the test cases we had discussed as part of Test Design Techniques.

Test Condition: Travel Date validation. Ticket booking is allowed for next one year. Assume that today's date is 18-Sep-19

TC ID	Test Case	Test Steps	Input /Test Data	Expected Result	Pass/ Fail?
	Format Checking		09/20/2019	Error	
			20/09/2019	Accepts	
	EP :		20/07/2019	Error	
			20/09/2019	Accepts	
			20/12/2020	Error	
	BVA (Assume Today is 29-Aug-16)		Previous date - 17/09/2019	Error	
			Today's Date - 18/09/2019	Allow?	
			Tomorrow's Date - 19/09/2019	Accepts	
			One year -1 - 17/09/2018	Accepts	
			One year later - 18/09/2020	Error	
			One year + 1 - 19/09/2020	Error	

Test Condition: Fly From and Fly to locations are Mandatory

TC ID	Test Case	Test Steps	Input /Test Data	Expected Result	Pass/ Fail?
	Fly from field Mandatory		Blank	Error	
			Vadodara	Error message- if no flight from Vadodara	
			Ahmedabad	Accepts	
	Fly to field Mandatory		Blank	Error	
			Vadodara	Error message- if no flight to Vadodara	
			Ahmedabad	Error	
			Mumbai	Accepts	

Test Condition: Name can contain only characters. Class is Mandatory and can contain only one of the three possible values

TC ID	Test Case	Test Steps	Input /Test Data	Expected Result	Pass/ Fail?
	input type - Only Characters allowed		Ramesh123	Error	
			ramesh	Accepts	
	input Length – up to 20 characters		Ramesh Maganlala Kashiparekh	Error	
			Ramesh M Kashiparekh	Accepts	
	Mandatory		Blank	Error	
	Mandatory		Blank	Error	
	Valid Class		Economy	Accepts	
	Invalid class		Second class	Error	

Test Conditions: Number of tickets need to be entered and should be between 1 and 10.

Technique: EP and BVA

Test Case ID	Test Case	Test Steps	Input /Test Data	Expected Result	Pass/ Fail?
	Mandatory		Blank	Error	
	Input Type - Numeric only		Two	Error	
			2	Accepts	
	Range (EP) - 1 to 10		0	Error	
			5	Accepts	
			15	Error	
	Range (BVA) 1 to 10		0	Error	
			1	Accepts	
			10	Accepts	
			11	Error	

Discount Calculation Rule: If the tickets are booked 20 days in advance, you get 5% discount. All the people who books more than 3 tickets gets additional 5% discount

Technique: Decision Table

TC ID	Test Case	Test Steps	Input / Test Data	Expected Result	Pass/ Fail?
	Ticket not booked in advance of 20 days and Number of tickets < 4		Travel Date = 5 days after Number of tickets = 2	Discount = 0	
	Ticket booked more than 20 days in advance but Number of tickets < 4		Travel Date = 20 days after Number of tickets = 3	Discount = 5%	
	Ticket booked less than 20 days in advance but Number of tickets > 3		Travel Date = 19 days after Number of tickets = 4	Discount = 5%	
	Ticket booked more than 20 days in advance and Number of tickets > 3		Travel Date = 20 days after Number of tickets = 4	Discount = 10%	

Requirement: Unregistered user can view flight details but cannot book ticket. Once registration is done, application displays login page.

Technique: State Transition

Pre-Condition	Test Case ID	Test Case	Test Steps	Input -Test Data/ Action	Expected Result	Pass/ Fail?
Unregistered User		Viewing Schedule does not change the state		Action View Schedule	Application displays schedule but does not allow booking	
Unregistered User		Behaviour changes after registration		Action: Register	Application Takes you to Login screen	
Unregistered User		Unregistered user tries to Login (Invalid UID, PWD)		Login	Application gives error message	
Registered User		Registered User tries to login (with valid UID, PWD)		Login	Application display User name and allows booking	

6.2.4 Test Execution and Defect Management

Generally Unit and Integration testing is done in the development environment by the developer themselves. So, the execution does not require lot of care and planning. However Validation and System Testing is done in a different test environment where latest version of the entire application is installed, the required set up needs to be done before testing. In order to carry out the execution effectively, it has to be planned properly.

6.2.4.1 Test Execution Process

Following chart shows steps being taken during execution phase.

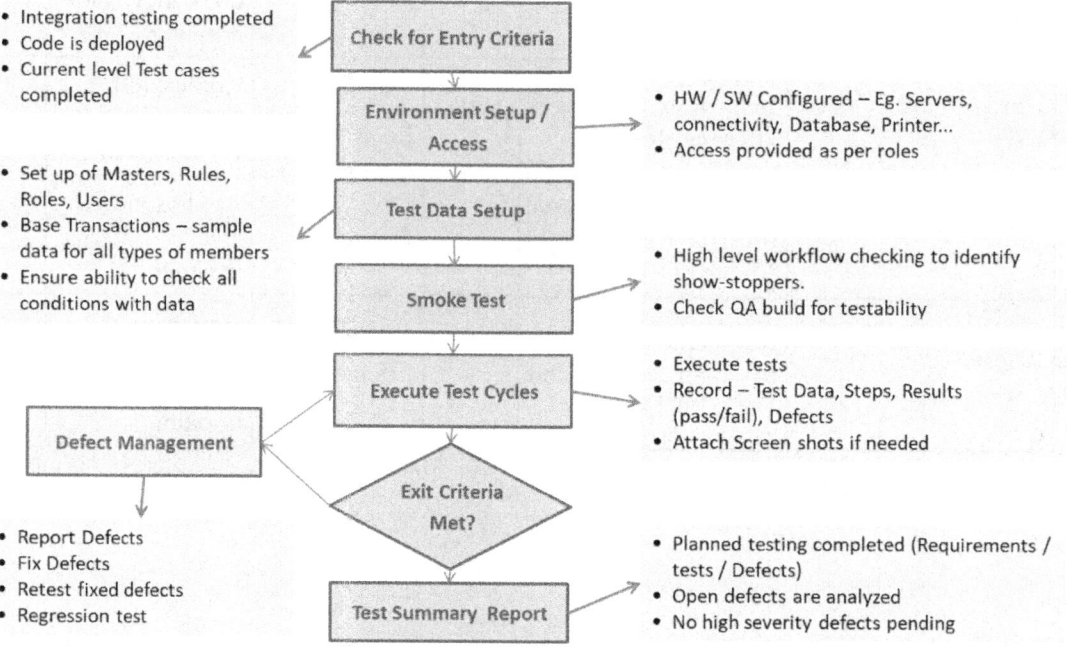

Let us understand each step in more details

1) **Check for Entry Criteria:** As part of this step we ensure that all the phases required to be completed before we start system testing are really completed.
   a) For example, Unit and Integration testing are completed and most (if not all) defects are fixed.
   b) All the test cases are designed and ready to be referred during execution. Test Procedures are developed if not yet developed
   c) Latest version of the code is integrated and deployed in the environment
2) **Environment Set up done** and Required access given to the users (Testing team)
   a) Required configuration is done for hardware and software. Database set up is done, Connectivity if required is established

b) Users are created as per the user roles played by the testing team members and required access given to all the users (testers). Access is also given to other required resources if required

3) **Test Data Setup:** This is important so that different conditions can be checked with these data
   a) All masters are setup with some test data. For example, Flight details between some locations are made ready
   b) Charge master is set for all travel classes as per business requirements
   c) If testing is done only for some specific transactions such as cancellation of ticket, then some data for base transaction may also have to be kept ready
   d) If the testing is to be done for enhancement or changes in the functionality, production data can also be copied to test environment so that time can be saved.

4) **Smoke Test:**

Here very high level testing is done just to ensure that user is able to move from one step to other and there are no show-stoppers. The objective is to check if the build received for testing is testable or not. For example various menu options work, clicks on buttons are possible. Business rules or expected results are not checked but we only ensure that detailed testing will be possible. Many times if environment set-up or data setup is not done properly then we face some issues and we may unnecessarily waste time during testing. This is also known as testability checking

5) **Actual execution of test cycles and Defect Management:**

Only after we ensure that proper setup is done, we start execution of actual test cases. We use the test cases as designed in the test design phase.

For each test, we bring the application state to pre-condition, follow the steps mentioned, input the actual data as specified and observe the system response. If we find that the actual result we get while running the application is different than expected result, we conclude that there is a defect in the system and the step is marked as 'Failed'. The root cause could be wrong configuration, failure of test environment, corrupted data or even wrong test case itself. However if the root cause is really an issue in the software, it is known as a defect. Such defects are reported by testing team, fixed by the development team and closed by testing team after retesting. While reporting the defect we provide all the details such as steps followed, data entered etc. In some cases we may also attach screen shots showing result. This process may be repeated many number of times till all or most of the defects are fixed.

The defect is also known as incident, problem, issue or bug.

It is practically possible that during the process of this testing phase some requirements may change or some new defects get introduced. It is hence advisable to run more than one test cycles. How many cycles are required will depend on criticality of application, defects found and any other criteria decided. Many organization plan for 3 cycles for business applications.

6) **Check the Exit criteria and do test closure activity – prepare test summary report:**

It is practically impossible or very difficult to come to a stage where there are absolutely no defects in the application. At some point of time, we have to stop testing keeping in mind budget, time and quality level. So, organizations will come up with some criteria and team can decide to stop execution cycles and move application to production if those criteria are met. The criteria could depend on various factors such as criticality or the functionality, timeline available, market situation and potential impact.

For example criteria could be

a. There are no known critical defects (High severity) pending to be fixed
b. Not more than known 10 medium critical defects available
c. There could be 30 known low critical or only suggestion for improvement type of defect pending

Functional, Regression and non-functional testing if required are done during this phase and continues till defined criteria are met for the project.

Please also note that test execution could be manual and/or automated.

Test Cases for Login Page

Let us revisit the test case we have written for testing login page.

TC ID	Preconditions (If any)	Test Condition / Scenario	Test Steps	Input /Test Data	Expected Result	Actual Result
TC_01	The application is invoked and login page is displayed	To validate the login page with null password	Enter User Name	User Name=InputVar1		
			Enter password	Password= Inputvar2		
			Press LOGIN Button		Result Var1	

Test datasheet for the above test cases.

TC ID	InputVar1	InputVar2	Resultvar1
TC-01	'Mark'	Blank	Warning Message "Please Enter User name and Password"
	Blank	Patni1234	Warning Message "Please Enter User name and Password"
	CODES	XYZ	Warning Message "User Name or Password in invalid"
	Blank	Blank	Warning Message "Please Enter User name and Password"
	JIM	Pass123	Home Page displayed

This test case has three steps. The test case (all three steps) will be executed 5 times for each of the above data sets. The response from the application to be matched with expected result, and if the actual result does not match with the expected result then we can consider that the test case has failed for the specific data set and application has a defect.

In a current outsourcing and offshorization scenario, development team and testing teams may not be from the same company and may be operating from different geographical locations. Hence a very formal process is followed. In many cases screen shots at the end of each step is taken for all test cases or at least for failed test cases. Such details are useful to ensure that all the steps are properly followed and development team can clearly understand how the system was behaving when the test case was failed.

6.2.4.2 Content of Defect Reports

As we have seen, defect report should have all the information that can help above users. The details however may vary from project to project and organization to organization.

Following list covers various details that could be part of defect report

Defect ID - A unique number to each defect. This will help to identify the bug record. A bug-reporting tool will generate this automatically each time you report the bug.

Defect Summary – A short description of the defect.

Defect Identification Date - The date on which the defect is found.

Reporting Date – The date on which the defect is reported. This generally may be same as Defect Identification Date but sometime the defect may have been reported on a different date.

Detailed description – A detailed description of bug clearly mentioning the steps to reproduce the bug. It also includes how application should behave on above mentioned steps and what is the actual result coming on running above steps i.e. the bug behavior

Version - The product version if any. Many times multiple versions of the application are in production/testing and defect may come on any of the versions. The developer needs to know in which version the defect came.

Severity – determined based on impact of the defect on functionality of application. Possible values of severity field are

- Critical – Bugs that can cause very serious consequences due to system crash or some show stoppers or some security breach or wrong calculation/processing.
- High – If the bug could cause some malfunctioning with some manageable cost like slow performance of losing some data (but could be recovered) etc.
- Medium – If the bug can cause some minor impact such as truncation of names, inconsistency in look and feel
- Low – If the bug is of cosmetic type and do not impact the system operation or functionality. Such as spelling mistakes, alignment related issues etc. There could also be some recommendations for UI improvements

Note that severity type could vary from application to application.

Priority – Indicates when bug should be fixed? Generally set from P1 to P5. P1 – high ("fix the bug with highest priority") and P5 – low (" Fix when time permits"). Severity of defect may also impact priority.

Reproducibility – Some defects appear 'sometimes'. If your bug is not reproducible it will be difficult to get fixed. You should clearly mention the steps to reproduce the bug. Do not assume or skip any reproducing step. However if in some case defect cannot be reproduced easily, one need to clearly mention that.

Environment - Mention the hardware platform where you found this bug. The various platforms like 'PC', 'MAC', 'HP', 'Sun' etc. Also mention the OS (Operating system) where you found the bug. Operating systems like Windows, Linux, UNIX, SunOS, and Mac OS. Mention the different OS versions also if applicable like Windows NT, Windows 2000, and Windows XP etc. This may not be required if the testing is done in single environment.

Type / Category: The defects may be categorized under different categories as per company requirements. It could be as per SDLC phase or as per Functional grouping or as per type of requirement such as functional/security etc..

Application/Module: Name of application or module for which the defect found

Person responsible: If you know which developer is responsible for that particular module in which bug occurred, then you can specify email address of that developer. Else keep it blank this will assign bug to module owner or Manger will assign bug to developer.

Reported By – Name of the tester who is reporting the defect. This help if developer needs some clarification about the defect from the tester.

Attachments – One can attach some files with the defect to give some more information or screen shots if any.

Name and the contact information of the tester

Tentative fix date – the date by which the defect should get fixed. This would mostly be set by development team

Resolution details – Details of the action taken to correct the bug

Status – It indicates what is the current state of the defect. When you are writing the defect in the defect report or entering it in any tool then by default the status is 'New'. Later on bug goes through various stages like Fixed, Verified, and Reopen etc as explained in next section.

6.2.4.3 Users of Defect Reports

While reporting defect, it is critical that all the important details are provided in the defect report so that various users can understand clearly.

Test Team Lead: He/she needs to review defects before assigning to developer & reassign defects among testers. Defect count details help him to estimate the retesting effort and also understand performance of his/her team members based on defect related metrics such as Defect Acceptance Rate. If many defects are getting cancelled and closed, it is assumed that the testing team members did not have proper understanding of the functional requirements

Development / Maintenance Team Lead: They deal with application defects. He/she will review the defect and assign to concerned developer to resolve. So, he/she should be able to quickly and clearly understand software version and component for the issue, criticality and priority of the defect (Is it halting further testing) etc. It will also help him/her to estimate approximate effort required for fixing the defects and also understand performance of his team / team members based on some metrics such as Defect age (number of days the defect remained opened), Defect Density (number of defects per size of code) etc.

Developer/ Maintenance Engineer: Involved in Analyzing, verifying and resolving defects. So, he/she should know version, environment and possible root cause of the issue.

Management: They are interested to know overall health of the project at a given point in time. So, Individual defect details are summarized into specific manner that provide overall status, and quality of product. Some such reports may include

- Application module wise, severity wise defect summary of open and closed defects
- Category wise severity wise open and closed defects
- Expected dates for fixing and closing of high severity defects

6.2.4.4 Defect Management

Defect Management is also very important during execution phase. The flow chart provided below describes how the defect changes it's' status based on various actions taken and then ultimately closed

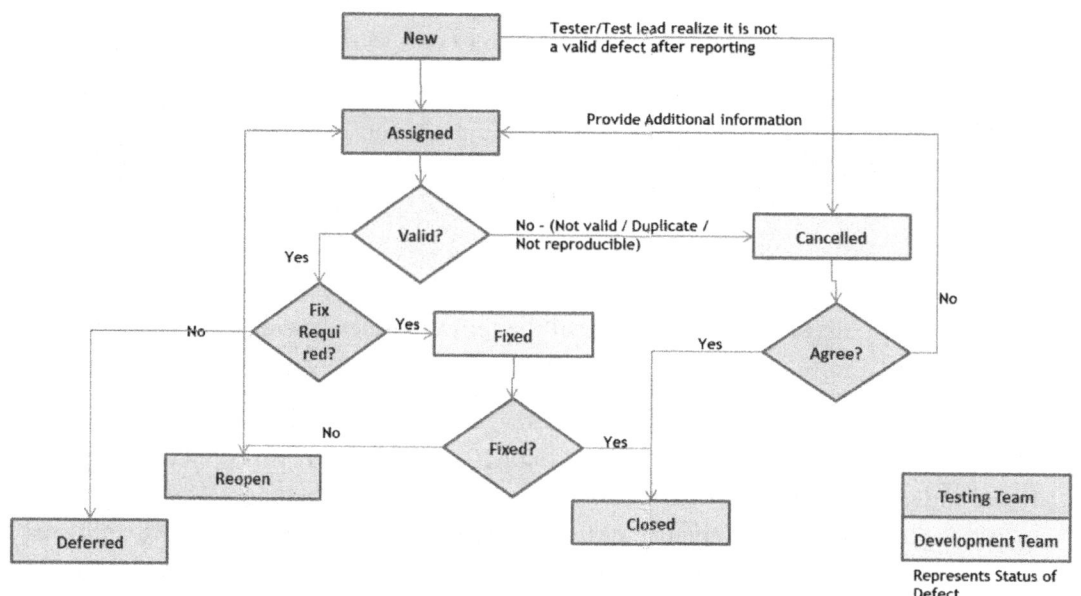

New – When a Defect is logged and yet to be assigned to a developer. Generally for smaller team, tester may know which developer should be assigned the defect but for larger team, Project Manager or Development Lead will decide.

Assigned – indicates that the developer who would fix the defect has been identified and has started analysing and working on the defect fix.

Duplicate – Manager or Developer will update the status of a defect as "Duplicate" if this defect was already reported earlier.

Cancelled – This status indicates that the developer is not considering the defect as valid due to any of the following reasons

    a) Not able to reproduce

    b) Not a valid defect and the expected result is as per requirement

    c) Test Data used was invalid to test the specific functionality

d) Defect referring to the Requirement was not part of the current scope from the current release

e) Details provided not clear/additional information needed

f) Is a new requirement or change which was not yet communicated.

Deferred – Defect fix has been held back because of time or budget constraints and defer the defect till next or future release.

Fixed – Developer has fixed the defect and has unit tested the fix. The code changes are deployed in test environment

Reopen – Status is changed to "Reopen" by a tester, when a tester finds the defect is not fixed or partially fixed.

Closed – Tester verifies the defects in "Fixed" status and once they find the defect is fixed after retesting, they change the status to "Closed". This is the last status of Defect Life Cycle. Cancelled defects may also be closed if tester agrees that it was a wrong defect.

6.2.4.5 Defect Management Tool

In a real life situation where large number of people are involved in a project or development team, testing team, business team are sitting at different location, it is critical to ensure that all the defects are properly documented, communicated, fixed, retested and closed.

Providing all the defect details accurately, summarizing them as per management need and tracking the status of each defect will be very difficult if entire defect management is done manually. There are many defect management tools available in the market. Many Test management tools like Quality Centre from HP or Test Manager from IBM also provides features for Defect management. There are also some open source defect management tools. Mantis is one such defect management tool. Refer to following screen shot to understand how defect related details are captured by tool like Mantis

ID	Project	Category	View Status	Date Submitted	Last Update
0008834	mantisbt	email	public	2008-01-30	2012-10-19
Reporter	striker69				
Assigned To	dregad				
Priority	normal	**Severity**	major	**Reproducibility**	always
Status	resolved	**Resolution**	no change required		
Platform		**OS**		**OS Version**	
Product Version	1.1.1				
Target Version		**Fixed in Version**			
Summary	0008834: Database query failed. Error received from database was #1406: Data too long for column 'body'				
Description	Seems that the email feature has changed in version 1.1.* from version 1.0.8. The emails are now inserted into the DB and then read back to be processed. When inserting the data in the DB, we get the error in the Summary. This happens on cases with lots of notes. I have looked at the DB (MySQL 5.0.27) and the datatype of column 'mantis_email_table.body' is LONGTEXT. Any hint on how to fix this?				
Tags	email, utf8				
Attached Files					

Benefits of Tools

Different tools may have different features but following primary feature are provided by almost all the tools.

    a. Built in validation checks
    b. Reduced Turnaround Time and other communication issues
    c. Available - 24x7
    d. Maintenance of history
    e. Generation of summarized information, metrics
    f. Ability to quickly search on specified criteria
    g. Multiple attachments
    h. Online/ real-time status through queries/reports

Many additional features may be provided by some of the popular tools

    i. Proactive notification when no action taken for a defect on due date
    j. Involvement of translator for translation when needed
    k. Understand number of items on which actions to be taken
    l. Change Request approval process

As mentioned above, one can derive many benefits with the help of tools. It will not only reduce effort but with real-time generation of report, it can help management to have improved project control.

6.3 Test Plan

As you can see, testing project itself is a very intense activity involving multiple stake holders, resources, tools and of course considerable amount of time. This is a full-fledged project by itself and hence need to plan properly. So, the testing project manager would prepare and document a detailed plan that would cover at least following sections.

Scope: Describes what is in scope and what is out of scope. So, it will include list of applications, Modules, Functionalities, Testing Objectives and types within the scope and outside the scope.

Strategy: Describes how testing will be done. Will it be only manual or automated also? Which techniques to be used and at what level the testing should be done?

Milestones: Describes start and end dates of various phases / tasks (Refer STLC phases)

Quality Gates: Describes how quality of testing activities will be ensured through various reviews. At what stage a detailed status review should take place based on which some decisions may have to be taken for the continuation of the project.

Entry/Exit Criteria: Describes what are the preconditions to enter into a specific STLC phase and what should be completed to go to the next phase. For example, on what basis one would say that requirement analysis phase or test design phase is completed?

Resource Requirements: Provides details of what hardware, software and human resources required. Number of testers required would depend on total size of the project (eg. Number of test cases), Expected defect density and productivity.

Roles and Responsibilities: Describes who will be playing various roles and what they are responsible for.

Communication: Describes how communication will happen between various teams and how status of the project will be reported

Defect Tracking and **Resolution Process:** This section describes process to be followed for Defect tracking and resolution.

Risk Management: Describes all potential risks which can impact quality or timeline of the project and what steps to be taken to mitigate the same

Assumptions: Describes all the assumptions taken while planning

Let us understand some of the important sections in detail with example.

6.3.1 Testing Scope: Example

Category	In Scope – Example	Out of Scope - Examples
Boundary - Applications, Modules, Functionalities	Registration, Booking modules, … in scope	Payment module, not in current scope
Domain - Specific regions, customers, products	Testing to be done only for flight bookings	Bookings for railway, … out of scope at present
Type/phase of testing	Functional, Regression and Security Testing in Scope	Performance & Load testing will be out of scope
Specific Inputs/Outputs	All reports generated will be part of scope	Testing whether sms goes to various customers will be out of scope due to……
Specific Activities	All testing activities will be part of scope except test planning.	Test planning will be done by customer manager, so will be out of scope for test team.

6.3.2 Testing Strategy

Testing Strategy covers how part. It describes testing approach/techniques be used to ensure maximum coverage of requirements and finding maximum possible defects within limited time. It also includes prioritization

The strategy aims to answer following questions

- What Level of testing to be applied along with methodology and tools
- Which Testing Techniques to be used? Can we reuse some artifacts or define new ones.
- Will Risk based testing Approach be taken? If yes, what are the considerations?
- Can automation be done? If yes, then which part and how much?
    - Are there any existing automated scripts that can be leveraged?
    - Is maintenance required on existing scripts?
    - What standards will be followed for Automation scripting
- Which tools to be used and for what? – Eg. MS Project for Project tracking, HP QC (Quality Center) for all test artifacts and defect management, Selenium for Test automation etc

SW Testing Project Execution Process

6.3.3 Milestones and Timelines

This section provides **planned start and end dates** for **each milestone** within SW testing lifecycle phases. If there are multiple projects or applications impacted within release, milestones are provided for each such project and application

Sample:

Module	Milestone Name	Owner	Planned Start date	Planned End Date
App1	Business requirements Delivery	Mukesh	31-Aug-20yy	31-Aug-20yy
App1	Functional Requirements Delivery	Mukesh	6-Sep-20yy	6-Sep-20yy
App1	Requirement Upload	Mukesh	5-Sep-20yy	10-Sep-20yy
App1	Test Strategy	Varun	4-Sep-20yy	10-Sep-20yy
App1	Test Case Completion	Varun	5-Sep-20yy	11-Sep-20yy
App1	Test Case Review (AD/Bus.)	Varun	12-Sep-20yy	13-Sep-20yy
App1	Code Drop Date	AD	20-Sep-20yy	20-Sep-20yy
App1	Functional Test Execution Completion	Vinita	22-Sep-20yy	5-Oct-20yy
App1	Regression Test Execution Completion	Maitry	8-Oct-20yy	26-Oct-20yy

These Milestones are tracked very closely to ensure that overall project is not delayed because of delay in any of the milestones

6.3.4 Quality Assurance Gates

This covers how the **quality of Testing will be assured**. Various internal external **reviews** happen at each stage with various stakeholders to ensure proper coverage and quality.

Generally in Quality Assurance meetings, various teams and their respective leads/managers are involved as given below.

BSA – Business System Analyst. Generally BSA is part of development team and is responsible to document function specification document

BA – Business Analyst. Generally BA is part of Business team and is responsible to document and provide business requirements of the project

QA – Quality Assurance Team

AD – Application Development Team

Following is an example for one such project

Verification Technique	Used in this release? (Y/N)	Phase	Owner and Participants
Business Requirements Walkthrough	N	Analysis	Lead – BSA/BA Participant(s) – QA Lead, AD PM, AD Lead Developer
Functional Specification Walkthrough	Y	Analysis	Lead – BSA/BA that authored documents Participant(s) – QA Lead, PM, AD Lead Developers Optional – AD Lead Developers, A Leads, QA Analysts
Functional Specification Ambiguity Review	Y	Design	Lead – QA lead that performed Ambiguity Review Participants – BSA, BA, Business, PM, AD Lead Optional – AD Lead Developers, QA Leads, QA Analysts
Functional Test Design Walkthrough	Y	Build	Lead – QA Peer Designated in Role Participants –QA Manager, QA leads, Analysts
Regression Design Walkthrough	N	Build	Lead – QA Peer Designated in Role Participants –QA Manager, QA leads, Analysts
Defect Tracking Review Meetings	Y	Test	Lead – QA Lead or Manager Participants –QA Manager, QA Leads, Analysts, AD Developers, UAT Manager, Project Manager

6.3.5 Entry / Exit Criteria

This section provides criteria under which you start a specific testing phase or type criteria when you consider completion of testing type or phase

Test Phase / Type	Entry Criteria (Acceptance Criteria, if within the Test Phase)	Exit Criteria (Completion Criteria, if within the testing phase)
Smoke Testing	N/A	N/A
Functional Testing	Unit and Integration Testing completed as per criteria	Functional Test Cases • 100% of planned test cases executed • 95% of planned test cases passed • 0 Urgent or High Defects • Business deferral of any medium or low open defects
Regression Testing	Functional Testing has been completed as per exit criteria above.	Regression Test Cases • 100% of planned test cases executed • 99% of planned test cases passed • 0 Urgent or High Defects • Business deferral of any medium or low open defects.
User Acceptance Testing	Test results report to include End-to-End Testing is 100% completed. No Urgent Defects	• Functional Testing results reviewed and approved. • Regression Testing results reviewed and approved • End to End Testing results reviewed and approved. • There are no severity 1 defects open. • UAT results evaluated for Go/No Go decisions

6.3.6 Resource Requirements

All the resources such as people, hardware, tools etc. required for the project are identified and listed in this section.

Resource	Description & Quantity	Owner	Considerations/ Other Details
Subject Matter Expertise			
People			
Hardware			
Software			
Tools: / Quality Center			
Tools: MS Project			
Automation			
Test Environments			

6.3.7 Communication - Status Reporting

This section covers various status reports to be prepared and submitted to various stakeholders during the project.

Types of Reports

- **Progress reports** – This provides details of the progress of various activities being carried out against the planned progress.
- **Automation Report** – It provides progress of the automation creation and execution activity.
- **Defect Reports** – This provides list of all the defects at a given point of time along with status
- **Defect Aging Reports** – It provides number and list of open defects as per their age. Age is calculated based on defect open date and current date.
- **Release Metrics Reports** – It provides metrics and related analysis for various metrics calculated (coverage, Productivity, Quality etc.)

Frequency

The above mentioned reports may be generated every **day** or every **week** and some reports may be generated every **month**.

Project Health Indicator

Depending on status of the report, health indicator is decided and provided as per guidelines below.

- **Green** – Health Good; everything on track – Reporting weekly
- **Yellow** – Health OK but cautionary – Reporting 2 – 3 times a week
- **Red** – Health In trouble- missing milestones – Reporting daily

6.3.8 Defect Tracking and Resolution Process

This section describes process to be followed for Defect tracking and resolution.

Example :

- All defects will be reported through Quality Center (Test/Defect management tool) within XX days
- All project stakeholders, including UAT participants, will be required to have access to Quality Center to view and respond to defects assigned to them.
- Developer(s) are responsible for updating Defect Status's within XX days.
- Defects summary will be provided within the daily and weekly QA Status Report.
- Defect Review meetings will be scheduled weekly in the initial stage and daily during the last four weeks of testing.
- Defect turnaround will be jointly determined by the QA and Development Lead.

6.3.9 Risk Management

It covers list of all possible risks along with mitigation plan such as

Risk/Issue	Likelihood	Impact	Mitigation strategy
Delay in Code delivery	Medium	Slippage in QA Milestones	Plan for tasks not dependent on Code
Changes in requirements during testing	Low	Rework with potential impact on quality and timeline	Implement change management process
Environment/system outage	High	Slippage in timeline	Keep schedule buffer. Keep track of all outages in QC

6.3.10 Assumptions

This section provides all the **assumptions taken to carry out the project**. It can include dependency on various external factors or any requirement of taking deviation from standards due to various reasons.

Examples

- Testing team will start regression testing along with functional testing in order to meet timelines
- Test environment will be set-up by Development team with all necessary changes
- Development team will help in preparing Test Data required for functional and Regression testing
- It is assumed that Development teams will be doing proper unit and integration testing to assure required code quality before system testing starts
- Not more than xxx defects are expected in code.
- All Queries will be resolved within two working days

6.4 Summary

We discussed in earlier chapters that Tesing is important and we need to do testing at different levels of development phases applying various techniques. Quality of testing process and activities is very important and hence a well-defined process needs to be followed. We also need to quantitatively measure some testing and process related parameters which are known as Metrics. We discussed **Coverage Metrics** (Design coverage, Execution coverage, Automation coverage), **Productivity metrics** (Test case creation, execution and automation productivity), **Process Metrics** (Defect Removal Efficiency, Defect Acceptance Rate) and Project Metrics (Schedule Variance, Effort Variance, Effort distribution). Analysis of these metrics data helps to understand the actual quality and status of the testing and helps in taking timely corrective actions. They are also useful for planning and estimation of similar future projects.

We subsequently discussed SW Testing Life Cycle Phases covering Requirement Analysis, Test Design, Test Case Construction and Test execution with Defect Management

Requirement Analysis process uses guidelines we discussed in chapter 2. To make the process effective, we need to understand the business and functional requirements from all the angles, Itemize the requirements to the granular level, distinguish testable and non-testable requirements, Identify ambiguities if any and verify our understanding from the customer.

As part of **Test Design** process, we look at the test basis (itemized requirements) and **derive test conditions.** Then we apply various test design techniques and develop test cases. Initially high level test cases may be prepared without providing exact input values for different fields and at a later stage detailed test cases are prepared providing actual values for input fields. Test cases are then organized in proper sequence to form **Test Procedures.**

The project enters into **Test Execution** phase once the test design is completed and code is deployed for the testing. Within this phase **(a) Entry criteria** is checked (Previous level testing already done, code is deployed and detailed plan is also ready) **(b) Environment setup** is done (configuring hardware, establishing connectivity, providing access etc) **(c) Test data** set up is done (as per the pre-condition set for various test cases), **(d) Smoke testing** is done to just ensure that there are no show-stoppers and then **(e) Test Execution** is done using test cases already developed. During execution, defect found are reported using **Defect Management** Tool. Subsequently we discussed Defect Management process in which different teams change the status (from open to close/differed/cancelled). Defect report provides all the necessary information required by various users of the defect report and summary.

We then discuss that it is important for tester to know overall **Test Project Plan** which includes Scope of work, Strategy, Milestones with timelines, Quality Gates, Entry/Exit Criteria, Resource requirements, Roles and Responsibilities of various human resources playing various roles, Communication plan, Defect Tracking and Resolution Process, Risk management and Assumptions.

6.5 Exercise

Sr	Question
1.	Explain meaning and purpose of metric using example
2.	Explain any four metrics with examples
3.	A metric that determines % of Test cases executed is known as _____ Options: (a) Test Design Coverage (b) Test Execution Coverage (c) Automation Coverage (d) Test Case Creation Productivity
4.	Explain Defect Removal Efficiency metric in brief
5.	Explain Requirement analysis phase from testing perspective
6.	Any requirement which cannot be tested at a given point of time is known as _____ requirement
7.	Give any two examples of non-testable requirements
8.	What are the differences between Ambiguity & Defect (any two)?
9.	One requirement can have multiple test conditions / test cases. True / False?
10.	One test case may have multiple test steps. True / False?
11.	A set of input values, execution preconditions, expected results and execution post conditions, developed for a particular objective or test condition is called _____
12.	Describe what is generally written as pre-condition in a test case
13.	Explain test case template with suitable example
14.	While preparing the test design, what should be done to establish traceability
15.	There is a program that takes two inputs Product code and quantity, takes price of the product from the database and displays cost of the product and discount, and final cost after discount. 10% discount is given if the quantity is 10 or more. Prepare test case in the test case format with all the detailed step
16.	What is the entry criteria for test execution (What should be completed before test execution for system testing starts)?
17.	Explain Smoke testing in brief.
18.	Explain what are the statuses that a Defect can occupy?
19.	If Development team is not able to reproduce the defect, they will change the status of the defect to _____

20.	If testing team finds that the defect is actually not fixed or reoccurred even if development team mentioned that it is closed, testing team will change the status of the defect as _____
21.	State when the defect will be considered as Differed?
22.	State any 5 features provided by Defect management tool
23.	State any 3 advantages of using defect management tool
24.	What are the key expectations of Development/Maintenance Engineer from the defect report?
25.	State at least 6 important attributes of the defect report (Provide at least 6 different details provided by testing team while reporting defect)
26.	Testing team cannot change the status of the defect to 'Fixed'. True or False?
27.	Development team can change the status to 'Closed'. True or false?
28.	What are the phases of SW testing life cycle?
29.	A login form takes user name and password data as input in two text boxes and Checks for valid user name and password. Enters home page if user name and password is valid Else it displays error message Write Test Cases for above requirement in a standard test case format (Test Case ID, Precondition, Test Condition, Test Steps, Input/test data, Expected Result)
30.	One of the entry criteria for Functional testing is: - Code is delivered and successfully promoted to the Functional/System Test Environment as described in Master Test plan. True or False?
31.	This is not one of the entry criteria for Functional testing: - Functional/System test planning is detailed, reviewed and approved within the Master test plan. True or False?
32.	Explain how to design and execute test cases with suitable example

7 SW Test optimization – Test Automation and Risk Based Testing

In earlier chapters, we learnt SW testing types, levels, techniques and project execution processes (STLC phases). This builds foundation of SW testing. Let us now understand some of the advance topics on Software testing.

As discussed earlier, SW testing does require good amount of effort to ensure complete coverage and accuracy. However most SW projects have constraints in terms of time and effort for multiple reasons

- Overall budget for SW project is not enough to take up cost of all the testing types, activities and coverage.
- Even if sufficient budget is provided, development activities many times consume more than expected budget and time requiring reduction in time and effort for testing
- The quality of software is worse than expected requiring more testing cycles but deadline cannot be extended

It is hence important to identify various means to reduce the effort without compromising much on the quality. We will discuss following aspects to optimize our efforts.

- Test Automation
- Risk Based Testing (RBT)

7.1 Test Automation and Automated Testing

7.1.1 Introduction

In simple terms, using other software tool to test the developed software application is known as automated testing.

There are ready to use software testing products / tools available in the market which allows creating various scripts for testing the software application.

Most of these tools have capability to perform very similar tasks that a human being is performing to do manual testing. It involves opening a browser, opening an application, login, open a specific page (Eg. Ticket Reservation) and entering values in various text boxes, select specific option from available options or clicking a button or a link. It can also verify whether the application is responding correctly as expected or not.

We need to create scripts using tool so that it can do such operations.

The process of creating scripts using these tools is known as **test automation** and using the scripts to test the application is known as **automated testing**.

Definition: Test automation is the use of special software (separate from the software being tested) to set up test preconditions, control the execution of tests and then comparison of actual outcomes to predicted outcomes and report

Commonly, test automation involves automating a manual process already in place that uses a formalized testing process.

Note that our intention is to get high level understanding of test automation meaning, standard feature provided by various tools and the overall process. So, you may have to refer other documents/books and manual of corresponding tool you may want to use to actually automate your tests.

7.1.2 Test Automation Tools

There are many commercial and open source tools available in the market and newer tools continue to be developed. Different tools are available for different testing types and objectives. So, there are tools available for functional testing, Performance and Load testing, Security testing and also User interface testing. Following are some of the popular tools on functional testing

Commercial tools:

    a. HP Quick Test Professional
    b. Borland SilkTest
    c. Compuware TestPartner
    d. IBM Rational Functional Tester
    e. ….

Open Source Tools:

    f. Katalon Studio (which is built on Selenium)
    g. Selenium
    h. Watir
    i. FIT/FitNesse
    j. …

Open Source Unit Testing Tools:

    k. jUnit
    l. nUnit

7.1.3 How the tool works?

In order to imitate human being for executing some steps, the automation tool must understand various objects first.

Everything which is visible in an application such as Label, Textbox, Button, Image, Checkbox, Radio button, Dropdown, Hyperlink, etc. is known as "**Object**".

Automation is nothing but identifying such objects and taking actions on that object. The action could include enter text, click, move mouse over, or change any attribute of the object.

So, automated script for Login functionality need to

- Open the browser and maximize it
- Enter specific url in the browser to open the application's login page.
- identify text box for UserID and enter specific User ID say 'Admin',
- Identify text box for Password and enter specific password say 'admin12',
- identify Submit button and Click it.

Please find below small portion of the Login script developed in Katalon Studio tool.

1. WebUI.openBrowser('')
2. WebUI.maximizeWindow()
3. WebUI.navigateToUrl(GlobalVariable.a_url)
4. WebUI.*setText(findTestObject*('Registration object/Page_THIMS Log in / input_User_ID'), 'admin')
5. WebUI.*setText(findTestObject*('Registration object/Page_THIMS Log in / input_User_Passwd'), 'admin12').
6. WebUI.*click(findTestObject*('Registrationobject/Page_THIMS Log in / button_Sign in'))
7. WebUI.verifyElementPresent(findTestObject('test_login/Page_THIMS Log in/p_User Name or Password is Incorrect'), 0)

Study the above statements of the login script. You can notice that the first 2 statements are used to open and maximize the browser. The 3rd statement is used to navigate to specific url. Notice that here global variable is used. The value of the global variable is set in a specific data sheet where all the global variables are defined.

In statements 4 and 5, WebUI.setText command is used to set text in the text box. It contains two parameters. First parameter is an object and 2nd parameter contains the text to be set in the object.

Similarly you can notice in the 6th statement, the click action to be applied on the button object.

The 7th statement is to verify that the object with error message 'User Name or Password is Incorrect' appears because the password entered is actually not correct and we are expecting application to display a dialog box with this message.

In order to do such scripting, one has to learn scripting language supported by the tool. The tool/supported scripting language provides many such commands to take various actions (very similar to the one taken by human being) and also for verification.

Additionally, tools also provides many features as described below

1. **Record and playback features**

It allows users to interactively record user actions and replay them back any number of times. You have to activate recording in the tool by pressing the 'Record' button and then run the application under test. Whatever action you take on the application are recorded and a script will be directly generated. For example, take following action on login page after pressing 'Record' button on the tool.

- Open Brower
- Enter url for the application
- Enter User ID
- Enter Password
- Click Login button

Once recording is completed, you can stop recording by clicking Stop button. The tool will automatically generate statements in scripting language for each action you have taken. You can the save the script for future use.

When you play back the script, same operations are then performed by the tool.

Note that while recording, the objects are automatically identified and saved in the object library. If you need to identify objects which are not involved in recording session, then you need to manually identify those objects and save in the object library. All tools provide mechanism (sometime known as object spy functionality) to do that. Some tools may support multiple scripting languages.

The automation script can be enhanced to incorporate verification statements that compare actual results with expected result

2. **Programming capabilities**

In addition to recording feature, the tools also provide programming feature that allows you to modify the recorded scripts or create a new script for some or more of the following aspects

- **Setting up of test preconditions** – eg. Open browser, login and click the menu option which will open the registration form which you want to test.
- Incorporate various **programming constructs** such as If then else, Loop etc – There could be situation in which you need to provide some additional details only if some specific values added in previous fields. For example, while booking the ticket, if number of passenger traveling are 3, then you need to take passenger name, age and gender three times. The tool provides this facility to include for loop which will be executed three times.
- **Parameterize** the inputs **and** take data from the data source

    Instead of hardcoding input values in the script itself, you can use variable whose value can be read from excel or data based table. The objective is to be able to pick different values at run time or use. Parameterization can also be done for checkpoints. It Reduces Time and Effort

- **Incorporate Verification points.** The tool can capture various html elements and their properties that can be used for comparing with expected outcome.

    For example, on entering valid User ID and Password, the application should display home page and on entering invalid User ID and Password, the application should display a specific message. So, one can write a command to check whether specific error message element exists or not. Similarly many verification commands are available to read and compare text of the label, font colour, font size or alignment etc and even compare two values.

- **Report test results** without human assistance. When the script is executed, the tool reads the command and accordingly take various actions on the browser (for Web application) and prepares a log showing execution of each step. Similarly it maintains the outcome of each verification and accordingly putting the status whether the test case has passed or failed.

So, Using various commands one can

- test the **existence of UI elements** based on their HTML tags,
- Check for specific content,
- Check for broken links, input fields,
- selection list options,
- submitting forms, and table data

Apart from the basic features provided above, different tools provide many other features as described below.

- Support multiple browsers and platforms.
- Minimal Script development effort (excel like input instead of scripting command).

- Supports **Data Driven** Testing (use different data sheet/Excel or database table to store data and pick the data while execution). Develop and use data files with set of variables and corresponding values for data driven testing
- Allows **Reusable functions (also referred to as keywords).** For example, you want to ensure that all the labels of all the forms should have standard height, width, font size and font colour, you can create a reusable function to receive the label object, verify all these parameters and pass on the result back to the calling script. This can reduce lot of coding to be duplicated in different scripts.
- Clubbing of test scripts to make test suits for End-to-End scenario testing. For example login process may be required for almost all the test cases (particularly based on various use case scenarios). So, one can have separate scripts for Login, Book Flight, Make Payment, Print ticket etc and club them in different test scenarios as per requirement.
- Exception handling and reporting. With this feature, you can specify whether you want to continue further testing or want to stop execution or even perform some other task if test case fails.
- Detailed (Test case wise) and Summary wise **HTML reports** which can be customized
- Set up global variables which can be used for some standard details.

7.1.4 Automation Process

There are three main steps involved as part of test automation

1) Creating Test scripts

    - Recording a session on a site or application.
    - Modify the Tests as per the requirements.
    - Insert **checkpoints** into the test.
    - Broaden the scope of the test by replacing fixed values with **parameters**.

2) Running Tests

    - Run your test to check the site or application.
    - Run a test to debug the test.

3) Analyzing Test Results

    - View the test results in the Test Results window.
    - Analyze defects detected during the test run.

7.1.5 Test case selection for automation

It is also important to note that developing testing scripts using these tools also require effort and the scripts developed should also be correct. Automation hence should be used carefully after considering pros and cons of the same. Following are the high level guidelines.

Test automation is useful for

- Tests that need to be **run frequently** for every build of the application (sanity check, regression test). There is no point in automating tests which are going to be executed only once or twice because test automation (creating scripts) itself takes time.
- Tests that use multiple data values for the same actions (data driven tests). Tests which are executed multiple times with different dataset can also be good candidates for automation. For example, you want to login with different combinations of User ID and Passwords. Instead of repeating same steps (in script) for each user ID and Password, variables can be used in the script and different combinations of User ID and Passwords can be stored in database or Excel. Automation tool can run the same scripts for all the combinations of data.
- Testing that would be difficult to perform manually or tests requiring great deal of precision. Scientific applications or any other such applications that require very accurate results may be difficult to test manually or even if done, there are more chances of human error. Such test cases if automated can be used with accuracy.
- Supporting Agile and extreme methodologies requiring high regression. These approaches require lots of regression testing of previously built functionalities as you add more and more functionalities to the system. Automating regressions tests would help better coverage
- Other than testing tasks such as – Test Data creation, Comparisons etc. If you want to create say 1000 transaction in the system. You can use automated scripts to insert data rather than typing them manually.

Test automation not used to automate

- Exploratory tests – as the objective is simultaneous learning (exploring) and testing. If such tests are automatically performed, one cannot explore the functionalities in detail. And without knowing actual functionalities, it is not possible to develop scripts.
- Test that will never fail – Why to test when it is always going to pass? There could be very simple tests and having known that these tests are not going to fail once tested in the beginning. Such tests may not be executed again and again and hence automation of such tests not required.
- One of Tests – as it does not pay back investment in automation
- Usability tests – The objective can be best checked by the end users themselves.
- When application UI changes frequently. Most test automation tools are UI based tools and operate in the same manner as actual user. The automated scripts will have details of

the layout and customer is not expected to make any changes in to that. Every time UI changes, the automated script will need to be changed. This requires lot of effort. It may instead be better to execute such tests manually until the UI is almost final. Please note that many tools provide very effective methods of identifying objects and some level of changes in UI can be absorbed without making changes in the scripts.

7.1.6 Automation Benefits

Executing same tests again and again is boring and time consuming. It creates fatigue resulting into error and lower coverage. This is where automation provides lot of benefits as compared to manual testing

- Time consuming
- Low Coverage
- Human resources
- Inconsistent Results
- Error Prone

- Speed – 10 to 100 times faster than human
- Wider testing Coverage
- Save Time – Frees people
- Consistent Quality and Output
- Reliable – no error
- Reusability, Frequent execution
- Save Cost

Automation requires time and skills. Also the test cases should be very detailed covering <u>each</u> and every input field, actions and expected results.

7.2 Risk Based Testing

We already discussed that we can categorise our test cases in two main high level categories **Test-to-pass** test cases and **Test-to-fail test cases.** Generally Test-to-Pass test cases should get higher priority than test-to fail test cases.

Risk is the possibility of a negative or undesirable outcome. In the future, a risk has some likelihood between 0% and 100%. The potential consequences or impact is an important consideration affecting the level of risk, too

We can classify risks into project risks (factors relating to the way the work is carried out, i.e. the test project) and product risks (factors relating to what is produced by the work, i.e. the thing we are testing).

Risk based testing is other technique used to ensure minimum impact on the quality with limited amount of effort and time. The primary objective in this technique is to focus on areas which are more critical (or risky) as compared to areas which are less risky. The process of identifying level of risk is known as risk analysis. The risk analysis is done on Requirements, technical aspects and people aspects and then a strategy is prepared. The process involved, aspects considered and deliverables at the end of each these phases are shown below

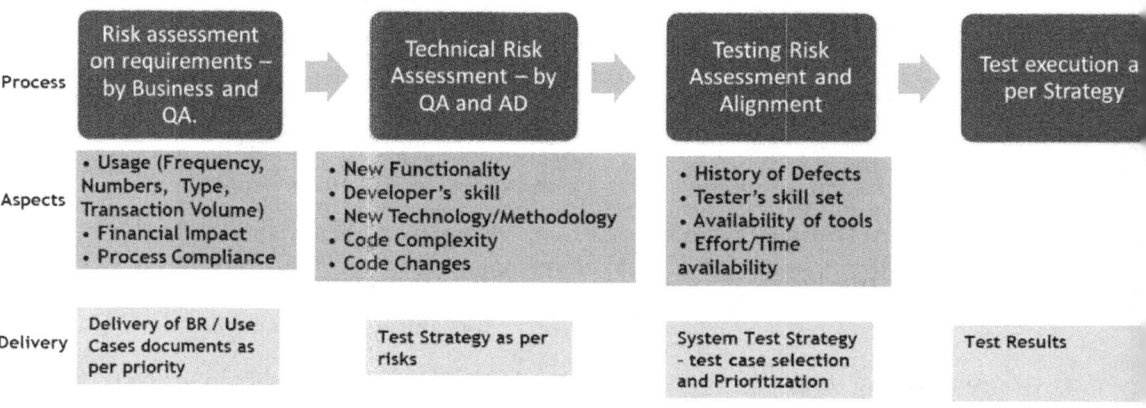

Based on the above analysis, the test cases are categorized into following four catagories

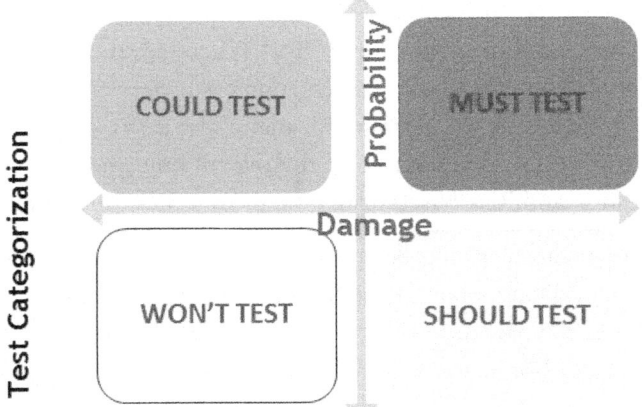

As an example, we would ideally follow the procedure of testing valid partitions first, then invalid partitions, then valid boundaries and finally invalid boundaries.

However, test objectives can help us decide what to test. We may do testing for valid partitions only. If you want to find as many defects as possible as quickly as possible, you may start with boundary values, both valid and invalid. If you want confidence that the system will handle bad inputs correctly, you may do mainly invalid partitions and boundaries. Your previous experience of types of defects found can help you find similar defects; for example if there are typically a number of boundary defects, then you would start by testing boundaries.

The risk based testing provides many **benefits** as listed below

- You can give up tests (do not execute) you worry about the least with low impact on quality so that the time and effort can be reduced but overall quality is not much impacted
- Pick the right tests out of the infinite possible tests reducing effort
- Since you prioritize the tests based on risk analysis indicating which are must test, Should Test, Could Test and won't test, the likelihood of discovering high severity defects are faster to resolve ("find the scary stuff first")
- Make smart release decisions. With this approach, the analysis and test results can help us deciding when to release the product - "release when risk of delay balances risk of dissatisfaction".
- Risk-based testing involves both

    mitigation - testing to provide opportunities to reduce the likelihood of defects, especially high-impact defects - and

    contingency - testing to identify work-around to make the defects that do get past us less painful

7.3 Summary

SW testing requires good amount of time and effort. There are many reasons because of which some functionality which was earlier running properly may stop working properly due to changes done in the system. So, many test cases which passed earlier may have to be executed again. This adds up to the overall time and effort required for testing. Automated testing and Risk based testing helps to reduce both time and effort.

Test Automated testing means carrying out testing using some other tool in the similar manner as done by human being. Many open source and commercial tools are available in the market. The tools can identify object and take required action on the object in the same manner as we do. For example, I can open browser, it can input some text in the text box, click a button or link. It can also verify availability of objects on the screen and compare values. Most tools provide record-play feature in which all the actions taken by human being to test a specific functionality are recorded by the tool and it then generates Automation Scripts. These automation scripts can be directly replayed or can be modified as per requirement and then executed. All tools have programing capabilities through which control statements (such as If..Then, Loops), include parameters for taking data from external files and can also incorporate verification points. Scripts generates test results after execution. So, it is possible to quickly create automation scripts for many regression test cases, Modify the scripts, add checkpoints and use parameters to read data from external source. Run the tests and analize the results. Automation is best suited for test cases which are run frequently, or which has same steps but uses multiple data sets, or test which requires high precision and can also be used to generate large number of data in the system. Since automation also require time and effort, it can not be used for exploratory tests, tests which will never fail, usability tests. Automated testing helps executing large number of tests very fast and hence it becomes possible to cover large number of regression test cases.

It may still be possible that team do not have time to execute all the test cases (manual or automated). Under such situation, risk based testing can be applied in which first of all test cases are categorised into 'Must be', 'Should be', 'Could be' and 'won't be' categories and execution is prioritised accordingly. The categorization depends on assessment of requirements – usage, financial impact, compliance requirement etc or Technical assessment considering criticality and newness of functionality, Skill level of developer, code complexity etc and also based on testing related risk assessment considering history of defect, effort / time available. Risk based testing helps in optimizing effort where time and effort is reduced without compromising much on quality.

7.4 Exercise

Sr	Question
1.	What is test automation
2.	Explain benefits/reasons of test automation
3.	For which type of testing, test automation is most useful?
4.	Automation should not be done for test cases that does not fails. Is it true?
5.	Give examples of commercial and open source test automation tools
6.	Explain Automation process for software testing optimization
7.	Explain Risk based testing with suitable example

8 Testing Types

Software testing types are based on specific requirement type or Objective which includes

1) **Testing of a Function** (Functionality Testing)

   The function of a system or component is *'What it does' or 'what it is supposed to do'*. Functional Testing covers all the functions and features specified in the high-level design and demonstrate that the system works correctly in a production-like environment. Functionalities and features specify what the system should do or how it should work. This includes different transactions being carried out by different users of the system.

   So as part of this testing, we test registration process, Ticket booking process etc and within that we test various features of the system such as - it allows payment through credit card, Debit card or Net Banking and so on. We also check that the system does required validations for all inputs and throws proper error messages for wrong inputs. We also ensure that system accurately generates various reports helpful to customers (such as past travel history, Reprint of ticket etc). The result of each test would be whether it is passed (met the requirement) or failed (did not meet the requirement).

   So it is aimed to verify

   - Business Processes; rules and constraints
   - Interfaces with other systems including manual system
   - User Interface (Forms, Reports)

   All the test design techniques we learnt (White Box, Black Box and Experience based) are primarily used for Functional testing. Please refer section 6.2.3

   In the current scenario of globalization, many applications are used by users across the world and / or many application products are developed in generic way so that its functionality can be used internationally or the product can be customized easily to meet local functional requirements when implemented in different countries. So, apart from basic **Functional Testing**, Functional testing also includes **Internationalization Testing** and **Localization Testing**

2) **Testing of Software Product Characteristics (Non-Functional Testing)**

   It covers quality characteristics of the system. It is *'How well it does'* or *'How fast it does'*.

   This includes **Performance** (Response time), **Usability** (How attractive it is and how easy to use) or **Security** (How much secure it is). Such issues if available do not provide good experience to the user even if the system works functionally well (correctly). The result of the test would not be passed or failed but would be in terms of the **extent to which** the system is fast or secured or usable.

It also includes **System management issues**: Installation, Configuration, Portability

3) **Testing Related to Changes**

Every system undergoes some or the other changes due to various reasons. Some functionality hence may need to be tested again and again to ensure that the changes have not impacted the previously working functionality and defects are fixed properly. Otherwise something which was working earlier may not work properly after change. This is also known as **Regression** Testing.

Testing activities are organized based on the testing type (Objective) at each level.

We will discuss each Testing Type that meets each Requirement Type in greater detail in subsequent section

8.1 Functional Testing

Functionality: The capability of the software product to provide functions, which meet **stated** and **implied** needs, when the software is used under specified conditions. [ISO 9126]

Function – **A function is described as a set of inputs, the behaviour, and outputs.**". It refers to actual operation/process such as Registration, Booking, Ticket printing etc

So, **Functional testing** considers specific behaviour of a function describing **a set of inputs, the behaviour, and outputs** as expected from specifications.

There are only two possible outcomes for each test – **met or not-met**. So, this requires a very clear expected result. The results generally depend on actual product (or code of the product) and not **on environment**.

Functional testing is done in all **phases/levels** such as unit testing, Integration testing, system testing and acceptance testing and generally using Specification Based techniques. Even experience based techniques also used. Some people consider Functional Testing and Black-Box testing same but it is not true. Functional testing is generally done using black-box test design techniques, even non-functional testing is also done using black-box.

8.1.1 Bases for Functional Testing:

The expected functionalities and features are either described in the specification documents. However, some functions/functionalities may not be documented and are 'Assumed' or 'Implied' to be provided by the system. All these processes and rules to be tested whether documented or not documented.

Let us understand some aspects based on which the functionally testing is done.

As part of functional testing both customer-specific requirements and standard rules are considered. We have already discussed standard rules in section 6.2.2.

Customer / Project Specific Functionalities.

Most functions/functionalities and rules are explicitly described in Requirement Specification, Function specification or Use Case documents. The specification documents may also include business rules related to various functions and processes. For example, business rule for cancellation says that cancellation can be done only before 24 hours of travel time.

The **testing objective** is to verify that each functionality and feature of the **software application / system** operates in accordance with the **specifications**. To check that it delivers **what** is expected.

Some of the examples include Discount policy, Fee waiver policy etc.

> Platinum Card members do not have to pay any reservation charges
>
> If (booking is done for return journey or number of seats booked are four or more) and gold Platinum card member, you get 10% discount
>
> All registered members are sent sms for reservation in addition to sending email.

8.1.2 Functional Testing Process

Test cases are derived based on analysis of functionalities and related rules defined in specification documents for component or system.

- **Provide Input data to the system with the help of user interface** (Graphical User Interface, Command Line Interface or Application Programming Interfaces)
- All field level, form level and transaction level validations are performed as per the rules / requirements specified in function specification document.

  This is to ensure that only valid inputs get into the system. If the inputs are not validated the output will be wrong even if all the processes are correctly performed.

  Also ensure that Proper **error messages** displayed when wrong inputs provided.

- **Execute related processes** – Applications may automatically execute some processes or one may have to instruct the software – for example pressing a specific button or selecting a specific menu option
- **Check output** – The output may be on
    - GUI – Screens or
    - printed report/document
    - or any other output such as email, Message, or any other devices.

Even if input values are correct and processes are correctly implemented, the software functions used to display information on the output device may not be correctly implemented.

All applications implement rules by ensuring that the data supplied to the application comply with those rules. Applications also need to ensure that changes made to the data should not result in a loss of data consistency thereby maintaining the Integrity.

8.1.3 Testing of Error Messages

While system may work well to ensure that erroneous inputs not provided, the system is expected to display helpful and useful message to the user if any erroneous inputs provided or there are any unexpected environmental issues.

The error message should precisely indicate that the action / data is invalid and it should provide some specific indications as to how the problem may be resolved with next steps and if possible let users pick from a small list of possible solutions.

Error messages should also be consistent across the application

Error Message Validation

- Look for missing error messages
  Validate that the
    - Error message appears when the order referred to does not exist

- *Warning* Message pops up when the mail containing an attachment is closed and that attachment is still open
- When the input value is too big.
* Look for misplaced error messages

    Insure that the expected error message does occur and provides the user with helpful information.

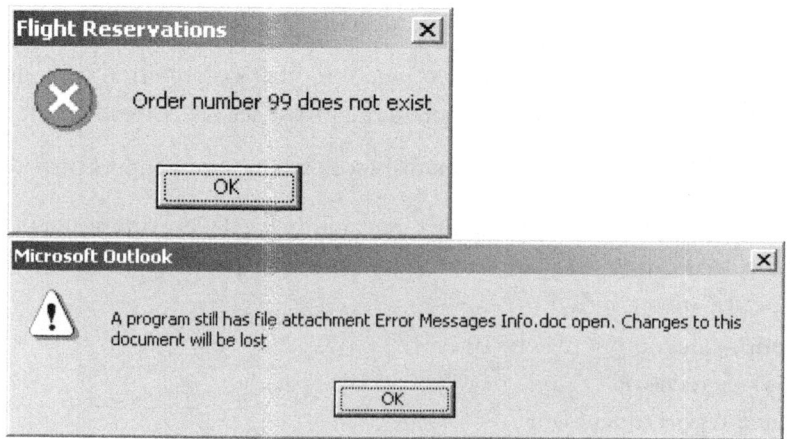

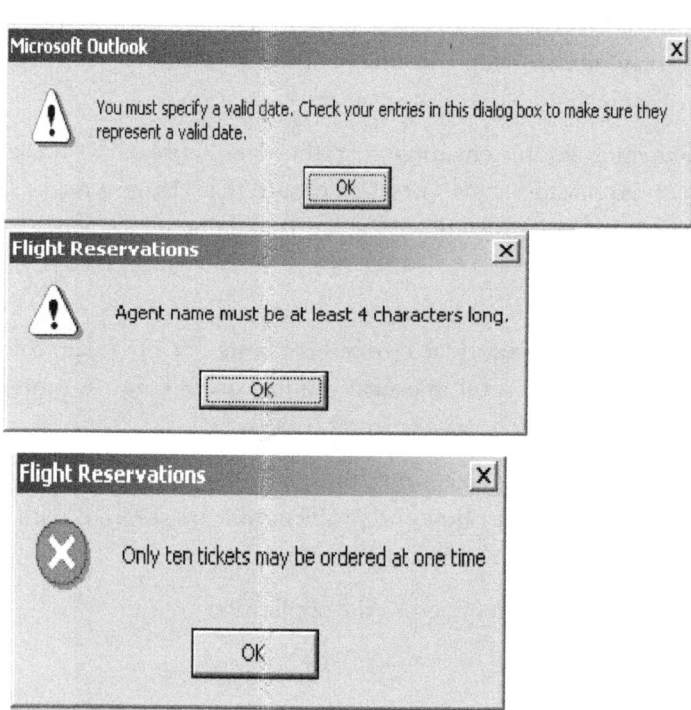

Ensure that Error Messages are displayed When software components interact with other components (hardware or software) that are subject to errors or faults, the calling software component must handle errors and recover properly

E.g.

- Remote connections being dropped
- security denials
- Performance problems
- No such messages should appear: "Error 949 - Unknown Error"

Check for a shared database content that is unexpected. As other systems begin to interface and update the shared database, initial data purity assumptions may be violated.

Check for the Disk being full

8.1.4 Report Validation

Reports

- Give a written account of something
- Convey information about an event or situation
- Present oneself as having arrived somewhere

Reports are generated after some business processing is done.

There could be different users for different types of reports – Textual, Graphical, and Pivot charts

OP Registration Report

Period : 11/04/2019 To 12/04/2019 Run Date : 30/04/2019

Sr.	OP ID	Date	ID	Name	Contact No	Doctor	Ref. Doctor	Case Type	MLC Type	User
1	3058	11/04/19 02:23 PM	329	DHARMISHTHABEN PRITESHBHAI THAKKAR [F/36Y] SMVS PROMOTIONAL / OTHERS	1103531414	Dr. Hcmpnshp Parmar		NEW		thims
2	3059	11/04/19 02:34 PM	13	NEW VIP PA [M/20Y] SMVS PROMOTIONAL / EMPLOYEE SELF	2222288888	Dr. KZTPN PATEL		NEW		thims
3	3060	11/04/19 04:25 PM	100	DAYALU SWAMI [M/36Y] SMVS PROMOTIONAL / SAINT / MUKT	8989888888	Dr. Spndcp Rathod		NEW		thims
4	3061	12/04/19 10:13 AM	39	RASHMI PATEL [M/25Y] SMVS PROMOTIONAL / OTHERS	1234577777	Dr. DR CHPNDRZS PATEL		NEW		thims
5	3062	12/04/19 10:46 AM	121	CHETNABEN OZA [F/57Y] SMVS PROMOTIONAL / OTHERS	1054101111	Dr. Spndcp Rathod		NEW		thims
6	3063	12/04/19 05:56 PM	954	MANUBHAI ZAVERBHAI PATEL [M/70Y] SMVS PROMOTIONAL / OTHERS	9999999999	Dr. BHPGYPdhpn Patel		NEW		hasmukh

OP Registration Report

Period : 11/04/2019 To 12/04/2019 Run Date : 30/04/2019

Summary

Doctor	Patients
Dr. BHPGYPdhpn Patel	1
Dr. DR CHPNDRZS PATEL	1
Dr. Hcmpnshp Parmar	1
Dr. KZTPN PATEL	1
Dr. Spndcp Rathod	2
Total	6

User ID : thims Print Date & Time: 30/04/2019 05:03 pm

Note: The sample report shown above is not from Aireline reservation system. However it can demonstrate how the layout etc are considered while generating report.

Elements important for testing reports

- Content - Data printed on the report should match the expectation. It should not happen that you want to print list of passengers registered today but it displays list of passengers travelled today.
- Right data printed in the report? The content should be correct. For each column
- Report for the right selection – period, category. If the period selected is one day, all the data of only that date should be displayed. If it is a period, then all the data only from hat period should be displayed.

- Data reported up to date (data source's status)? Many reports display details as per status of the entities. For example, if we need to display all passengers who registered till yesterday then passengers registered today should not come.
- Summations and calculated data derived from databases
- Accuracy of Totals – Group total, pager total, report total
- Schema – The structure of the report should be as expected

Format & layout

- Report formats are the columns, headers and footers on a page.
- Report Width / number of characters per page
- Lines per page, Spaces between columns
- Top/Bottom/Left/Right Margins
- Page Numbers
- Date and Time stamp

Summary page

- Position of various objects/graphs/pictures etc
- Record formats are the fields within a record.

8.1.5 Localization/Internationalization Testing

Applications today are used across the world. However every country's language, culture, currency, taxes and standards are different. Applications hence should take care of some of the key aspects so that when the applications are accessed by people from different countries, they still get fill of the local culture and norms.

Key Aspects: At lease following key aspects should be considered for testing.

Formatting, Special characters, Currency, calculation, shipping options

Language issues: Even if functionalities are working fine, many language related issues may come as described below.

- **Text Expansion** – Improper Wrapping, truncation, Removal of other object from screen
- **Hot keys and Shortcuts** – May have to provide different keys and hence to be tested
- **Computation on characters** – String functions, Sorting, Search
- **Reading Style**: Reading left-to-right and right-to left
- **Text in graphics**. – Icons, images etc

In general Text should be outside of code and not hardcoded in the program.

Data Formats: Apart from language, one need to ensure that the formats are also changed as per the country. Below are some standard aspects for which data formats may vary from country to country and hence need to be verified.

- **Measurements**: Meters Vs Yards
- **Numbers: Comma, decimal or space separator,**
- **Currency symbol and position of symbol** – Before amount or after amount
- **Date: Order of month, day year. Long and short formats**
- **Time: 12 hours or 24 hours** eg. 3:30 Pm vs 15:00
- **Different calendars:** and starting day of the week. Standard holiday lists
- **Addresses:** Format of postal code / Zip codes format: 380 052 vs T2N OE6
- **Telephone number format: separators used** – Parentheses Vs dash: (411) 444-2121
- **Different paper and envelop sizes**: US letter vs A4 in India

Many of these aspects could be easily taken care by regional settings in the operating systems. However one has to see that there is no impact on display/print meaning etc.

Internationalization (i18n) is a process of designing a software application so that it can be adapted to various languages and regions without engineering changes

Localization (L10n) is a process of adapting internationalized software/ modifying application for a specific region or language by adding Locale-specific components and translating text. Localization translates the product UI and occasionally changes some settings to make it suitable for Local region.

For example

In Islamic Banking, bank cannot pay interest on the customer; instead they charge a nominal fee which is termed as "Profit"

Calendar used for loan repayment as they can use any of the two calendars, one with 365 days and other with 354 days.

Testing Objective is

- To detect potential problems in application design that could inhibit/hinder globalization.
- Makes sure that the code can handle all international support without breaking the functionality that would cause either data loss or display problems.
- Ensure that areas affected during localization, UI and content is as per local need. Verifying how correctly the application is changed / adopted to the target culture and language
- Culture/locale-specific, language specific and region specific areas are taken care of

Hence testing should take care of each field for correct translation that the layout remains proper after translation.

8.2 Non-Functional Testing

This covers testing of the quality characteristics, or non-functional attributes of the system (or component or integration group). The objective is to check how well or how fast something is done. We may use scale of measurement for example time to respond.

We will cover Usability, Efficiency (performance, load, and stress), and security testing in some more detail.

This testing **may not be very straight forward** and may require large amount of resources, data, specific configurations and some tools.

The results may not only depend on the product but also on the environment. Non-functional testing can be done at all levels but is generally done as part of system testing and in Acceptance testing.

8.2.1 Usability Testing

Usability Testing is to determine the extent to which the software product is understood, easy to learn, easy to operate and attractive to the users under specified conditions. [After ISO 9126]

In the highly competitive environment, experience of the end users using the application is very important. It is likely that many applications providing excellent functionality may not be used by the users if it is difficult to navigate, requires multiple screens to be traversed through or multiple buttons to be pressed to carry out a task.

> **User Interface Testing:** The means with which the user interacts with the program/application is called its User Interface or UI. With these UI, users give inputs and receive outputs. Very sophisticated Graphical User Interface (known as GUI) are now available and application should be developed with good GUI which makes users job very easy.

Usability means effectiveness, efficiency and satisfaction with which specified users can achieve specified goals in a particular environment (ISO 9241-11).

> **Effective**: User is able to accomplish goal completely.
>
> **Efficient:** Accomplishes the goal **quickly**.
>
> **Satisfaction–** User enjoys the experience.

So the key aspects to be considered for any application are as given below

> **Interactivity** – Are Pull down menus, buttons etc are easy to understand?
>
> **Layout** – Is it easy and quick to find content? Consider navigation mechanisms, Placement of content.
>
> **Readability** – Is the Text well written? Is Graphic presentation Understandable?

Aesthetics – Look and feel – Consider layout, colour, typeface and related characteristics

Display characteristics - optimal use of screen size and resolution.

Time sensitivity – Ability to use, acquire important features, functions and content

Consistency – the layout characteristics are consistently used in all the programs of the application. For example, Short keys and menu selections, Terminologies used, Placements of buttons such as OK and Cancel, and even size, font and colours used for all controls are consistent.

Flexible: It provides more options and ways to accomplish the same tasks. It provides ability to skip some steps which are not important for some users. Also there could be different ways to enter data and see the results (Eg Type the data, Copy Paste from other place, Import / Export, Voice to text conversion etc).

Error Handling: Consistent and easy to understand error messages for wrong data inputs

Online Help: Provision to guide the user to understand each data inputs, separately marking mandatory fields, steps to accomplish a specific task and availability of FAQs where required. Online help is indexed and searchable. Ideally natural language queries are best.

Personalization - Web application tailor itself to the specific needs of different user categories or individual users?

Many of the aspects may be tested along with the functional testing for widely used applications; Most product development organizations give lot of focus on usability testing. Proper testing should also be done for static websites for usability.

Sample Test Cases

ID	Test Condition	Login	Registration	Reservation	...
U01	Are the text box width for all the text boxes same?				
U02	All the fields are aligned properly				
U03	There are no spelling mistakes in the page title and labels				
U04	The Tab order of various fields are correct from top to bottom and from left to right				

ID	Test Condition	Login	Registration	Reservation	...
U05	Font colour and size for all fields are same				
U06	Font colour of labels and entered text is different but consistent				
U07	Check that any error message displayed are in red colour				
U08	The sequence of fields aligns to normal business requirements.				
U09	Menu options and captions for pull down menu and buttons are self explanatory and do not create any confusions				
U10	The icons used or pictures used are relevant				
U11	Check that frequently used options are separately shown as per usage pattern				
U12	Check that required validations are done instantly.				
U13	Check wherever standard options are expected, System provide Select control rather than expecting user to enter				
U14	Ensure that each invalid field entry displays sensible error message that says why the given input is invalid and what user should do to correct				
U15	Ensure that only relevant functionality related menu options or links or buttons are displayed as per access				

ID	Test Condition	Login	Registration	Reservation	...
	rights of the user				
U16	Ensure that each hyperlink jumps to the correct destination/opens correct window Links are underlined and mouse pointer changes when when itis over the link				
U17	Check that users navigational bar and home buttons available on each screen				
U18	Check that the text used in the pages / forms are latest as per the audience level with no spelling mistakes. Note that spell checker will not check spelling of the text used in images				
U19	Check that popup of graphic images are correct				
U20	Check that the layout is responsive by reducing and enlarging the size				
U21	Ensure that there are no orphan pages (which are part of website but there is no way to reach there)				
U22	Check that all the graphics are named correctly, loads properly (or displays proper message when not loaded)				
U23	Check that the text wrapping is done properly around graphics				
U24	Check Loading performance on dial up or slower network (that user				

ID	Test Condition	Login	Registration	Reservation	...
	may be using)				
U25	Check other objects like Scrolling marquee, text changing advertisement, internal site searches work properly				
U26	Ensure that the graphics dynamically changes as per requirement based on defined conditions (such as Time of Day, User preference, or previous action taken by user) or as per details stored in database				
U27	Ensure that general layout is good with no long scrolling pages, no non-standard link colours and url reflects human readable names reflecting nature of content				

Note that U15 could be considered as security related but as part of security, option may be displayed even if specific user not allowed but when the user selects an option, system display error. From usability perspective it is an additional step for the user and hence an issue.

Similarly for displaying error message when invalid input is given is part of functional testing but message should be proper and consistent which is more of usability testing and hence U14 part of usability.

There are tools available for checking standard look & feel requirements such as font size, font colour etc. However only human being can bring out some other issues based on how they feel when they use the application.

So, specialized test labs are used and rigorous process are used to get quantitative and qualitative data on the effectiveness of user interfaces. In some cases, representative or actual users are asked to perform several key tasks under close observation, both by live observers and through video recording. The users evaluate the product based on their experiences during and at the end of the sessions.

Accessibility testing: Testing to determine the ease by which users with disabilities can use a component or system. This includes **Visual Impairments** (colour blindness, extreme near or far sightedness, dim vision etc.) **Hearing impairment** (Partially or completely deaf people may not be able to hear onscreen videos audible help or system alerts). **Motion Impairments** (There may be people who lost motion control of their hands or arms and hence cannot use keyboards / mouse properly). It is important that widely used applications have multiple options so that it is easily accessible by these kind of partially disabled people. Applications should take advantages of operating system features such as

- StickyKeys – Shift, Ctrl and Alt keys stay in effect until next key is pressed.
- FilterKeys- prevents Brief, repeated (accidental) keystrokes from being recorded
- ToggleKeys – Plays tones when Caps Lock, Control Lock or NumLock modes are enabled.
- SoundKeys-Creates a visual warning whenever the system generates a sound
- ShowSound tells the programs to display captions for any sounds or speech they make
- HighContrast – set up the screen with colours and fonts designed to be read by the visually impaired

So, if the application is expected to be used by partially disabled people, testing should be done to ensure that above features are incorporated in the system as applicable.

Software Testing Types

8.2.2 Performance, Load, Stress Testing

Performance is the behaviour of the system w.r.t. expectations for time & resources utilization.

Performance testing is the process of testing to determine the performance of a (components of a) software product under specific environment.

In today's competitive environment, response from the application for any request must be fast enough to maintain the interest of the end user. If you are booking a ticket through a specific website, and if it takes more than 10-20 seconds to get confirmation on your request, you may not continue to use the same application in future and would look over to other options. Poor response time could be because of environment, internet traffic or many other reasons also, but one need to ensure that the required environment set up, the application design, coding, data access etc are done in efficient manner so that response to the end user is within required time.

There are three **Key Aspects** responsible for the poor performance

Response time: The time elapsed during input arrival and output delivery. Generally average time and worst case values are of higher interest.

Throughput: The number of tasks completed per unit time. Indicates how much work has been done within an interval.

Utilization: The percentage of time a hardware component (CPU, Channel, storage, file server) is very busy

Hence the primary **objectives** of performance testing are

- Application maintains **acceptable response time** and **reliability** by increased user traffic. Eg. After selecting flight, application displays seating chart within 3 seconds
- If not, **Identify which components are responsible** for performance degradation and what usage characteristics cause degradation to occur

Load testing: A type of performance testing conducted to evaluate the behaviour of a component or system with increasing load, **to determine what load can be handled** by the component or system.

Objective is to test the system through constantly and steadily increasing the load on the system until it reaches the threshold limit

Most of the applications are accessed by multiple users – sometimes thousands of users simultaneously. More the number of users, more will be the load on the application. Application performance under normal environment when accessed only by single user may respond very quickly but as the number of users increases, the load increases and performance starts degradation or sometimes the application may even crash. For example, Higher Secondary board exam registration. One must have noticed that towards the last few days of the registration completion date, the application response time is degraded. Similarly when examination results are announced, all the students tries to connect to the application and many students are not able to access.

So the Objective of Load testing is to ensure that Application handles extreme load without unacceptable operational degradation.

The Expected load and the specified transactions on the system may vary from application to application.

Please note that number of simultaneous users may be much less than total number of registered users. The count of users simultaneously accessing application may also depend on time of the day, day of the month or a season. All such parameters need to be considered while carrying out load testing.

If you expect on an average 300 users access the application simultaneously but during peak time 800 users Simultaneously access the application, and the expected response time to be within 5 seconds, we need to ensure that response time is within 5 seconds when the load is up to 300 users and may degrade by 1-2 seconds only when the load is up to 800 users. However even for the load of 500 users if the performance degrade below 10 seconds, one must report it as bug. We need to understand load profile of the application before carrying out load testing

Load profile: A specification of the activity which a component or system being tested may experience in production.

> Example: Around 500 users will login at a given point in time: Start with 5 users and 5 users added every 5 seconds. 50% of the users will be viewing the flight details, 20% will be viewing their ticket status and 20% will be booking tickets, 10% will generate various reports

A load profile consists of a **designated number of virtual users** who process a **defined set of transactions in a specified time period** and according to a predefined operational profile.

Stress Testing is a type of performance testing conducted to evaluate a system or component at or beyond the limits of its anticipated or specified workloads, or with reduced availability of resources such as access to memory or servers

Stress testing involves subjecting the program to **heavy loads or stresses** that demands **resources in abnormal quantity, frequency, or volume** and analyze the **maximum limit** of concurrent users the application can support.

The objective is to see what happens when the system is pushed beyond design limits and try to break. For example

> Generate 5 interrupts when the average rate is 2 or 3

Average 10 users added every 2 seconds (instead of 5 users every 5 seconds)

Increase input data rate (An agency has automated ticket booking process and every ticket is booked in 1 second instead of 5 minutes)

Test cases that require maximum memory

After this testing one would come to know

- Whether the system degrades gently or does the server shut down
- Whether appropriate messages displayed? E.g. Server not available
- Are transactions lost as capacity is exceeded?
- Are certain functions discontinued as capacity reaches the 80 or 90% level?

The goal of the stress testing is to analyze behaviour of the application after failure. The system should not compromise the security of sensitive data and should come back to normality along with all its components even after the most terrible breakdown.

Performance, Load and stress testing involves extensive planning and effort for the definition and simulation of the workload.

If 5000 users access only static pages, they all may get good response time but if all of them submit a reservation transaction at the same time, the response time may vary drastically as it requires significant amount of processing on the server side.

Note that actual response time depends on Network and Product issues both. You can improve product performance only to certain level. Required steps may have to be taken to improve Network.

Tools: It is practically impossible to do load/stress testing manually. Hence there are many tools available in the market, which generates load on the system with multiple virtual users as per defined load profile and check the output. Some of the popular tools available in the market are as given below.

HP – LoadRunner, IBM – Rational Performance Tester, Apache Jmeter, LoadUi, OpenSTA

Sample Case study:

An ecommerce web site conducted a survey and the findings are as given below.

- Transaction response time is acceptable to the users if it does not exceed 5 seconds
- 20% users may cancel their transactions if the response time is beyond 5 seconds but less than 10 seconds
- 50% users may cancel their transactions if the response time over 10 seconds

The company had estimated that the number of transactions would rise by 25 to 30% in next 6 months and would like to learn whether

- they are able to maintain the response time below 5 seconds or not.
- At what point if time the system will start deteriorating drastically
- If the transaction growth increases beyond expectations, upto what level the system will be able to take the load and will not break.

Performance, Load and Stress testing can help to answer these questions.

8.2.2.1 Typical Performance root causes

There are memory related issues that one can find while doing unit testing such as **memory leaks, memory fragmentation and overwrites**. These kinds of issues can become root cause for many other issues to occur and can take lot of time to resolve if not found early in the life cycle. Memory leaks are **most common types of defect and difficult to detect**

Memory leak occurs whenever a program loses track of memory (due to incorrect memory management)

In Object Oriented programming, Memory leaks occurs if a program fails to free objects that are no longer in use.

Let us try to understand this with an example of a function below

```
void read_file(char*);

void test_read(bool flag)
{
    char* buf = new char[100];        - 100 bytes are allocated every time the function is called
        if (flag) {
            read_file(buf);
            delete [] buf;            - However the bytes are released only if the condition is true
        }
}
```

The code allocates 100 bytes of memory every time the test-read function is called but does not release the same when the argument flag as false. So, if the function is called say 100 times with flag as false, 100*100 bytes would be occupied unnecessarily. This is memory leakage.

If a program continues to leak memory, **its performance degrades**. Its runtime memory footprint continues to increase and it spends more and more time in swapping and can eventually run out of memory.

Finding Memory Leaks

There are different signs that indicate that the application might be leaking memory.

- Application is throwing an Out Of Memory Exception.
- Applications responsiveness is growing very sluggish because it started swapping virtual memory to disk.
- Maybe memory use is gradually (or not so gradually) increasing in Task Manager.

You can spot a memory leak when you detect an unexplained increase in either committed system memory—memory used by various applications—or in memory owned by a specific application.

One can do **Repetition testing** – Doing the same operation again and again. This could be as simple as starting and closing the program again and again – repeatedly saving and loading data again and again. We may be able to find bug only after some iterations (Sometimes hundreds or thousands of times).

One can also use system command that displays memory usage by each application. One can conclude that there are issues if the allocated number is unexpected or has grown unexpectedly.

There are also Memory leak detection tools which help to identify

- memory allocated but not de-allocated
- uninitialized memory locations

Example of tools : jProfiler, IBM Rational Purify, BoundsChecker, Valgrind, ParasoftInsure++, Dr. Memory

Memory Fragmentation

Fragmentation occurs when a large chunk of memory is divided into much smaller, scattered pieces

If memory is fragmented because of frequent allocation and de-allocation of memory, application's performance can be degraded drastically.

Memory Overwrites

Once a block of memory has been allocated, it is important that the program does not attempt to write any data past the end of the block or write any data just before the beginning of the block. Even writing a single byte just beyond the end of an allocation or just before the beginning of an allocation can cause disaster. It is a possible candidate for turning on overflow buffers.

Memory overwrites occur when too little memory is allocated for an object and when program attempts to write large data into the memory allocated, some data may be written past the allocated block which probably used by some other object. This results into memory corruption and intermittent failures. So program may work correctly some times and fail at other times. Such issues are difficult to find using black box testing techniques.

Database tables not Indexed as required.

Most business applications will need to access data from the database with hundreds of tables and sometimes millions of records within tables. Depending on the conditions used for accessing data, system will take time. The time required would be less if there are indexes available on the required table columns. One may need to refer database material to understand these features.

As part of the design reviews, one should check for such requirements.

8.2.3 Security Testing

Let us understand first the meaning of some key terms

Security: Attributes of software products that bear on its ability to prevent unauthorized access, whether accidental or deliberate, to programs and data.

Vulnerability: This is a security related weakness in the application which if gets exploited can cause threat.

> From coding perspective **buffer overrun** is considered to be most common problem that can easily cause security issue. Buffer overrun occurs when you try to assign large value to a memory location with smaller size. It will not only fill the destination string but then continue overwriting the values stored in other local variables and sometime even the content of the executable code also.

Security testing: Testing to determine the security of the software product. A process that determines that confidential data stays confidential (i.e. it is not exposed to individuals/ entities for which it is not meant) and users can perform only those tasks that they are authorized to perform.

Examples of security breaches.

You may come across many examples similar to the ones given below

- *Heartland Payment Systems* - Attackers were able to steal more than 130,000,000 credit card records - *January 2009*
- CBI website hacked by Pakistan Cyber Army - December 2010
- One of the customer databases of *McDonald's* was hacked. The Hacker was able to grab e-mail addresses, mailing addresses, phone numbers, birthdates, and other information of people who signed up online for special promotions - *December 2010*

Impact of unsecured applications:

Insecure applications may result very negatively as provided below

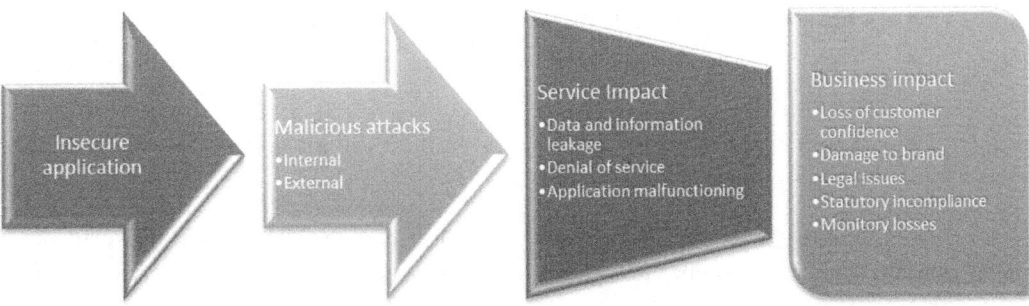

Hackers may want to gain access to the application either because of

1) only curiosity, or

2) want to use some features even though not authorised (or not paid money) or

3) want to destruct the operations or

4) want to steal some information/data for their own purpose.

The first two reasons not very harmful but the last two reasons could impact a lot. The hacker can enter a super long password, stuffed with hand-written assembly code instead of alphanumeric ASCII characters and override the intended password validation and possibly gain access to the system. Buffer overwritten however depends on compiler, OS and CPU but hackers may know it. There could be many library functions prone to buffer overrun. It is advisable to use safe string functions which take care of these issues. As a developer/tester, we need to ensure that buffer overruns do not occur.

There are multiple ways on which the hackers can attack the applications as given below. We will understand each of them in little more detail.

1. Password cracking
2. URL manipulation
3. SQL Injection
4. Cross site scripting
5. Spoofing

So the Objective of security testing is to verify that **protection mechanisms** built into the system will protect it from improper **penetration,** to discover the vulnerabilities of the web application

So as part of the testing process, the testing team executes test cases that challenges the program's security mechanism expected to be implemented such as

- One should not be able to break the operating systems memory protection mechanisms.
- One should not be able to break DBMS's data security mechanisms.
- A user should not be able to deny the functionality of the web site to other users,
- A user should not be able to change the functionality of the web application in an unintended way etc.

Implementing all the mechanism of protection may not be feasible however developer should make the system such that the penetration cost for the hackers would be more than the value of the information that will be obtained by them.

Software Testing Types

Let us now see the potential threat in little more detail.

1. **Password Cracking:** is the process of recovering passwords from data that have been stored in or transmitted by a computer system

   One can **Guess** a username/ password or use some **password cracker tool** for the same.

   Lists of **common usernames and passwords** are available along with open source password crackers.

   If username or password is stored in cookies without encrypting, attacker can use **different methods to steal** the cookies and then **information stored in the cookies** and use.

   As part of testing, we need to ensure that it is not easy to guess the password; it is not easy to crack the password. We need to ensure that the system implements mechanism to ensure that passwords follow certain criteria and users are forced to change the password at some predetermined frequency.

2. **URL manipulation:** is the process of altering the parameters in a URL (Uniform Resource Locator). Internet user to access a Web site that has a complicated URL by entering a simpler URL

   Some web applications communicate additional information between the client (browser) and the server in the URL for authentication or fetching data.

   So, The URL can make it possible to send parameters to the server by following the file name with a question mark and then data in ASCII format. A URL is then becomes a string of characters with the following format:

   http://target/forum/?cat=2

   In this we are passing parameter cat=2. By manipulating certain parts of a URL, a hacker can get a web server to deliver web pages he is not supposed to have access to. For example, user changes the text as below

   http://target/forum/?cat=6

   As part of testing, we should check that server does not accept the changes such done in the url.

3. **SQL injection**

   The process of inserting SQL statements through the application user interface into some query that is then executed by the server (Eg direct MySQL queries are executed on database by accepting some user inputs.). Attacker can inject SQL statements or part of SQL statements as user inputs to extract vital information from database.

   Input Passenger Name:User inputs : anything' OR 'x'='x';

Let us assume that the original SQL in Program is SELECT * FROM *Passengers* WHERE *Passenger_name* = 'InputValue';

Where InputValue = anything' OR 'x'='x;

So the constructed SQL would be: SELECT * FROM *Passengers* WHERE *Passenger_name* = 'anything' OR 'x'='x';

The 'x'='x' clause is guaranteed to be true and will result in returning every item in the member database. Even entire query can be inserted like this.

So, Special characters from user inputs should be handled / escaped properly. Entering a single quote (') in any textbox should be rejected by the application.

For testing purpose, one can create temporary table and attempt to insert into it or update or delete some data from that table (it is risky to use any live/active table which has live data).

If the tester encounters a database error, it means that the user input is inserted in some query which is then executed by the application. In such a case, the application is vulnerable to SQL injection

4. **XSS (Cross Site Scripting):**

   When a user can **inject code (inserts HTML/ client-side script) in the user interface** of a web application and this insertion is visible to other users, it is called XSS.

   Attacker can use this method

   - To execute malicious script or URL on victim's browser.
   - To use scripts like JavaScript to steal user cookies and information stored in the cookies

   So, Any HTML e.g. <HTML> or any script e.g. <SCRIPT> should not be accepted by the application.

5. **Spoofing:** The creation of hoax (fraud) look-alike websites or emails by creating of TCP/IP packets using somebody else's IP address. Routers use the "destination IP" address in order to forward packets through the Internet, but ignore the "source IP" address. That address is only used by the destination machine when it responds back to the source

Security Testing Vs Functional Testing

Functional Security testing checks for:

- Role based privileges and access control to modules, functionalities, screens and fields
- Password usage guidelines
- Invalid links (outgoing/internal/broken)
- forward/backward link to ensure that they represent to the correct page
- Validations in each fields in the forms or web pages

Non-Functional Security testing covers following:

With the help of a hyper links is it possible-

- To access restricted resources like documents?
- To insert any piece of code that could do the damage?
- To upload any executable program?
- Client side validations in each fields-
- Properly validated fields - can they be bypassed
- Even a single Quote- ' - can do the damage
- Error pages can reveal sensitive information

8.2.4 Compatibility Testing

Compatibility / Interoperability Testing: The process of testing to determine the interoperability of a software product.

The objective is to ensure that the product works properly on the different platforms, applications and devices in its environment

Platforms/Hardware considered are

- Operating systems and their versions (Windows, Mac OS and Linux)
- Mobile Operating systems (IOS, Android, Windows, BlackBerry…)
- browsers (IE, Chrome, Firefox…)
- Databases
- Other Software Components
- Devices (Mobile devices, ATMs, Tablets…, POS, any other relevant)

The general approach used for compatibility testing is as given below.

- Identifying areas of risk in terms of product compatibility
- Preparation of a Compatibility Test Plan, which specifies the tests to be carried out
- Creation of platform and scenario matrices to test the product
- Carry out Testing
- Reporting results

Parameters and Generic Scenarios for test - samples

Parameter	Description
Page Load Time	time taken for all pages to load fully
Accessibility	Tabs, Tab Order, Headings, Rollovers, Scroll bars, Table presentation,
Cookie Handling	application behaviour after clearing cache
Data Verification	Accurate data is displayed
Data Entry	data can be entered into all fields; and application handle invalid inputs.
Email Links	able to send an email on clicking the Email link
Images	Images are displayed properly in terms of size and alignment
Links (Navigation), Back Link	All the links are Navigating properly including third party sites

Look and feel, Resolution	All pages, contents, messages, images etc.
Documents	handle uploads/downloads of csv, doc, pdf, txt, xls files

Compatibility Testing also should take care of Backward and Forward Compatibility, Data Sharing – Export / Import compatibility. Compatible with standard Word, Excel formats when allowing some object in to your application. Allowable image formats, Allowable video formats, voice formats etc

8.2.4.1 Compatibility testing of Mobile Applications

Mobile application **testing** is a process by which application software developed for hand held **mobile** devices is **tested** for its functionality, usability and consistency

Hardware: device including the internal processors, internal hardware, screen sizes, resolution, space or memory, camera, radio, Bluetooth, WIFI etc

Application testing: Application Functionality and appearance

During testing, following aspects are taken into consideration.

- **Different range of mobile devices:** with different screen sizes and hardware configurations like a hard keypad, virtual keypad (touch screen) and trackball etc.
- **Wide varieties of mobile devices** like HTC, Samsung, Apple, ...
- **Different mobile operating systems** like Android, Symbian, Windows, Blackberry and IOS.
- **Different versions of operation system** like iOS 5.x, iOS 6.x, BB5.x, BB6.x etc.
- Different mobile network operators like GSM and CDMA.
- Frequent updates – (like Android- 4.2, 4.3..iOS-5.x, 6.x) –

Basic Difference between Mobile and Desktop Application Testing:

- On the desktop, the application is tested on a central processing unit. On a mobile device, the application is tested on handsets.
- Mobile device screen size is smaller than desktop.
- Mobile devices have less memory than desktop.
- Mobiles use network connections like 2G, 3G, 4G or WIFI where desktop use broadband or dial-up connections.
- The automation tool used for desktop application testing might not work on mobile applications

Mobile App Testing – Types

- **Usability testing** – To make sure that the mobile app is easy to use and provides a satisfactory user experience to the customers
- **Compatibility testing** – Testing of the application in different mobiles devices, browsers, screen sizes and OS versions according to the requirements.
- **Low-level resource testing:** Testing of memory usage, auto-deletion of temporary files, local database growing issues known as low-level resource testing.
- **Performance testing**– Testing the performance of the application by changing the connection from 2G, 3G to WIFI, sharing the documents, battery consumption, etc.
- **Operational testing** – Testing of backups and recovery plan if a battery goes down, or data loss while upgrading the application from a store.
- **Installation tests**– Validation of the application by installing /uninstalling it on the devices.
- **Security Testing** – Testing an application to validate if the information system protects data or not.

Mobile App Testing – Strategy: It is practically impossible to consider all the available varieties and options available in the market. So, one need to build a strategy based on requirements.

- **Selection of the devices** – choose the devices that are widely used.
- **Emulators** – system that runs software from one environment to another. It duplicates the features and works on the real system environment without changing the software itself
    - Extremely useful in the initial stages of development,
    - Allows quick and efficient checking of the app.

8.3 Regression Testing

The system may undergo changes before it moves to production or even after it moves to production because of various reasons as described below.

- In order to fix the defect, the software is changed (the way it functions, the way it performs (or both) and it's structure). In this case, we execute the test again to confirm that the defect is really fixed. This is confirmation testing (and re-testing). Note that the test is re-executed exactly in the same manner as it was done earlier using same environment, input steps and data. If the test passes, we know that the defect is really fixed but it is likely that while making the changes in the software to fix the defect, the developer has introduce some other defect which was not earlier there.

- The software may have to be modified not only for fixing the defects but due to other reasons also for implementation of newer features and / or changes in business rules, changes in government norms.

- In an iterative or agile development approach smaller functionalities are implemented and newer functionalities added requiring some changes in the implemented software.

Every time system undergoes any change, it is likely to disturb functionality already developed and tested. So, even if it was working earlier, may not work now as per expectation.

Regression testing: Testing of a previously tested program after doing modification, to ensure that defects have not been introduced or uncovered, as a result of the changes made. So, regression testing is performed when the software or its environment is changed.

Objective – The objective of Regression testing is to ensure the **reliability** of each software release by checking that **changes did not introduce any new errors** into the system

Regression testing is very similar to confirmation test, where we do re-testing of previously executed test cases. The primary difference is that in case of confirmation test, the test had failed previously whereas in case of regression tests, the tests might have passed previously.

Regression testing is **applied to** the **system in production** undergoing changes or the **system in development** undergoing changes.

Since testing requires time and effort it will not be feasible to execute all the test cases again and again, most organizations identify some sample test cases from the entire set of test cases which are termed as regression test cases (and the entire set is known as regression test suit). So, the regression test suit will be a **subset** covering all functions **of full test suit.** Whenever system undergoes some changes, some test cases from the available regression suit are identified based on possible impact analysis and re-executed.

It is assumed that if the changes have affected the specific function, error should come while testing some sample test cases. It is better to test few test cases from all functions rather than doing extensive testing only for some functionality and doing no testing for some other functionality.

Generally detailed impact analysis is done based on the changes and possible impacted functionalities are identified. Some more test cases are selected from those areas.

Tests for software **components that have been changed.** Almost all the test cases are selected from the functionalities which are actually changed. The changes in requirements would need some new test cases to be added or some test cases to be changed.

Regression testing is also suggested when some aspects of the environment changes. For example, when a new DMS version is introduced or new version of compiler is used.

Since these test cases are executed multiple number of times in the project life, they are best suited for automation and are generally **automated** using relevant automation tool.

It is important that the regression test suit is maintained continuously. New sample tests should be added from newer functionalities added and the existing tests should be modified if related functionalities changed. Similarly some tests from the suit can be eliminated if related functionalities removed from the system or even because tests have not found a defect for a long time.

8.4 Summary

At a high level, Software testing can be divided into two types – **Functional and Non-functional**. Functional testing is done to test functional requirements and we try to ensure that system is doing **what** it is supposed to do and it is not doing what it is not supposed to do. We discussed all the techniques in details which can be applied for functional testing in previous chapters. Apart from that we covered Testing of error messages, Report validation and Localization/internationalization testing in this chapter which are also considered to be part of functional testing.

As part of **Error message testing** we try to ensure that proper, relevant, and helpful error message appear at right time at right place. Also the style approach and content provided in all error messages follow specific guidelines so that they are consistent for all types of errors that could appear in entire application.

Similarly as part of **report testing** we try to ensure that right content for right period or right categories as expected accurately appear in the report and also ensure that the report format, margins, layouts, spacing, report heading, column headings, calculated numbers, System date and page number etc are correctly displayed at a right place.

We then discussed **Localization and Internationalization testing** for the application that is expected to be used by users across the world. We need to ensure that the system is designed in such a manner that it can be easily customized without any engineering / design changes to the system for various countries and cultures. So, we try to ensure that there are no issues due to language change (Text expansion, usage of Shortcut and Hot keys, evaluation of string functions, or text used in graphics are taken care of). Apart from that we also try to ensure data formats are correctly used as per local country requirements – such as date & time format, currency symbol, comma and decimal separators for numbers.

Non-functional testing on the other hand focuses on other characteristics of the software and we try to measure to what extent the system satisfies those characteristics.

As such any characteristics other than functional aspects of the system is covered under non-functional testing, but we covered some important testing types such as Usability, Performance, Security and Compatibility testing.

Usability testing is done to ensure that the system can be understood, learned and used easily, effectively, efficiently with satisfaction not only by normal users but also by people who are physically impaired. So, we consider various aspects such as interactivity, layout, readability, aesthetics, display characteristics, consistency, flexibility etc during this testing.

Performance Load and Stress testing is done to ensure that the response time, throughput and resource utilization is within acceptable limit. **Load** testing is done to ensure that performance does not degrade beyond a certain limit even if the load is increased to highest possible level. **Stress** testing is done to evaluate the maximum limit stress the system can support and ensure that system does not crash or does not compromise on security of sensitive data. Memory leaks, memory fragmentation, overwrites or not having index even if some conditions are used for fetching database records are some of the key causes of performance related issue.

Subsequently, we discussed security testing which is done to determine the security of the software product. As part of this testing we try to act like a hacker and see whether system can be penetrated with various possible attacks such as Password cracking, URL manipulation, SQL injection, Cross site scripting or spoofing.

Since many systems are used directly by end users (general public and not just company employees), they should support all (at least most popular) platforms available in the market. So, We need to do **Compatibility testing** to ensure that it support various operating systems, browsers, databases and devices. Focus is given to some potential issues such as page load time does not degrade, tabs and tab order works, data displayed accurately, email links still work properly, images are displayed properly, documents can uploaded / downloaded and look and feel or screen resolutions are not impacted.

Lastly we discussed about **Regression testing** we need to do for all functional and non-functional requirements to ensure that they continue to work as expected even after making some changes or in the system due to changes in rules or process or even fixing defects. All the test cases prepared are evaluated (for criticality / potential impact) and set of important test cases are identified as regression test cases. Most of these test cases (based on impact analysis of change) for every release due to change either manually or automated.

Software Testing Types

8.5 Exercise

Sr	Question
1.	Provide 2 important aspects to be checked while testing a report
2.	Provide 2 important aspects to be checked while testing a Error messages
3.	_____ testing is done to check that if an application response time is 3 seconds when 300 users are accessing the same and may be impacted only little (1-2 seconds) if say 800 or more users access at a given point of time
4.	Name any 3 types of possible attacks on the system
5.	Provide 4 key aspects to be checked during Usability testing
6.	What is regression testing? Why it is important?
7.	_____ testing is subjecting the program to heavy volumes of data for e.g. an operating system's job queue would be filled to full capacity
8.	In _____ testing, a considerable load is generated as quickly as possible in order to analyzed the maximum limit of concurrent users the application can support.

9.	Match the following:
	
	1. Beta testing A. Stress testing
	2. Response time B. Exploratory testing
	3. Aesthetics C. Acceptance testing
	                             D. Performance testing
	                             F. Usability testing

10.	Explain non-functional testing in general and list down any non-functional testing with examples
11.	Regression testing is used to ensure _____ of application after each maintenance / enhancement release
12.	Which types of tests are covered under regression tests?
13.	What are the objectives of the performance testing?
14.	Name five objectives of usability testing
15.	Explain types of testing done as part of user interface validation
16.	Which are the main testing types
17.	Provide at least 3 key aspects of localization testing
18.	Briefly describe in couple of lines 5 possible attacks requiring security testing
19.	Explain with example how SQL injection can could be used to extract vital information from database
20.	Checking layout, readability is part of _____ testing
21.	_____ and _____ testing are two major testing types which

	are based on requirement types.
22.	_____ testing type refers to qualitative aspects of the software where the outcome may not be Met or Not Met but the extent to which the requirement met.
23.	When should you do regression testing? Why?
24.	Describe Error Messages validation with example
25.	Write a note on Compatibility Testing
26.	Write Note on Usability Testing
27.	Discuss Localization and Internationalization testing with suitable example
28.	Explain Performance and Load Testing with suitable example
29.	Write a note on User Interface Testing
30.	Compatibility Testing is a non-functional testing. True/False?

9 References

(1) Software Engineering by Roger Pressman
Foundation of Software Testing – ISTQB Certification by Dorothy Graham, Erik van Veenendaal, Isabel Evans, Rex Black

(2) Standard glossary of terms used in Software Testing - ISTQB version 2.1

(3) Software Testing Principles and Practices – by Srinivasan Desikan, Gopalswamy Ramesh

(4) Software Testing Techniques and Applications – by Arun kumar Khannur

Made in the USA
Coppell, TX
04 May 2021